THE WORST MEDIEVAL
MONARCHS

In memory of
Keith Humphrey
1952–99

THE WORST MEDIEVAL
MONARCHS
INCOMPETENT, EVIL AND
TYRANNOUS KINGS

PHIL BRADFORD

PEN & SWORD
HISTORY

AN IMPRINT OF PEN & SWORD BOOKS LTD.
YORKSHIRE – PHILADELPHIA

First published in Great Britain in 2023 by
PEN AND SWORD HISTORY
An imprint of
Pen & Sword Books Ltd
Yorkshire – Philadelphia

ISBN 978 1 39908 305 8

A CIP catalogue record for this book is available from the British Library.

Typeset in Times New Roman 11/13.5 by
SJmagic DESIGN SERVICES, India.
Printed and bound in the UK by CPI Group (UK) Ltd.

Pen & Sword Books Limited incorporates the imprints of Atlas, Archaeology,
Aviation, Discovery, Family History, Fiction, History, Maritime, Military, Military
Classics, Politics, Select, Transport, True Crime, Air World, Frontline Publishing,
Leo Cooper, Remember When, Seaforth Publishing, The Praetorian Press,
Wharncliffe Local History, Wharncliffe Transport, Wharncliffe True Crime and
White Owl.

For a complete list of Pen & Sword titles please contact
PEN & SWORD BOOKS LIMITED
George House, Units 12 & 13, Beevor Street, Off Pontefract Road,
Barnsley, South Yorkshire, S71 1HN, England
E-mail: enquiries@pen-and-sword.co.uk
Website: www.pen-and-sword.co.uk

or

PEN AND SWORD BOOKS
1950 Lawrence Rd, Havertown, PA 19083, USA
E-mail: uspen-and-sword@casematepublishers.com
Website: www.penandswordbooks.com

MIX
Paper | Supporting
responsible forestry
FSC
www.fsc.org   FSC® C013604

Contents

Acknowledgements

I first began thinking about the reputations of medieval kings twenty years ago, when I wrote an MA dissertation on 'The Tyranny of Edward II', so it has been a real pleasure to come back to the subject and to write this volume. I am very grateful to Gwilym Dodd for his encouragement with this project, his generosity in discussing some of the topics considered, and for his advice and comments on earlier drafts. Owain Bell, Richard Gill and Luise Horrocks all kindly read the entire work and provided helpful feedback. Doug Chaplin generously took the photo of King John's tomb and commented on the text. All remaining errors are, of course, my own.

I owe a considerable debt to two people who are no longer with us. That MA dissertation, and my subsequent doctoral thesis, were supervised by Mark Ormrod. His early death in 2020 deprived the field of medieval history of one of its great scholars. All those who were his students and colleagues remember above all his kindness and encouragement. He profoundly shaped my development as a historian across two decades, for which I am immensely grateful. I am sure that he would not have agreed with everything I have written in this book (I can imagine his gently questioning look upon reading one or two sentences), but he would have been endlessly supportive and generous. Further back still, my uncle encouraged my love of history as a child. Many of the questions addressed here echo the debates he would have with me in my teens, although he would be amused to see how far my opinions have changed and developed in subsequent years, especially about King John. Having so supported my desire to study history, he sadly died shortly before I took my 'A' levels. It has taken nearly quarter of a century, but the dedication of this volume reflects my gratitude to him for his encouragement and nurturing of my passion for history.

Preface

In the United States of America, frequent surveys are taken to rank the country's presidents. Academic historians are questioned about the effectiveness of each president, judged on various criteria, with a league table summarising the combined findings. The 'best' president is normally found to be Abraham Lincoln, with George Washington and Franklin Delano Roosevelt usually vying for second and third place, then Theodore Roosevelt and Woodrow Wilson usually making up the top five. There is less consensus about the 'worst' president, although in recent years James Buchanan has tended to receive that dubious honour, with Franklin Pierce, Andrew Johnson and Warren Harding (and lately Donald Trump) keeping him company at the bottom of the league.

The validity of this exercise is questionable. For all the careful methodology and criteria, it is exceptionally hard to compare George Washington, who began as leader of eleven eastern states in a pre-industrial age, with Barack Obama, presiding over a transcontinental nuclear empire. It is perhaps notable that the top five were all warriors, having either come to the presidency on the back of military success (Washington and Teddy Roosevelt) or presiding over some of the most significant wars in US history (Lincoln, Wilson and FDR). The passage of time can also have an impact, with Richard Nixon and George W. Bush viewed increasingly less negatively than in the immediate aftermath of their time in office.

It is also telling that these surveys of expert historians differ markedly from polls of the wider public. The likes of Washington and Lincoln are, of course, deeply embedded in United States culture and mythology, so can usually be found in the top ten of popular surveys. The general public, however, tend to opt for presidents they can remember, which gives John F. Kennedy and Ronald Reagan much greater prominence. Obscure, nineteenth-century nonentities like Millard Fillmore never have a hope. A 2011 Gallup poll, for example, had as the top five Reagan, Lincoln, Bill Clinton, JFK and Washington. Admittedly the sample size was small (only 1,015 adults), but it does show the role memory plays in these surveys. The high positions afforded Reagan and Clinton may also have reflected the ideological polarisation in US politics, people in 2011 looking back nostalgically to recent heroes of their parties.

Across the Atlantic in the United Kingdom, there is far less of an appetite for this kind of exercise. For British prime ministers, the few academic surveys that have been done tend to restrict themselves to the twentieth century onwards, or even the period after the Second World War. Winston Churchill, Clement Attlee, David Lloyd George and Margaret Thatcher normally head the table, with the unfortunate Anthony Eden propping it up. Once again, successful war leaders dominate. No one seems to care much about the relative merits of eighteenth- and nineteenth-century figures like the marquess of Rockingham or Viscount Goderich, which makes the approach very different from that in the United States.

When it comes to the monarchy, such rankings are not even attempted. In part, that is because in a constitutional monarchy the sovereign excites far less popular passion than a president or prime minister, given that they are not typically responsible for the success or failure of an administration and its impact on everyday lives. There is also the issue of time, the impossibility of comparing the rule of William I in an age of motte-and-bailey castles with that of Elizabeth II in the space age. Finally, there is the problem that the further back in time one goes, the more monarchs there are in what is now Britain. The sovereign has only been king or queen of the United Kingdom since 1707 (and even the meaning of that changed in 1801 and again in 1922). Before that there were separate monarchs of England and Scotland (albeit the same person after 1603), and further back still those two countries were split into smaller kingdoms. How does one compare Æthelwulf, King of Wessex in the ninth century, with Victoria, queen-empress of a quarter of the globe in the nineteenth century?

Nevertheless, there is an interest in the various monarchs of the British past and their relative success. In the 2002 BBC show *100 Greatest Britons*, the top hundred were chosen by popular poll. Their number included eleven sovereigns who ruled in all or part of what is now Great Britain: Elizabeth I (7th), Alfred the Great (14th), Victoria (18th), Elizabeth II (24th), Boudica (35th), Henry VIII (40th), Henry V (72nd), Robert Bruce (74th), Richard III (82nd), Henry II (90th) and Edward I (94th). With the possible exception of the last two, there must be a strong suspicion that these are mainly the most memorable of monarchs (for various reasons) in the twenty-first century. That the entirely legendary King Arthur ranked 51st on the list tends to reaffirm this view. Assessment of monarchs therefore seems to rely above all on their place in popular memory. Those in the list above either defined eras (Elizabethan, Victorian) or contributed in some way (usually militarily) to national mythologies. If the question of who was the best monarch in British history is unanswerable, the main candidates are usually fairly obvious. No one is likely to choose Henry VI of England or James V of Scotland. Assessments are generally rooted in the memory of the monarch's significance in the national myth, rather than in detailed knowledge of their reign.

In some ways, however, the question of their success becomes more relevant in the pre-modern era, when monarchs were genuinely 'in charge' and actually ruling rather than merely reigning. Four of the top hundred in the 2002 poll were medieval monarchs and although Richard III is a controversial inclusion, most academics would probably see Henry II, Edward I and Henry V as among the most successful kings of the Middle Ages. Henry II is credited with responsibility for establishing the common law, Edward I both with legal reform and for the conquest of Wales, Henry V with the greatest successes of the Hundred Years' War against France. There are problems and nuances in all these cases, but that is how they are popularly remembered. Throw in Edward III and maybe (depending on who you ask) Richard I, and there is the pantheon of England's 'best' medieval kings.

How about the other end of the performance table? Perhaps wisely, the BBC has never done an equivalent '100 Worst Britons', but there are definitely monarchs who are remembered as failures or worse. Unlike US presidents, where those ranked worst are generally the ones people cannot remember, 'bad' monarchs have left a much greater impression on English/ British consciousness. King John and Magna Carta, and Charles I being separated from his head, are well-known parts of the national story. There is a general sense of their 'badness', even if nothing is known of the details. Whether monarchs can be easily divided into 'good' and 'bad', any more than British premiers or US presidents, is a legitimate question; the differing contexts and circumstances always prevent too easy a comparison. Yet we live in an age when there is a popular desire for such clear-cut categories, where lists of best, worst, most evil and so on abound in television programmes made to fill ever more channels. Whatever the legitimacy of the question, we cannot avoid the fact that people do divide leaders (and many other people and things) into such categories. While the relative positions can change over the years, once someone acquires a negative reputation in such exercises, it can be very hard to shift.

This book looks at a small group of those who have acquired enduringly negative reputations. Taking the five 'worst' English kings of the Middle Ages, it examines how their reputations were acquired and shaped, and whether they are deserved. The selection is, of course, no exact science. Every king chosen here would find some defenders, even if only one (Richard III) would seriously polarise opinion. More contentious are those omitted, although some aspect of almost every king's reign would probably merit inclusion. The only serious additional contender is Henry VI, who was indeed a disastrous king, but he spent so much of his two reigns as a minor, mentally unbalanced, or under the control of others that he is enormously problematic. Since the focus is on worst kings rather than worst reigns, Henry is overlooked in favour of those who actively exercised their kingship and in various ways brought about their own unhappy demise. This is not an exercise in rehabilitation or special pleading; all five monarchs featured were demonstrably failures in different degrees. It is instead an examination of why they came to be viewed as failures and how they were cast as the lasting villains of the medieval story.

Introduction

Eighteen men sat on the English throne between the Battles of Hastings (1066) and Bosworth (1485). None was an unqualified success. Even those who have generally had a good posthumous reputation encountered crises and opposition at times. Medieval kingship was a difficult art and no one could always get it right, especially during a long reign. Yet some kings were less successful than others. Of the eighteen who wore the medieval crown, five have traditionally been seen as particular failures. Whether fairly or not, Stephen, John, Edward II, Richard II and Richard III have been judged as the worst monarchs of the Middle Ages.

Four were obvious failures by one clear standard: they lost their thrones. John died in the middle of a civil war he was losing, Edward II and Richard II were both deposed, and Richard III was killed in battle. Stephen alone died peacefully in his bed, but only after almost two decades of civil war, leaving his throne to his opponent. Holding onto the crown, being accepted as rightful king and passing on the throne to a son were critical for a medieval monarch. All five failed, albeit in different degrees and for different reasons. Interestingly, none of the five were expected to be king at the time of their births, but that cannot explain their failures. Edward II and Richard II became heirs as young children, when their older brothers died. Stephen and John took advantage of unclear laws of succession. Only Richard III unambiguously usurped the throne. Yet legitimate heirs, opportunists and usurpers alike could lose their crowns through bad kingship.

That raises an obvious question: how do we determine what good and bad kingship was? Society's standards and values change over time, so historians of the twenty-first century are not judging a king in the same way as one of his medieval contemporaries. If we talk of these five as the 'worst' monarchs of the Middle Ages, we have to understand how they acquired that reputation and how opinions have fluctuated across the centuries. We need to know what contemporary expectations of a king were and how contemporary writers judged whether or not a particular king had met those expectations.

There is a popular myth, grounded in half-remembered stories of Henry VIII beheading anyone he fancied (especially his wives) and filtered through memories of the absolutist European monarchies of the seventeenth and eighteenth centuries, that medieval kings were all powerful. The Hollywood and Disney version of medieval monarchy turns kings into caricatures of the Queen of Hearts, able to scream 'off with his head' and be instantly obeyed. The reality, in England as in most European monarchies, was very different. Yes, kings were powerful, but as the old adage goes, great power brought great responsibility. Kingship was contractual. The king was given the power to rule, seen as chosen for that role by God himself, but he had a duty to his subjects. He had to undertake his office in accordance with their expectations and the more general expectations of what a king was. If we judge a king a failure, we need to be clear about the standards we are judging him against.

Expectations of Medieval Kings

In medieval thought, the realm was often likened to a body (hence the term 'body politic'). Most often in this analogy, the king was the head, the most crucial part of the body which directs the rest. A headless body, after all, is not viable. Although originating with Plato, the body metaphor in Christian Europe drew on the New Testament version, specifically chapter 12 of the first letter to the Corinthians, which nuances the picture. St Paul observed that the body relied on its many parts working together and that 'the members of the body that seem to be weaker are indispensable'. The king, as head of the body politic, needed the other parts in order to exist as head of a functioning state. Kings did not exist in isolation, nor could they simply ignore the rest of the body. From this basic model derived many of the theoretical expectations which underpinned medieval kingship.[1]

Mirrors and Manuals

One of the most influential political thinkers of the Middle Ages was the twelfth-century Englishman John of Salisbury, who became Bishop of Chartres in France. His *Policraticus* drew, naturally enough, on the Bible, but also on Roman law and ancient writers. One of its most important features was an explanation of the duties and responsibilities of kings. Since a king's power came from God, John explained, his subjects had an obligation to obey him. However, the king had a corresponding obligation to his subjects to rule in accordance with the law. A king who did not do this and who failed to rule according to divine law was a tyrant. Tyrants, as far as John was concerned, could and should be killed once all alternatives had failed.[2]

The later Middle Ages thus had a working definition of tyranny, but it was problematic. Originally, the term 'tyrant' had been fairly neutral in the Greek world, although had assumed ever more negative connotations. By the time John wrote, a king who was a tyrant was effectively a despot ruling contrary to (divine) law and not meeting his obligations to his subjects. In reality, there was often little agreement about when that point was reached. It is notable that when Edward II and Richard II were deposed, the official records carefully avoided calling them tyrants. Explicit accusations of tyranny against medieval English kings are rare and typically date from after a king's disgrace and death. John of Salisbury's ideas may seem clear and tidy, but confronted with the messy reality of political life, medieval writers were hesitant about applying them, something modern commentators sometimes overlook. Tyranny was usually in the eye of the beholder.

John of Salisbury's work shared features in common with a genre known as Mirrors for Princes. These were manuals or guidebooks advising rulers or their heirs how to rule wisely and correctly. There are numerous examples from across Europe from Antiquity onwards, some of which were aimed at rulers in general, others of which were targeted at particular individuals. One influential text, for example, was Giles of Rome's *De Regimine Principium* (*On the Rule of Princes*), written in the later thirteenth century for Philip IV of France. Notable English texts include those written by William of Pagula for Edward III and by Thomas Hoccleve for the future Henry V.[3]

All these 'mirrors' drew on a mixture of Biblical and classical examples, but ones aimed at specific individuals also made use of the relevant context, along with local examples and historical warnings. Although these were idealised pictures, reflecting the views of particular authors, they demonstrate that there was a clear theoretical understanding of how a king should perform his role and the responsibilities he had to his subjects. A sovereign entrusted with rule by God was expected to heed both divine law and the warnings of history.

Coronations and Promises

Subjects' expectations of their rulers can also be found in their coronation oaths.[4] A coronation was the essential ceremony which made a king a king. Until the thirteenth century, the new king's reign began on the day he was crowned. While the rules of succession remained unclear, acting quickly and persuading an archbishop to crown him was a means of securing the throne:

Henry I, Stephen and John all became king in this way. This changed when Henry III died in November 1272, as his heir was on Crusade in the Holy Land. Edward I was proclaimed king a few days after his father's death, but not crowned until August 1274. From then on, reigns began immediately upon the death of the previous king. As it became accepted that the crown passed to the reigning king's eldest son, the pressure for a swift coronation receded. Seven months elapsed between Edward II's accession in July 1307 and his coronation in February 1308, although the later medieval gap was typically considerably less than this. Before 1066, the place of coronations varied. However, Edward the Confessor (crowned at Winchester) poured considerable resources into Westminster Abbey, where he was buried. Seeking association with the Confessor, both Harold II and William I were crowned in that abbey. Thereafter, Westminster became the accepted coronation Church.

As it was a religious ceremony in a Church, coronations usually took place on a Sunday, unless they happened on a major Christian festival, as was the case for William the Conqueror (Christmas Day) and John (Ascension Day). It is important to recognise the overtly Christian nature of a coronation, for kingship was held to be a divinely-instituted office. The act of anointing the sovereign with holy oil was a conscious echo of a practice found in the Old Testament.[5] Biblical precedents had a major role in the ceremony, as a reminder of the sacred nature of kingship. A king was believed to be set apart by God through his anointing, something reinforced by the various regalia (such as the crown, orb and sceptre) with which he was invested. As God's anointed, the king had a right to expect the loyalty and service of those he had appointed to rule.

However, that did not give a king unlimited power or allow him to do anything he wished. Precisely because he held a sacred office, the anointed king had a responsibility to those from whom he had been set apart. He was meant to be a Christian ruler, overseeing his people wisely like King Solomon in the Old Testament. For this reason, he had obligations which were laid out in the coronation oath. In his oath, the king swore to do three things: maintain the peace of Church and realm; administer justice; and rule fairly and mercifully. Additionally, four twelfth-century kings issued 'coronation charters' setting out their commitment to just rule and promising to reform the bad practices of their predecessors. In 1308, when Edward II was crowned, an additional clause was added to the oath in which the king promised to uphold the laws chosen by the people.

These were the sacred promises kings made and the theoretical standards to which they were held. Of course, interpretation varied widely. Maintaining peace, for example, mattered only domestically; disturbing peace outside England was perfectly acceptable if done in the name of a good war of conquest. No medieval king could claim to have met these standards all the time. A monarch could survive occasional transgressions, but consistently falling to keep his oath placed him in trouble.

Counsel and Consent

That the king did not have unlimited power is shown most clearly by the fact that he was required to seek advice from his leading subjects, including their agreement to taxation and other matters. Medieval England was not, of course, a democracy. The king's 'natural' advisors were the nobility and he was expected to listen to their views and spread his patronage widely among them. Relying on too narrow a group, concentrating rewards in too few hands, led to accusations of favouritism, and royal favourites were not popular. They were even more unpopular if they were foreign or viewed as lowly men raised above their station. Trouble arose when a particularly powerful lord or a significant group of nobles felt alienated. Evil counsellors were an occupational hazard for a medieval monarch, but the charge was levelled most against kings who failed to be attentive to the nobility as a whole. English kings were not omnipotent, but were expected to listen to and work with their nobility in governing the realm. The wisest realised this and cooperated with the nobility in a common cause. The more foolish concentrated too much in the hands of certain favourites and usually suffered the consequences.

Additionally, the question of subjects' consent was complicated by the fact that the king of England did not merely rule over the territory now recognised as England.[6] The Scottish border remained fluid until Berwick-upon-Tweed was finally settled in England in 1482. Various medieval English kings claimed overlordship over Scotland, some more forcefully and successfully than others. Until Calais was lost in the mid-sixteenth century, the English sovereign also ruled over parts of modern France. Sometimes these parts were extensive and greater than the lands under the direct control of the king of France. From Edward III to George III, the English/British monarch actually used the title 'King of France', although only Henry VI was ever crowned as such and even he failed to make his title a reality. English control of areas of Wales gave way to a complete conquest under Edward I at the end of the thirteenth century. From Henry II's reign, Ireland was claimed by the kings of England, although the land under effective English control there varied widely. The Channel Islands and the Isle of Man also had direct and complex relationships with the English crown. As

xv

a result, the king had to take account of customs and procedures for advice in other areas where he ruled, which could at times create tensions with his English subjects. Balancing these competing expectations was not easy.

Anglo-Saxon kings had had councils of their leading nobles and churchmen (both bishops and abbots), a practice which continued throughout the Middle Ages. These were the king's inner circle who advised him and helped him with key decisions. From the thirteenth century, these councils met alongside or in addition to parliament, another body of which the king now had to take heed.[7] The membership of parliament was highly fluid in its first century or so, but by the end of the fourteenth century had coalesced into a House of Lords (comprising all bishops, the abbots of major monasteries, and all nobles summoned personally) and a House of Commons (with two representatives from each county and a variable list of towns, plus representatives of the lower clergy). The House of Lords remained the more important in this period, but crucially, it became established that taxation could not be granted without the consent of the representatives in the Commons. The king was meant to live from his own means, taxation granted only to support extraordinary expenditure such as a war to defend the realm.

Parliament confronted a king with the concerns of his subjects. Even in times of domestic harmony, people sought justice and reform from their king. While this could be done through the courts, the king was the fount of justice and from Anglo-Saxon times his personal verdict was often pursued by those with the means to do so. From the thirteenth century the concerns of individuals and the wider community are reflected in the petitions presented to the king in parliament. These are a reminder of the continuing pressure on a medieval king to balance the competing needs and desires of his subjects. Into the middle part of the fourteenth century, these were most frequently private petitions, submitted by an individual or small group seeking redress for some complaint. While private petitions continued to be presented, from the reign of Edward III (1327–77) common petitions became much more significant than before. These contained either a single petition or a list of grievances agreed by the members of what became the House of Commons. Usually they touched on matters of national or regional significance. In addition, the clergy, who were part of parliament but also had separate assemblies called convocations, would occasionally submit their own list of complaints known as *gravamina*. A wise king saw the importance of addressing these petitions and seeking to provide justice in parliament.[8]

Obviously these petitions covered a wide range of subjects, but there are recurrent themes throughout the later Middle Ages. One is dissatisfaction about corrupt or inadequate royal officials, such as sheriffs and judges. Part of the king's duty for administering justice was ensuring that his representatives acted fairly, but complaints that they did not were ubiquitous. Extravagance or corruption in the royal household was often criticised. Another common complaint was about taxation. Kings were meant to raise taxes only in time of need, such as to prosecute a war against a foreign threat. Periods of heavy, repeated taxation (such as during the opening phase of the Hundred Years' War in the 1330s) brought vociferous complaints, especially when the money seemed to be squandered. Subjects had a clear sense of how a king should perform and were quick to let him know when they felt he was not meeting his obligations. From the mid-fourteenth century, there was a clear trade-off between parliament accepting its duty to grant necessary taxes if the king accepted his responsibility to provide justice. The wise king worked with parliament to ensure that both his and his subjects' needs were met. Successful kings worked with parliament, not in opposition to it. Counsel and consent were integral to successful kingship.

Protests and Depositions

Precisely because the king was God's anointed, the political community often shied away from the extreme step of removing an unsatisfactory ruler. Not until 1327 was a monarch deposed for inadequacy, with a second occasion following fairly swiftly in 1399. The depositions of Edward II and Richard II were the culmination of lengthy processes in which they had repeatedly fallen out with leading nobles and shown themselves unfit to rule. The most comprehensive critique of royal failings is found in the formal records of these depositions. By their nature, these are atypical because they seek to justify the momentous step of removing a king. While containing much information on how the two had failed to meet expectations, most kings faced less thorough dissection of their kingship.[9]

Short of this, there were times when the usual processes were deemed insufficient and strong opposition was aroused. Instead of removing the king, at least at first, opponents often sought major reform. Sometimes they produced written protests outlining their demands. On other occasions, we have the text of the reforms as agreed between the king and his opponents, such as Magna Carta (1215), the Provisions of Oxford (1258) and the Ordinances (1311). Such 'agreements' were essentially forced on a king who had little alternative; it is notable that all three of these examples were later repudiated by the same monarchs who conceded them. Nevertheless, we can glean important information about the concerns of the king's leading subjects from these texts. They tell us much about how they thought a king was failing in his office and what they felt needed to be done about this.

Although several of these documents have come to be seen as significant landmarks in English history, it is important to remember that they were very much a response to particular circumstances. They were not an immortal, theoretical statement of liberties. Some of the demands in them are very specific, even vindictive, such as the banishment of named men in Magna Carta or Piers Gaveston in the Ordinances. Nevertheless, they do reveal some of the other expectations medieval subjects had of their king. Most crucially, many opposition movements raised the issue of advice and advisors. Criticising the king directly was often avoided; instead, his choice of advisors would often be attacked.

Many people, at least among the landed and politically active, thus had a clear sense of what kingship entailed. A king was expected to maintain the peace and protect his subjects from foreign attack (hence the heavy criticisms of Edward II when he failed to deal with Scottish raids in the northern counties). He was meant to listen to his advisors, not rely on too narrow a circle or those deemed unfit to advise, and provide remedy and justice. In return, he could expect loyalty, service and taxes when necessary to undertake his core duties. English kingship was contractual and if a king failed to fulfil his obligations, people did not suffer in silence. They knew what a king was for and what he should do. A king had to fulfil his side of the bargain if he wanted loyal subjects and a peaceful realm.

Judging a King: Medieval Chronicles

We are not only reliant on theoretical views and official documents when assessing how a king was viewed. The most influential contemporary verdicts on medieval kings are found in the chronicles of the time.[10] Although these are invaluable for historians, who use them extensively, they represent the views of a limited group rather than the population at large. Until the fifteenth century, the majority of these were written by monks, with most others by secular (non-monastic) clergy, so obviously tended to have a clerical perspective. Most are in Latin and some in Anglo-Norman French, with English more common towards the end of the Middle Ages. Unlike the modern mass media, chronicles would not have influenced large numbers of people, given how many people were illiterate and how few copies of these works existed in accessible locations. The audience for most chronicles was intentionally limited to the writer's monastery or a close circle; only a handful were copied and distributed widely. Nevertheless, they were not secret documents, with evidence of certain kings sending to monasteries for chronicles to consult for historical information, as Edward I did when trying to assert his claim over Scotland in the 1290s. It is likely that most monasteries would have kept a chronicle and what we have today represents only a proportion of the total once written, since many have been lost over the centuries (and some survive only in later transcriptions made before fire, flood or theft carried off the original). For all those caveats, the chronicles are colourful works which do preserve contemporary viewpoints and help us understand how a king was judged at the time. Notably, however, these were not in any sense 'official' works, as was the case in other countries. In France, for example, the chroniclers at the great abbey of Saint-Denis, north of Paris, effectively served as the justifiers and glorifiers of the monarchy. This was never the case in England. While some writers may have strongly supported a particular monarch, it was not because they were employed to do so. Chronicles were not official history, even if they often incorporated official views.

The term 'chronicle' encompasses a large variety of works. Some were 'universal histories', beginning with Adam and Eve and tracing the story to the writer's own day, where recent history is almost an appendix to the sweep of the human story. Others were extremely limited local histories of an abbey and its own affairs, with external events barely allowed to intrude into the narrative. Still others were national epics, repeatedly reworked and extended. Many of these works were derivative and copied down the centuries. There are some chronicles which cover only a single reign, or even just part of a reign. Often, they are detailed and well-informed, the best sources we have, although frustratingly, the authors of the most important are usually unknown. The *Vita Edwardi Secundi* (*Life of Edward II*), the Westminster Chronicle and the Crowland Chronicle are arguably our most valuable individual narrative sources for the reigns of Edward II, Richard II and Richard III respectively, but are all anonymous. It is clear that their authors were close to the centre of government and in a position to comment with authority, which suggests that people in key positions did keep records or journals. How many have been lost is an unanswerable question, but in a way these are the anonymous, medieval versions of cabinet ministers' diaries, casting light onto the processes and disputes underlying the official record. While invaluable, such chronicles are rarely strong on opinions and feelings in the provinces. Although they provide insights into kings which are lacking from the more general monastic chronicles, they have to be supplemented by more local works, which survive very unevenly.

Chroniclers wrote for reasons which are difficult for the modern, secular world to understand. That they wrote with a particular agenda is no surprise. Much modern journalism is written with a distinct slant, reflecting the opinions and prejudices of the writers, however the contemporary world might like to deceive itself about its objectivity. But where the modern author is likely to approach their judgement in political terms (Conservative or Labour, Democrat or Republican), medieval writers framed their opinions in religious terms. Theirs is a world full of omens and portents, in which God's judgement is shown through supernatural happenings. His approval is found in auspicious signs, his disapproval in the likes of plague, flood and military defeat. These were Christian writers who judged rulers by the Christian standards of their time.

One of the key standards, perhaps the one least comprehensible to the modern age, was how a king treated the Church. Chroniclers, especially monastic ones, were acutely sensitive to a monarch's attention to ecclesiastical liberties, how well he conformed to conventional expectations of piety, how generous he was towards religious institutions. Someone like King John, who spent much of his reign at odds with the Church, is treated with almost universal hostility by the chroniclers for this reason. They had little interest in his administrative efficiency, which has won him modern admirers, being far more concerned with the consequences of his clash with the papacy and the enthusiastic way he made use of the Church's revenues. John is unique among the five kings considered here, and probably among all medieval kings except William II, in the hostility his perceived impiety provoked. It is an important reminder of the different standards applied by medieval chroniclers. Politics and religion were inextricably linked in the Middle Ages, the separation we observe between secular and religious both impossible and incomprehensible. Deposition, death in battle or a painful end was God's punishment for a king failing to meet Christian standards of kingship.

Nevertheless, if the religious language and framework is alien to the modern approach, chroniclers still engaged in recognisable assessments of the success (or otherwise) of kings. It is very rare that a king is universally judged positively or (excluding King John) negatively in the chronicles. This is why it is important to know by whom, where and why a chronicle was written, for it helps us understand the criteria the author was using to judge the king. Often the disagreements among chroniclers reflect their main concerns: chroniclers writing in the North, for example, tended to be far more critical than their southern counterparts of kings who failed to deal with damaging Scottish border raids. Interpreting the views of chronicles on the success and failure of kings is thus something of an art form, for not all chronicles have equal value and we always have to keep authorship and motivation in mind. Some works which have been hugely influential can be historically dubious. For all that, however, the opinions contemporary chroniclers express about a king tend to agree in broad outline, even if not in all the specifics. The writers who did not see the five kings considered here as failures were outliers, dissenters from a generally negative verdict. Assessing the reliability of these verdicts has occupied historians ever since.

Judging the Judgements: Historians beyond the Middle Ages

In the first volume of his biography of Tony Blair, written while Blair was still prime minister, Anthony Seldon argued that 'all history is contemporary history' because all histories 'will always reflect the predominant concerns of the age in which they are written'.[11] Looking at how the reputations of medieval kings have fared since the end of the Middle Ages suggests that there is considerable truth in this assertion. They have been consistently reassessed and reimagined as social attitudes have changed. The criteria employed are often anachronistic and would have been unrecognisable to medieval writers. Kings have frequently become didactic examples serving the needs of a later age, heroes or villains in stories which are not really about them at all.

The Sixteenth to Nineteenth Centuries

Although the medieval era in England traditionally finishes in 1485 with the start of the Tudor period, in many ways Henry VII was the last medieval king. The true end of what became known as the Middle Ages came in the reign of his son, Henry VIII, with the upheavals of the Reformation. The break with Rome and the formation of the Church of England was a dramatic rupture, terminating centuries in which England had been subject to the papacy and part of a universal European Church. In religious terms, Henry never fully abandoned his Roman Catholic outlook even when he rejected papal authority. Strict Protestantism arrived with the reign of Edward VI (1547–53) followed by a restoration of Catholicism under Mary I (1553–58) and a return to a Protestant Church of England under Elizabeth I (1558–1603). Religion was thus a hotly-contested topic, which strongly influenced how figures from the past were viewed and used in arguments.

The verdicts of medieval chroniclers on kings became problematic. They had praised kings who were dutiful servants of the Roman Catholic Church, who played their proper part in Christendom, supported papal initiatives like crusades, and founded and financially supported monasteries. When the Reformation denied the authority of the papacy, separated the English Church from Rome and dissolved monasteries as hotbeds of corruption and iniquity, such praise became deeply problematic. Suddenly the history of English kingship was viewed through a new lens, one which did not flatter those monarchs who had conformed too vigorously to the religious habits of their time. This anti-Catholic backlash saw the first major challenge to the medieval chroniclers' verdicts on their kings, for the religious outlook and values of the sixteenth century had changed dramatically. Kings who had followed popes too slavishly were now condemned, those who had resisted them lauded. The medieval worldview was inverted.

Religion continued to be a divisive subject in the seventeenth century, with the fierce debates of James I's reign, the Civil War and anti-Catholic hysteria after the Restoration in 1660. Medieval kings also became propaganda tools in the bitter political debates of the century. Edward II and Richard II became warnings for Charles I and James II, Richard III's 'tyranny' a comparison for critics of Cromwell's alleged monarchical ambitions. Magna Carta was reinvented as a foundational document of English liberty to be used as a weapon against Charles I. Stuart historians struggled to break free of their own context in writing about the Middle Ages, but it is perhaps anachronistic to imagine that they wanted to. The key value of the medieval past was in the lessons and precedents they could draw from it to apply to the present.

The Enlightenment in the eighteenth century brought another angle, with growing scientific rationalism and scepticism about organised religion. This made the worldview of the medieval chroniclers, with all their supernatural happenings and divine signs, distinctly suspect. On the other hand, this was also the age of Church of England dominance, where all office holders had to be visible members of the established Church. Eighteenth-century historians, sceptics and dutiful Anglicans alike, were much less impressed by kings as paragons of (Roman Catholic) piety. The American and French Revolutions prompted reflections around questions of liberty and citizenship, with the bloodletting of the French Revolution and Terror leading to agonised reflections on kingship and tyranny. As the English-speaking world expanded, so people thousands of miles from England began to retell the stories of English kings in new ways which made better sense to them.

The eighteenth and nineteenth centuries also saw a particular interest in collecting, sorting and publishing medieval sources, chronicles as well as government records. Some sources were saved for posterity by this passion, copies preserving a text subsequently destroyed or lost. The 1838 creation of the Public Record Office in London made many sources easily available to scholars. One notable achievement of the Victorian era was the Rolls Series, in which many chronicles and other sources were made available in published form. No longer were those writing about kings largely reliant on the opinions of earlier historians. Now it was possible for far more people to examine the records and opinions of the time, forming their own verdicts. The result was some considerable shifts in opinion about certain kings.

The Modern Era

By the time Queen Victoria celebrated her Golden Jubilee in 1887, she nominally reigned over a quarter of the globe. Politicians and statesmen in London took great pride in the fact that so much of the world map was coloured red. Never mind, as British foreign secretary and future prime minister Lord Salisbury candidly admitted while carving up Africa with his European counterparts, that most of them had not the faintest clue where half of the places they were arguing over were. It was a reflection of the United Kingdom's prestige and civilising mission. In the late Victorian mindset, the British Empire was the pinnacle of history, in which a constitutional monarchy and liberal democracy (represented by the 'mother of parliaments') brought its benefits to the world, whether the world wanted them or not. History was reinterpreted as the onward march of progress towards the system of Queen Victoria, Gladstone and Disraeli, the unwritten (but self-evidently ideal) constitution of the United Kingdom.

Historians thus judged kings in 'constitutional' terms, based on how they had helped (or hindered) this march of progress towards Victorian perfection. Kings who were viewed to have granted great liberties, improved the law or boosted the role of parliament were viewed favourably; those who did the opposite were condemned. This was to judge medieval kings by anachronistic criteria which would have made no sense to their contemporaries, but this constitutional approach was enormously influential. The greatest name associated with this school of thought was William Stubbs, who was Regius Professor of Modern History at the University of Oxford (1866–84), before becoming successively Bishop of Chester (1884–89) and Oxford (1889–1901). His work, especially the three-volume *Constitutional History of England,* overshadowed historical scholarship well into the twentieth century: Winston Churchill's popular retirement project, *A History of the English-Speaking Peoples*, was published in the

1950s, when the former prime minister was in his eighties and harking back to the views of the late Victorian approach in which he had come of age.

If they did not accept Stubbs slavishly, most historians of the early twentieth century followed calmly in his enormous footsteps. History was still approached in constitutional terms. Ironically, although they were deplored for their actions, 'bad' kings were essential to the constitutional version of history, since their misdeeds forced their subjects to wring major concessions (such as Magna Carta) from them. Constitutional historians were deeply immersed in the original documents, but were often too busy trying to fit them into their story of triumphant advancement to see them in their original context. It is this approach which is so brilliantly satirised by Walter Carruthers Sellar and Robert Julian Yeatman in *1066 and All That* (1930). As the subtitle (*A Memorable History of England comprising all the parts you can remember including 103 Good Things, 5 Bad Kings and 2 Genuine Dates*) reveals, it is a witty play on the half-remembered 'facts' of school history. The subtitles of the main chapters in this volume are the titles of Sellar and Yeatman's sections on the relevant kings.

Two World Wars and Britain's loss of global status fatally damaged the underlying idea of the nation's history as a relentless onward march of progress. It persisted (and arguably still persists) very much longer in popular imagination, but historians ceased trying to fit the stories of England's kings (and queens) into a straightforward, linear narrative leading to an obvious conclusion. This involved trying to understand how a particular king fitted into the context of his own time, rather than judging him by universal or anachronistic later standards. There was also a marked shift away from 'top down' history, the story of the deeds of great men, towards a greater interest in 'bottom up' history, the story of societies and social trends. This was particularly the case for historians with Marxist leanings; after all, monarchy and nobility were prime examples of the system Marxism aimed to overthrow. The growth of feminism from the 1960s onwards challenged a male-dominated narrative, trying to restore women to their place in a story largely written by men, for men, about men.

However, for all the attempts to place monarchs in context and judge them by the standards of their own time, no historian can ever fully free themself of their own context. That influences the questions asked and inevitably colours the conclusions. Most historians recognise this, but it is incredibly hard to put aside the culture in which one is writing and that is reflected in the way opinions about kings are constantly changing. The reputations of medieval kings are continually reshaped by the shifting outlooks of later ages.

Shaping Popular Memory: Medieval Kings in Popular Culture

Historians alone are not responsible for how kings are remembered in popular thought. Since Tudor times, the lives and reigns of medieval monarchs have been retold and dramatised in fictional portrayals. Plays, novels, and more recently film and television, have brought new interpretations of past rulers to ever-changing audiences. While many are based on the work of historians, some have little in common with reality beyond the names, yet these can be among the most influential. As times and social culture have changed, so writers have had to find ways to tell stories to make sense to new audiences.

Nevertheless, the Tudor versions have never lost their influence. Four of the kings in this volume were the subject of plays in the Elizabethan era. While Christopher Marlowe's on Edward II has never had the same influence, it is impossible to overstate the impact William Shakespeare's work has had on popular impressions of English history. His play on King John is one of his less satisfying works which has never had quite the same appeal, but well into the twentieth century historians were still wrestling to free opinions on Richard II and Richard III from the Shakespearean version of history. Shakespeare's brilliance has been deeply problematic for historians, with generations of schoolchildren raised on a hunchbacked Richard III offering his kingdom in exchange for a horse. However historically inaccurate, there is a depth and appeal to Shakespeare's kings which made them immensely memorable. They have cast a shadow over all interpretations ever since.

Indeed, while there was a handful of additional works in the seventeenth and eighteenth century, and the epic contributions of romantic novelists like Walter Scott, it was not until the twentieth century that historical fiction became a popular topic for novelists. In the twenty-first century, supplemented by television and cinema, it has become big business. Writers of both books and films scramble to retell the stories, to find new angles, to bring to life hidden or neglected characters.

Far more than historians, novelists and screenwriters feel able to take liberties with how they portray medieval kings and their contemporaries. Novelists have a greater freedom to explore the hypotheticals and parts of the story for which there is little or no evidence. The best examples, such as the Cadfael novels set in King Stephen's reign, stick closely to known historical facts while creating a plausible fictional world around them. Precisely because this is fiction, it needs to speak to the culture for which it is written. Social movements such as feminism and gay liberation have allowed novelists and screenwriters to take different angles, approaching stories in ways which would never have been permitted in more censorious times. The worst examples, it is true, lapse into grotesque anachronism, transplanting the social movements of the 1960s onwards onto a medieval story in unbelievable ways. Yet good or bad, fiction has played a major role in forging the reputations of several medieval kings.

* * *

The reputation of a medieval king is thus shaped and reshaped over the centuries. Having seen how we view a king today depends on this evolutionary process, it is time to turn to the five 'worst' kings of the Middle Ages, to examine how they came to be viewed as such and whether their reputations are deserved.

Chapter 1

Stephen: A Dreadful Story?

> I do not know nor can I tell all the enormities nor all the tortures that they did to wretched men in this land. And it lasted the nineteen years while Stephen was king, and it grew worse and worse. [...] Wherever men tilled, the earth bore no corn because the land was all done for by such doings; and they said openly that Christ and His saints slept. Such things, and more than we know how to tell, we suffered nineteen years for our sins.[1]

This judgement, by a monk writing at Peterborough Abbey, is one of the most damning verdicts on any reign in English history. That God had turned his back on England and allowed such suffering was the strongest condemnation conceivable; God was so indifferent to King Stephen that he could not rouse himself to intervene. This evocative phrase has seeped deep into historical memory. Almost nine centuries have passed, but the king's reputation has never really recovered. For much of the twentieth century, these 'nineteen long winters', the age of Stephen and Matilda, were seen as a period of anarchy.

The chaos can be overstated. After writing this lament, the chronicler immediately proceeded to describe the remarkably successful time enjoyed by Peterborough Abbey during Stephen's reign. The whole of England did not spend nineteen years entirely consumed by violence. The chronicler was writing afterwards, knowing how things ended. His words employ dramatic licence to emphasise the official position of Stephen's successor Henry II, that Stephen was a disaster best forgotten. His reputation has never really recovered from Henry's campaign to obliterate him from historical memory. Stephen came to the throne in controversial circumstances which shaped his whole reign. Consequently, historians and novelists alike have repeatedly tried to work out what went wrong. Yet after nine centuries, their efforts have become as much of a stalemate as the war between Stephen and Matilda.

Stephen's Life and Reign

Stephen was born between 1092 and 1097, the third son of Adela, youngest daughter of William the Conqueror, and Count Stephen of Blois. His father died in battle in the Middle East in 1102, the title going to Stephen's elder brother, Theobald. A younger brother, Henry, trained for the Church and went on to become Abbot of Glastonbury and Bishop of Winchester; arguably the richest cleric in England, he was to be a major, controversial figure of his brother's reign. Stephen was sent to the court of his uncle, Henry I. It was not uncommon for noble sons to be sent to court for their education, but over the next quarter of a century, we catch only occasional glimpses of Stephen. His uncle favoured him, making him Count of Mortain and granting various other lands over the years. In 1125, he married Matilda, the heiress to the Count of Boulogne, soon assuming the title from his father-in-law. It seems to have been a happy marriage and becoming Count of Boulogne brought yet more sizeable estates in England. By the mid-1120s, Stephen was one of the most significant, wealthy landowners on both sides of the Channel, in favour with his uncle and a trusted member of the family.

Had history taken another course on the night of 25 November 1120, Stephen today would be no more than a minor actor restricted to specialist academic texts. That evening, Henry I and a royal party were sailing to England from Normandy aboard two ships. The first, carrying the king, made the crossing safely. The second, the White Ship, made a reckless exit from Barfleur with a drunken crew, hit a submerged rock and sank. All but a Rouen butcher drowned. Among the casualties was the king's sole legitimate son, William. Stephen should have been on that ill-fated voyage. Afflicted by illness, which the rowdy mood aboard can hardly have helped, Stephen disembarked before the ship set sail. This stroke of fortune would have enormous consequences fifteen years later.

King Henry was devastated and his dynastic plans in tatters. The king was desperate to avoid the succession of his nephew William Clito (son of Henry's oldest brother, Robert). The illegitimacy of his other sons would be an insurmountable obstacle to their succession. Infamous for the number of bastards he fathered (the exact number is disputed but is certainly more than twenty), Henry had only two legitimate children. Having been widowed in 1118, it was now imperative for the king to remarry. Henry duly took a second wife, Adeliza, in 1121. Yet with no child born of the union by the end of 1126, Henry had his barons and bishops swear that if he died without a male heir, they would support the succession of his daughter and lone surviving legitimate child. The widow of Emperor Henry V, she was known

2

(despite never having had an imperial coronation) as the Empress Matilda. To secure the future, in 1128 he married her to Geoffrey of Anjou, not a popular choice with his barons. His plans received a boost with the death of William Clito later that year, but Geoffrey and Matilda rapidly became estranged. Their quarrel was patched up in 1131 and their first son, Henry (the future Henry II), was born in 1133. Henry I may well have hoped that this secured the longer-term future of his dynasty, but he was now in his mid-sixties. It was far from clear that the nobility would respect his wishes once he was dead. Moreover, relations between Matilda's husband and father deteriorated and by late 1135, Normandy and Anjou were locked in a border war. When Henry I died on 1 December, possibly from an infamous surfeit of lampreys, his daughter was in Anjou.

Acting with a decisiveness which would rarely be attributed to him thereafter, Stephen crossed to England, secured the royal treasury, the crucial support of London and Winchester and, thanks to his brother Henry, the Church, and was crowned king. Normandy initially opted for his brother Theobald, but once the news arrived from England, Stephen was also accepted there as duke. Stephen's swift move fatally weakened Matilda's cause, for her cousin was now a duly crowned and anointed king, with the support of the Church. There has been considerable controversy about Stephen's seizure of the crown, but in many ways, there was nothing unusual about the succession in 1135. The previous four kings had all secured the throne against a potential or actual rival; the rules of succession were not fixed at this point and early mortality often wrecked succession plans. The precedent for an ambitious, quick-thinking man to win the throne was set in 1100, when Henry I took advantage of William Rufus' demise in a hunting accident in the New Forest. Stephen merely shadowed his uncle's path to power thirty-five years earlier. He was a grandson of the Conqueror, nephew of the previous two kings and a strong candidate in 1135. Certainly, he was considered a viable option. He could not have secured coronation otherwise.

The fact that he was a man also helped enormously. While kings' wives were perfectly acceptable as regents, queens regnant were a strange and unwelcome concept in the twelfth century. Where Stephen was vulnerable was the charge of perjury, for he had sworn to uphold Matilda's succession, and chroniclers did not hesitate to raise this issue once his reign had gone wrong, nor was Matilda shy to use the charge in attacking Stephen as unfit to rule. In 1135, while the possibility of his success remained, the barons largely quieted their consciences. The fact that the Archbishop of Canterbury crowned Stephen, despite himself having sworn the oath, gave a steer to others. Later would come the justifications to explain why they had broken their oaths to Matilda, with claims that these had been extracted under duress. Some chroniclers record that on his deathbed Henry I released his subjects from their oaths to Matilda, although others assert that he reiterated his support for his daughter. The oath would become part of the propaganda war later. For now, support for Stephen was pragmatic, a calculated gamble on the man in possession of crown and treasury.

Although in retrospect his reign looks like a see-saw struggle with Matilda, this was not necessarily inevitable at the start. Some initial turbulence was predictable; both William II and Henry I had faced opposition in their earliest years before enjoying largely peaceful reigns. There were signs of future problems with uprisings in Wales. The king had to march north quickly to deal with a Scottish threat to the northern counties, resolved in a treaty with the Scots at Durham. By Easter 1136, however, Stephen had the advantage of explicit papal support from Innocent II and in return had granted the Church its liberties. Nearly all the barons had reconciled themselves to his *fait accompli* and sworn allegiance. The main exception was Baldwin de Redvers, a supporter of Matilda who held Exeter Castle against the king and forced him into a three-month siege that summer. When the water ran out and the garrison was forced to come to terms, Stephen allowed them to depart unpunished, Baldwin heading to the Isle of Wight to cause more problems. The chroniclers were stunned. In his defence, this was not an unprecedented action, as Henry I had also allowed enemies to depart with honour after a siege. However, Henry had been firmly established on the throne. In Stephen's case, while it may have avoided bloodletting so early in the reign, it hardly gave anyone 'fear of the king, who should be as a roaring lion'.[2] Many probably had a considerably less intimidating beast than a lion in mind. While his actions look humane to us, by twelfth-century standards they made the king appear weak.

In 1137, Stephen made his only visit to Normandy as duke, spending the better part of the year there. Matilda's husband, Geoffrey of Anjou, was trying to take control of Normandy. Making little headway, he agreed a truce and Stephen crossed back to England, never to return. There had been challenges and with hindsight we can see the beginnings of the far greater crisis about to unfold, but as 1138 began Stephen could feel relatively optimistic. In the new year he rushed to deal with David I of Scotland, who was repeatedly harrying and invading the northern part of the realm. Stephen launched a retaliatory raid into Scotland. Later in 1138, the Archbishop of York would rally the northern troops and defeat the Scots at the Battle of the Standard, fought near Northallerton on 22 August. The resulting second

Treaty of Durham (1139) has been criticised by historians as conceding too much, but it can be defended (as it was by northern chroniclers) as a sensible response which secured the northern border.

More ominously in 1138, Henry I's illegitimate son, Robert of Gloucester, declared for his half-sister, the empress. Exactly why he chose this moment is unclear, but his defection emboldened others who had only superficially made their peace with the regime to defy Stephen. For most of the summer, the king appeared to be relentlessly dashing around firefighting, with his most notable failure being the inability to capture Bristol, Robert's base. Yet what appears to be wild hurtling around, reacting to events, can and has been justified as sound strategy. He managed to recapture Hereford and Shrewsbury from the rebels. In the former case, the garrison once more went unpunished, but in the latter the king's patience had run out and he displayed atypical severity by ordering the execution of the entire castle garrison. By the standards of the time, he was within his rights to take such action against those who had defied him and contemporaries welcomed this display of firmness. Other fortresses in the area surrendered rapidly thereafter. Meanwhile, over in Kent, a blockade by Stephen's queen helped bring rebel-held Dover Castle into submission. Towards the end of the year, Stephen created several new earls, almost doubling their number in England, perhaps to help him keep order in the localities.

In 1139, the civil war between the forces of Stephen and Matilda began in earnest. Before the autumn, Stephen had arguably been having a reasonable year, regaining castles like Ludlow, so only pockets of resistance like Bristol remained. A verdict in the papal court confirmed the Pope's support for Stephen's entitlement to the crown. The king had even survived a domestic clash with the Church, when he had arrested Bishops Roger of Salisbury (the face of Henry I's administration) and Alexander of Lincoln at a council in Oxford in June, with Bishop Nigel of Ely escaping to hide out in Devizes Castle before yielding. At issue was the question of their powerful castles, which the king forced them to surrender. Stephen's brother, Bishop Henry of Winchester, had been sorely disappointed not to become Archbishop of Canterbury but had been compensated by being named papal legate, effectively the highest ecclesiastical authority in England. He used this power to summon a council, either to hold his brother to account for his treatment of the bishops or allow him to prove his case, at which the king's representatives skilfully argued that there was no canon law justification for bishops holding castles and Stephen was vindicated. The wisdom of provoking this breach with the Church has been questioned, but there are credible allegations about the bishops' potential treason and even some contemporaries hostile to the king thought that his actions were justified.

At the end of September, though, Robert of Gloucester and Matilda landed in Sussex and sought safety in Arundel with Henry I's (remarried) widow, Adeliza. Stephen was besieging Baldwin de Redvers in Corfe Castle, but immediately dashed to Arundel. While Robert managed to escape to the West Country, Matilda was trapped. However, possibly acting on advice from his brother Henry, Stephen granted her a safe conduct and an escort to join Robert in Bristol. Some contemporaries were appalled, although others endorsed Stephen's action. Several modern historians have agreed that his decision, while problematic, was the most sensible, given the demands of behaviour towards a woman and the offence against Queen Adeliza any capture of someone in her protection would have entailed. Yet if the decision was the right one in the circumstances, it also made life much harder for the king.

With the empress now among them in person, certain Welsh and West Country lords defected to her cause, notably Miles of Gloucester and Brian fitz Count. Stephen laid siege to Wallingford, a critical location in the Thames Valley which was to be a perpetual problem for him, and recaptured Malmesbury and Trowbridge, but in early November the war turned ugly with the sack of Worcester by men from Gloucester. Forewarned, the citizens had taken refuge in the cathedral, where in the evocative image of the local chronicler 'the clergy chanted in the choir, children screamed in the nave; the cries of screaming babies and the grieving of their mothers gave the response to those singing the office'.[3] The local rivalries beneath the surface of the national conflict emerged as the citizens of Worcester blamed their commercial rivals in Gloucester, where the empress had her headquarters. The following year, the manor lands of Tewkesbury would be burned in retaliation. Personal feuds and local disputes played as much of a role as grand national ideologies about who should wear the crown.

After Christmas at Salisbury, Stephen headed into an 1140 where he was never still. 'To say where he was at Christmas or at Easter, is of no importance', opined Henry of Huntingdon, since 'there was no peace in the realm, but through murder, burning, and pillage everything was being destroyed, everywhere the sound of war, with lamentation and terror.'[4] Stephen's itinerary seems bewildering and breathless, as he criss-crossed the realm trying to quench the fires of revolt. We find him in Cambridgeshire, then Cornwall, then Gloucestershire, then Suffolk. If the South West and southern parts of the Welsh border remained the heart of the rebel cause, other parts of the country were not immune from trouble. Nottingham fell to

Robert of Gloucester in the autumn and was burned. It was not all doom and gloom. The empress' cause was hardly inspiring mass defections and in the late summer peace talks took place at Bath with Stephen represented by his queen and Archbishop Theobald of Canterbury. When these broke down, war resumed, the stage now set for the most dramatic year of Stephen's reign, 1141.

Towards the end of 1140, Earl Ranulf of Chester and his half-brother William de Roumare seized Lincoln Castle. Ranulf had been displeased by the second Treaty of Durham, which had denied him lands that he coveted, such as Carlisle, and so he became a major opponent of the king. When an embassy arrived from the citizens of Lincoln, complaining about their treatment by the brothers, Stephen travelled quickly from London to besiege the fortress. Ranulf escaped and sent word to Robert of Gloucester, the two men then marching on Lincoln with an army. On the morning of 2 February 1141, the feast of Candlemas, the king's candle broke and extinguished during the cathedral service, a very bad omen (at least in hindsight) to contemporaries. When the two sides met in battle later in the day, Stephen fought with great bravery, unlike his earls who fled, but was eventually captured. He was marched back to Gloucester and thence imprisonment in Bristol. Fortune (or God, for contemporary chroniclers) now seemed to have abandoned Stephen and be smiling on Matilda. It must have seemed as though she had won and peace would follow, a welcome prospect in parts of the realm afflicted by violence and disorder. Fortune (or God) had other ideas. By the end of the year, the positions of the cousins would be reversed.

By March, Matilda had received the homage of Bishop Henry of Winchester. Other bishops, including the Archbishop of Canterbury, proved less amenable than the king's own brother and sought permission to see Stephen in Bristol. There, with a graciousness which reveals much about his character but has left many commentators bewildered, the king gave them leave to swear allegiance to the empress. Secular lords proved less willing to change sides and come to her, while plenty of castles held out for the king. Matilda held court in the old royal centre of Winchester, where she adopted the style 'lady of the English', but she still needed to be crowned to confirm her triumph. When Geoffrey de Mandeville, the Earl of Essex and Constable of the Tower of London, switched to her side, the reluctant Londoners yielded and submitted to her. She moved to London in preparation for her coronation, but once there managed to throw away her advantage as the crown was within her grasp, alienating the Londoners through haughty behaviour towards them. London remembered the affable Stephen with fondness from his time as Count of Boulogne, when he had close trading links with the city, and many of its citizens remained Stephen's men at heart. Queen Matilda, Stephen's resolute wife, moved towards London with an army from Kent. At this, the Londoners took heart and on 24 June chased the empress and her followers from a banquet at Westminster, forcing them to retreat to Oxford. Whether Matilda's coronation would have been a final resolution is debatable, as there would still have been the problem of what to do with the other anointed sovereign in Bristol; unlike later in the Middle Ages, murdering him was not a viable option. Undoubtedly, however, a coronation would have made her position far stronger.

As she regrouped at Oxford, Matilda still had the upper hand, handing out titles and lands to shore up her support. Leading men continued to declare for her. She also had the support of her maternal uncle King David of Scotland, who actively supported her cause and was present to fight for her. However, one conspicuous absentee from Oxford was the Bishop of Winchester. Henry had skulked back to his cathedral city and by a somewhat opaque process in coming weeks, negotiated with the queen to change sides again. The empress marched on Winchester and by the second half of August, was besieging the bishop in his recently strengthened castle of Wolvesey. The queen then moved to Winchester and besieged the besiegers. In the resulting standoff, Winchester suffered considerable damage. In September, a force loyal to the king began moving on Winchester, burning Andover on the way. At risk of being cut off from safety in their West Country heartland, the empress' party hastily made their escape. Matilda reached Devizes safely, while King David managed to bribe his way out of capture three times on the retreat.

Robert of Gloucester was not so lucky and found himself a prisoner. He had a few weeks to reflect in captivity at Rochester, but in November, Stephen and Robert were exchanged. While an earl for a king might seem an unequal swap, Robert was simply too vital to the empress' cause to be allowed to remain in prison, since he provided the military support and leadership on which her struggle depended. The king was free and many of Matilda's new converts melted away. In some ways, it was almost as though the previous nine months had never happened, although key centres like Oxford remained in the empress' hands. Crucially, Stephen's focus on England meant he essentially abandoned Normandy, which Geoffrey of Anjou patiently conquered in stages until he took Rouen and was proclaimed duke in 1144, although the fact this process took several years shows that the Normans hardly flocked happily to his cause.

The king and queen had a resplendent Christmas court at Canterbury in 1141, but thereafter the effects of Stephen's captivity seemed to catch up with him. The first half of 1142 was quiet and the king disappears from view until Easter, although Nottingham was regained for his cause. In April, he was at York, but then he fell ill at Northampton. Only from the later part of the summer did he find a renewed energy. That autumn, he took Wareham and Cirencester before besieging Oxford. Matilda was trapped with a small force there and it was a measure of her weakness that no army came to rescue her. Instead, in the December snow, she escaped from the castle across the frozen Thames, camouflaged in white. Stephen regained Oxford, and Matilda's hopes of being queen were dead. Yet the fight continued. In 1143, Stephen tried to press home his advantage by taking the war into enemy territory. On 1 July, Robert of Gloucester surprised him at Wilton, and the king and his brother Henry had to escape. It was less dramatic, though scarcely less humiliating, than Matilda's escape from Oxford a few months earlier.

After Wilton, neither Stephen nor Matilda was able to make much headway. In September 1143, Stephen arrested Geoffrey de Mandeville and demanded his castles. When he surrendered them and was released, Geoffrey plundered Cambridge and seized the monasteries at Ely and Ramsey. Using these as his base, he spent much of 1144 in a guerrilla campaign in the Fens, until he died, excommunicate, from an infected wound in September. Yet Geoffrey was not fighting for Matilda. His cause was his own survival. This was the problem the two protagonists faced by 1144: the barons were weary of the struggle and increasingly unwilling to take up arms to perpetuate it. Matilda's exhausted side lacked the strength to take the fight to the king. Equally, he was unable to make any inroads into her West Country heartland. There followed three desultory years, with neither side really advancing. Stephen did successfully reclaim Faringdon in a siege in 1145, relieving pressure on Oxford. Late in the year, he had a propaganda coup when Robert of Gloucester's son Philip defected to his cause. This brought about further unsuccessful peace talks in 1146. In what was becoming something of a habit, Stephen arrested Earl Ranulf of Chester, demanding that he return all the royal castles he had seized. Naturally, Ranulf rebelled once he was set at liberty, although he was unable to take his most coveted prize: Lincoln.

In early 1147, Matilda's son Henry came back to England, although his unsuccessful trip is notable mainly for the story that Stephen paid off Henry's mercenaries for him so he could go back across the Channel. That summer, Robert of Gloucester launched one last campaign, targeting Hampshire, which fizzled out pathetically. In the autumn, Robert died. With him died Matilda's cause. Isolated in Devizes, the empress stayed just four more months in England. She and her husband had long been fighting separate wars; Geoffrey never showed the slightest inclination to travel to England to fight for his wife's crown. In February 1148, Matilda finally conceded defeat in her own bid for the English throne and sailed for Normandy, never to return. Her ambitions were instead invested in her son, Henry. The crown was Stephen's; from now on, this was a war for the succession, Henry backed by those of his mother's supporters who had been too zealous in her cause to be able to make their peace with Stephen. The civil war had become a question of whether Stephen's crown would pass to his son, Eustace of Blois, or Matilda's, Henry of Anjou.

In England, the king fell out with his Archbishop of Canterbury. Theobald went into exile in April and in September, England was placed under interdict, a sanction imposed by the Pope which banned nearly all Church services. The penalty had almost no impact because few of the English bishops had any desire to enforce it. Within weeks, Stephen and Theobald had made their peace, the archbishop even consecrating the first abbot of the king's new monastery at Faversham. Beyond this, little happened in the civil war in 1148 beyond inconsequential skirmishing. In 1149, Henry of Anjou returned to England and the 16-year-old was knighted by his great uncle, King David of Scotland, at Carlisle. Cumberland and the area north of the River Tees had effectively been absorbed into the Scottish orbit in recent years and with Stephen's troubles in the south, there had been all sorts of drama around the archbishopric of York and the bishopric of Durham.[5] Stephen travelled to York to head off a possible threat by David. Henry returned to the West Country, where Stephen and his son Eustace unsuccessfully tried to engage him in combat for some time, although one or other also had to deal with problems in the Midlands and East Anglia. When Henry returned to Normandy at the start of 1150, little had changed in England. In Normandy, however, Geoffrey resigned the ducal title to Henry. At some point around this time, Stephen attempted to have Eustace crowned as his successor, a practice familiar in France but unknown in England. Yet Pope Eugenius III inclined towards the Angevins (Matilda's party, named after her husband's duchy of Anjou) and refused permission, so the English bishops more than once declined to crown Eustace. It was a disappointed Eustace who crossed to France to ally himself with King Louis VII and make war on Normandy in vain.

The war had ground into a tedious stalemate because few of the barons were willing to fight for either protagonist. Several earls had made agreements among themselves to preserve peace locally. What conflict did take place was largely for personal advancement. In 1150 and 1151,

England was fairly quiet, Stephen's main action in both years being against Worcester. The first year, he plundered the city and set it ablaze. In the second, he began a siege of the castle, but left it to others to bring about a successful conclusion. In 1152, he was widowed, losing in his wife a great support and ardent warrior for his cause. Otherwise, it was a fairly dismal year of campaigning in which he captured Newbury but failed yet again to take Wallingford. Duke Henry was faring much better. His father died in 1151, leaving him Count of Anjou as well as Duke of Normandy. In May 1152, he married Eleanor of Aquitaine, just weeks after her marriage to Louis VII had been annulled. Louis was both furious and threatened, for the new Duke of Aquitaine now controlled far more of France than did the king of France, with Henry's territory stretching from the Pyrenees to the English Channel. Henry repelled further military action from Louis and by the start of 1153, was ready to resume the struggle for the English crown, crossing back to England.

In the first half of 1153, Henry made gains, but his progress was slow and nobles hardly rushed to support him. The weariness most felt about this endless conflict was shown graphically at Malmesbury in January and Wallingford in August, when chroniclers suggest that the royal and ducal armies simply refused to fight one another. A decisive victory seemed to lie beyond the grasp of either Stephen or Henry. One chronicler has a wonderful image of an instance when the two rivals sat alone on either side of a stream, complaining to each other about their respective troops. It was the Grim Reaper who intervened to help the cause of peace. In recent years he had claimed a succession of the protagonists of the time, some of whom may well have proved an obstacle to the eventual peace settlement. It was the death of the king's eldest son Eustace in August 1153 which was the most critical, for without his heir Stephen's main reason to keep fighting had vanished; his younger son William neither expected nor wanted the throne. At Winchester in November, peace terms were thrashed out. By this agreement, Stephen was to remain king for the rest of his life, then be succeeded by Henry, whom he adopted as his heir. The two spent Christmas together and after some slightly tense ceremonial appearances in early 1154 to prove that the civil war was definitely over, Henry returned to Normandy. For the first time in fifteen years, Stephen could rule as king of all England, yet he was able to enjoy his unchallenged kingship for only a few months. He fell sick at Dover, where he died on 25 October 1154.

There was no question about the succession and nearly two months elapsed between Stephen's death and Henry II's coronation. When Henry I had been laid to rest at Reading with pomp appropriate to a king, his successor had attended and acted as a pallbearer. Stephen received none of the ceremony granted to his uncle. He was taken to Faversham to be buried with his wife and son, but interment of the old king's corpse was scarcely noticed. Everyone was far more interested in the dynamic, youthful Henry II and the hopes he brought of a better, more peaceful future. Once Stephen lay in his grave, he could be conveniently written out of the official story. Even in death, he was not allowed to rest in peace. At the Reformation, Faversham Abbey was destroyed, his bones dug up and cast into a ditch.

Stephen through the Centuries

Modern views of Stephen have been heavily influenced by the Peterborough monk and his nineteen years of sleeping angels, even though his chronicle is brief, confused and far from the most valuable source for the reign. The author's argument that the reign was 'all strife and evil and robbery because the powerful men who were traitors immediately rose against him [Stephen]' has been equally influential, along with the picture of a land where barons built castles and used them as centres for robbery and 'unspeakable tortures' (so unspeakable that the writer describes them in detail). Yet while the reign is portrayed as an iniquitous time of suffering and godless misery, it was paradoxically a time when Peterborough flourished. Stephen himself is described as 'a mild man, gentle and good'. It is the barons who are held accountable for the horrors of these years, not the king.[6]

Henry of Huntingdon is a far more valuable source. From the outset, Stephen is described as 'a man of great valour and boldness'. More than once, Henry calls Stephen 'energetic', although at the siege of Worcester in 1151 this comes with a barbed qualifier: 'it was the king's habit to begin many things energetically but follow them up slothfully'. His great sin was reneging on his oath to support Matilda's succession and 'trying God's patience by seizing the crown of the kingdom'. The disasters of his reign were symbols of divine judgement; Stephen had acknowledged virtues but paid the price for his sins. However, Henry's narrative sums up 'a troubled and unfortunate reign of nearly nineteen years', far from the Peterborough tale of unremitting woe. While Stephen is criticised, Henry did not appear to like anyone very much, Matilda receiving a particularly savage review for her behaviour in 1141. Stephen may not have been a good king, but everyone else (including, with little appreciation of the irony, the very woman Stephen is attacked for supplanting) would have been worse.[7]

Although he wrote only about the first few years of the reign, William of Malmesbury was in his own opinion the finest historian since Bede. His *Historia Novella* was commissioned by Robert of Gloucester, which obviously coloured the work. Yet his lively text does not paint a stark picture of utter carnage. William does not deny the troubled state of things, stating in one of his more famous passages that 'there were many castles all over England, each defending its own district or, to be more truthful, plundering it'. Although Stephen obviously compares unfavourably to Robert and is accused of such things as succumbing to the 'poison of malice', William's view of the king is ambivalent rather than resolutely hostile:

> He was a man of energy but lacking judgement, active in war, of extraordinary spirit in undertaking difficult tasks, lenient to his enemies and easily appeased, courteous to all; though you admired his kindness in promising, still you felt his words lacked truth and his promises fulfilment.

William notes Stephen's affability, which made him popular, and attributes certain things to bad advice. The king may have been the enemy, but he is not depicted as evil incarnate. William's portrait, for all its limitations, is a nuanced one.[8]

Only one contemporary was unambiguously pro-Stephen: the *Gesta Stephani* (*Deeds of Stephen*), probably written by someone in the circle of the Bishop of Bath and Wells. Easily the most sympathetic chronicle until 1147–48, it thereafter attaches increasingly to Henry's cause. The *Gesta* has several regrettable lacunae, but its enormous value is the much more positive gloss it places on many events than other chronicles. It generally endorses Stephen's actions, even amid graphic tales of violence and disruption, which are the fault of others. The author provides some memorable images, not least when discussing Stephen's problems: 'it was like what we read of the fabled hydra of Hercules; when one head was cut off, two more grew in its place'.[9] Here is a salutary reminder that not all chroniclers saw the king as an abject failure; whatever else might be said about him, Stephen continued to inspire loyalty.

This selection from the chronicles shows that from the very start, there was disagreement about the nature and extent of the troubles in Stephen's reign. The struggle the chroniclers faced was trying to make sense of what God was up to and why he seemed arbitrarily to favour first one side and then the other. These were men who 'took sides, and clearly felt that a moral stance was not only appropriate, but also necessary'. It is important to note,

13

as those who take the chronicles at face value do not always, that their tales of woe are 'part of a wider European historiographical tradition, which deployed a specific terminology and imagery'.[10] The context is vital. Stephen is condemned by many for various decisions, yet for all their criticisms, contemporaries were also prepared to recognise qualities in him personally, including those necessary for kingship and, above all, bravery. Such diverse views are at the root of a historical debate which has never been resolved.

Henry II did his best to obliterate his predecessor's reign from the historical record, portraying himself as the successor of his grandfather. There was a good deal of propaganda involved here. Like all the best propagandists, Henry harked back to a golden age which was returning with his rise to power. Yet Stephen could not be so easily erased from history and the words of the chroniclers would be adapted and repeated in histories of the later Middle Ages. There would be bizarre embellishments as well, not least one found in the St Albans Chronicle, where in 1153 Matilda begs Stephen and Henry in turn not to fight as they are father and son, Henry the product of a liaison between Stephen and Matilda. Marjorie Chibnall has shown how this myth likely arose from Stephen's adoption of Henry as his heir at Winchester,[11] but the tale continued to circulate in later centuries and was taken up in modern times by novelists. From early on, the story was adaptable. Curiously, there was little comment on Stephen personally. In his immense *Polychronicon*, Ranulf Higden simply notes that Stephen was 'an active and daring man; but was crowned against his oath that he had sworn to the empress',[12] then tells the story of the reign, neither starting nor ending with a character assessment.

Stephen found no Tudor playwright to give him fame by rendering his story as dramatic entertainment (although in a later era, Keats would begin and leave unfinished just such a work). Yet the Tudor historical portrait of him, drawing on the medieval chronicles, would last in its basic form for almost four centuries. The Italian humanist Polydore Vergil made glaring errors in writing about the reign and repeated (with a disclaimer) the story that Stephen had seduced Matilda and was Henry's real father, but his portrait was extremely influential. The sketch of Stephen found later in the century in Ralph Holinshed's *Chronicles* is an almost identical English version of Vergil's Latin one:

> He was of a comely stature, of a very good complexion, and
> of great strength of body, his qualities of mind were excellent,
> expert in war, gentle, courteous, and very liberal; for though
> he continued all his time in a manner in maintenance of the

wars, yet he levied but few tributes, or almost none at all. […] Vices with which he should be noted I find none, but that upon an ambitious desire to reign, he broke his oath which he made unto the Empress Maude.[13]

Here are the virtues and the vice (usurpation) which formed the outline of character sketches of the king until Victorian times. It became the accepted portrait of the king, as found in Samuel Daniel, writing under James I:

> We never saw but a glance of him, which yet, for the most part, was such, as shewed him to be a very worthy Prince for the Government. He kept his word with the State concerning the relievements of Tributes, and never had subsidy that we find.
>
> But which is more remarkable, having his Sword continually out, and so many defections and rebellions against him, He never put any great Man to death. Besides it is noted, that not withstanding these miseries of War, That there were more Abbeys built in his Reign, than in an hundred years before, which shews, though the times were bad, they were not impious.[14]

After the bloodshed of the Tudor century, Stephen's clemency must have seemed remarkable. Even David Hume, writing in the eighteenth century what became a standard history for over a hundred years, echoed the now familiar view:

> England suffered great miseries during the reign of this prince; but his personal character, allowing for the temerity and injustice of his usurpation, appears not liable to any great exception; and he seems to have been well qualified, had he succeeded by a just title, to have promoted the happiness and prosperity of his subjects. He was possessed of industry, activity and courage to a great degree; though not endowed with a sound judgement, he was not deficient in abilities; he had the talent of gaining men's affections; and, notwithstanding his precarious situation, he never indulged himself in the exercise of any cruelty or revenge.[15]

From Vergil until late in the nineteenth century, this was the general opinion of Stephen: brave, merciful, able and likeable, but fatally damaged by his usurpation of the throne. There was little deviation from the portrait of his reign as a time of trouble and discord, with the preponderance of castles forming part of every commentary. However, the term which was to have such an impact and cause such debate in the twentieth century – 'anarchy' – slipped quietly into the discussion in the 1720s, little heralded at the time:

> The whole kingdom was divided, every city, county, and person siding with the king or the empress, according as they were swayed by passion or interest. The lords, nearest in neighbourhood and blood, fell upon one another in a cruel manner, burning the houses, and pillaging the vassals of each other, so that a terrible confusion was quickly spread over the whole kingdom. In this fatal anarchy, the barons, acting as sovereigns, graciously oppressed the people.[16]

This view would be taken up again some 150 years later, as attitudes towards Stephen changed with the new generation of constitutional historians. These moved away from the predominating view that Stephen usurped the throne to take the more practical view that it was up for grabs in 1135, but their reverence was for kings seen to have overseen an efficient bureaucracy and advanced administrative structures. Stephen never stood a chance, for constitutional historians viewed his reign as a time when the ultimate sin occurred: central authority failed and institutions collapsed. Slaughter and destruction were pardonable, a lack of government records was not. William Stubbs' verdict on Stephen was relatively benign: 'He was a brave man, merciful and generous, and had had considerable military experience; but he was gifted with neither a strong nor a clear head, and from the beginning of his reign neither felt nor inspired confidence'. The main disaster was the arrest in 1139 of the bishops who ran the government Stubbs so admired. Since, for Stubbs, the 'administrative machinery' ceased to function, the reign was presented as a time of anarchy. Stephen, however, was not blamed. The great villains of the piece were the barons, who 'were in earnest for their own interests'.[17]

Detailed modern study of the reign began with Stubbs' former student, J.H. Round, and his enormously influential 1892 book *Geoffrey de Mandeville*. Round had recently been the first to write about a capitalised 'Anarchy'. Although declaring that 'Stephen, as a king, was an admitted failure', Round fairly observed that 'Stephen's disadvantages were great, and that had he enjoyed better fortune, we might have heard less of his defects'. Round dissented from his mentor's belief that administrative machinery collapsed under Stephen. Nevertheless, Henry II's accession was welcomed because 'the evils of an enfeebled administration and of feudalism run mad had made all men eager for the advent of a strong king, and had prepared them to welcome the introduction of his centralising administrative reforms'. Here was Round's critique of the reign in distilled form: a weak king led to a feudal reaction which caused anarchy in the form of decentralised power. Feudalism and anarchy were inextricably linked. One can search the book in vain for an explanation of what exactly Round believed feudalism to be, but it is crystal clear that it is a bad thing. Mandeville was the evil baron *par excellence*, exploiting this feudal anarchy for his own selfish purposes.[18]

One other piece from this period which caused lasting damage to Stephen's reputation was an article by H.W.C. Davis, 'The Anarchy of Stephen's Reign'. The very title shows that 'the Anarchy' had become an accepted fact. Davis looked at the 1156 pipe roll (the central record of sheriffs' accounts), the first to survive since 1130, and the figures for Danegeld (a type of tax). These entries contained a category labelled 'waste', which Davis interpreted as showing the economic devastation caused in each county. As a result, he argued that there had been significant disruption in the Midlands especially, including in counties not otherwise known to have suffered badly. His arguments went unchallenged for almost eighty years, but from the 1980s a lively and still unresolved debate began over whether 'waste' should be interpreted as an administrative write-off rather than a reflection of conditions in Stephen's reign.[19]

The extent to which Round and Davis had become orthodox by the 1930s is demonstrated in the satirical retelling of *1066 and All That*:

> Stephen and Matilda (or Maud) spent the reign escaping from each other over the snow in nightgowns while 'God and His Angels slept'.
>
> Taking advantage of this lax state of affairs, the Barons built a surfeit of romantic castles, into which they lured everybody and then put them to the torture; nor is it recorded that the Sword was once sheathed, right to the bottom, during the whole of this dreadful reign.[20]

General textbooks echoed this consensus. Worse, Stephen had gradually become 'simple-minded' by the mid-twentieth century.[21] This is a particularly insidious consequence of the belief in 'anarchy' and government collapse. Historians and writers began to assume that these could not happen under an intelligent man, so decided Stephen cannot have been intelligent, evidence to the contrary notwithstanding. As late as the 1950s, Winston Churchill's Stephen was an entirely conventional late Victorian portrait, hardly surprising from the pen of a conventional late Victorian.

Yet like attitudes towards Churchill's beloved empire, views on King Stephen and his reign were undergoing a process of change and since the 1960s the king's reputation has ebbed and flowed as much as the struggle between him and Matilda. The first modern biography of Stephen, by R.H.C. Davis (son of H.W.C.), appeared in 1967. Davis is intensely critical of Stephen personally, summing him up as 'a man of great activity but little judgement' who was 'easily pleased with the appearance of success'. There was 'a strand of shiftiness in Stephen's character' because 'beneath the surface he was mistrustful and sly', master of a 'special technique of the contrived quarrel at court leading to a disingenuously sudden arrest' which characterised 'a king who would not keep his word'. As well as having little regard for his character, Davis had scant esteem for Stephen's administrative competence. He criticises the king for profligacy and dismissively notes without evidence that 'Stephen probably found the intricacies of chancery and exchequer so much double-Dutch'. Stress is laid on the level of destruction and the impact on royal revenues. Stephen's acts as king are generally seen as mistakes, especially in the early years (chapter three is titled 'Mistakes, 1136–1139'). King Stephen emerges not as an unfortunate victim of circumstances, but as one whose character defects and consistent inability to do the right thing were a direct cause of the descent into strife. It is a harsh, unfair portrait which sits uneasily alongside Stephen's obvious virtues. On the other hand, the barons emerge with their reputations partially redeemed. Davis radically reinterpreted their role in the reign, arguing that far from being the cause of the strife, they provided the solution by forcing the protagonists to come to a settlement.[22]

Two further studies quickly followed. Unsurprisingly, that by H.A. Cronne (1970) did not deviate hugely from the views of Davis; the two had worked together on printed editions of the sources and were colleagues at Birmingham. Oddly, for a volume with the subtitle 'anarchy in England', it is argued almost at the outset that anarchy is an inappropriate term and that government survived 'very severely tried, but nevertheless in some sort of working order'. Although there is much agreement with Davis, Cronne is unwilling to go as far in denigrating the king's character, observing that 'Stephen has never really ranked with the bad kings, the tyrannical and the infamous, for nature had not cast him for such a rôle'. In what may be seen as damning with faint praise, Cronne judges that 'Stephen hardly qualifies for inclusion in that select list of rulers who [...] exhibited ineptitude as monumental as it was varied; his talents did not extend to the larger lunacy.' He does flatly contradict Davis by noting that Stephen 'must have known something about the elaborate and relatively advanced financial machinery controlled by the exchequer'. Ultimately, however, Cronne is willing to go only so far in the cause of Stephen's redemption, deeming it 'right that Stephen should stand to judgement'. If he is less cruel than Davis and more willing to see some good, the verdict is still a condemnation: 'Weak men in politics are frequently far more dangerous than wicked ones.'[23]

John T. Appleby (1969) painted a rather different picture. He saw the refusal of the bishops in 1139 to surrender their castles as treasonous and Stephen as being within his rights to respond as he did, even if 'he might have used less spectacular methods'. The successful siege of Faringdon in 1145, barely mentioned by Davis, is here 'the greatest triumph of Stephen's career'. By 1147, the king 'had shown himself to be resourceful, courageous, and daring, and no mere weakling could have brought himself from Stephen's abject position after his defeat at Lincoln in 1141 to the height of power that he had reached by 1147', when 'the country was at peace, although it was a precarious peace at best, and there was no open challenge to his position in England.' This seems rather excessive, given that a fair chunk of his kingdom was out of his control. In conclusion, Appleby cautions that 'one should consider the alternatives to his rule' and that in those terms, Stephen 'made a better king than anyone else could have done who had a clear title to the crown'. Suddenly, however, after a generally positive summing up, the final paragraph is something of a contradiction. 'Stephen, in spite of every advantage of birth, education and the example of his uncle, simply was not a big enough man to be king of England in 1135. Neither was anyone else.' While the core thesis is that no one could have successfully followed Henry I, all that goes before suggests a more positive view of Stephen.[24]

All three studies, to some degree, challenged the appropriateness of the term 'anarchy', but throughout the 1970s and 1980s, 'anarchy' appeared unqualified with depressing regularity in titles, even in pieces which proceeded to question the term's validity, as if the concept were now too ingrained to be abandoned. There were those, notably C. Warren Hollister (a fan and later biographer of Henry I), who made a strident case for the retention of Anarchy, capitalised and without quotation marks, as a designation for Stephen's reign. As late as 1994, an important volume of essays could appear under the title *The Anarchy of King Stephen's Reign*.[25] Meanwhile, Davis' severe views on Stephen's character and inadequacies gained acceptance, reflected in a similar portrayal in the standard biography of Henry II, where Stephen is summed up as 'both ordinary and complex'.[26] Stephen had gone from being a basically admirable character but perjured usurper presiding over troubled times, to being a shifty character but legitimate claimant to the throne failing to control anarchy. His reputation was lower than ever.

Yet it had reached its nadir. This damning portrait was gradually questioned, until by the 1990s historians were ready for a new approach. Matilda was the subject of a desperately needed biography by Marjorie Chibnall.[27] The empress had fared even worse than Stephen at the hands of historians and this important reassessment of the evidence redressed the balance. In 1993, Keith Stringer made a careful effort to look at Stephen more sympathetically in the context of his own times, tackling the criticisms levelled by R.H.C. Davis, the third edition of whose biography had recently appeared. Stringer argues that 'when Stephen became king he faced problems that might have broken any ruler'. The ensuing problems on multiple fronts with 'an excess of enemies' reveal 'a more complex story than the oft-told tale of incompetent war leadership'. Stringer shows that the actions so bluntly labelled 'mistakes' by Davis can be interpreted differently, as sensible policy decisions given the situation at the time. He asks sensible questions about the pressures facing Stephen, the parallels between his acts and those of other kings, and the reality within which he operated. Stringer concludes that 'King Stephen's reign was not one of genuine anarchy', but instead a 'transitional period between the Norman and Angevin supremacies, when abnormal pressures meant that England experienced momentous changes in the way it was governed'. These 'abnormal pressures' would have led to conflict whoever took the crown in 1135.[28]

Jim Bradbury likewise looked far more positively at Stephen. He notes that Henry I's 'ruthless and often harsh treatment of his leading barons had aroused far more resentment than Stephen's measures ever would', but Henry was fortunate in having no main opponent around whom such resentment could coalesce. Notably, 'Stephen did act decisively in the years before the war began, and that should not be viewed as mistaken policy, but it did provoke opposition and helps to explain the formation of the warring parties'. Like Stringer, Bradbury shows how Stephen's so-called 'mistakes' are explicable and defensible in the context of contemporary thought and practice, generally achieving their aims. The peace after the Battle of the Standard, often criticised, led to most northern English barons staying loyal to Stephen throughout the civil war. Bradbury made two especially important points often overlooked. Since the initial rebellions were in the

West Country and East Anglia before Robert of Gloucester declared for Matilda, and these were also to be the main theatres of war, we must keep in mind the possibility of other causes of discontent in these regions. Moreover, 'nearly all the major writers who provide us with our information were based in areas at the centre of the troubles […] Inevitably they described the damage which they knew about, perhaps even were inspired to write because they were in the middle of such dramatic events.' Bearing this corrective in mind, 'not only was there not anarchy, but there was a properly organised and operating government even able to make improvements on the methods of its predecessors'. If Stephen was no great success, he did as good a job as could be expected in the circumstances.[29] The work of Stringer and Bradbury together did much for Stephen's rehabilitation. An article by Björn Weiler also looked at the question of usurpation in a wider twelfth-century context, especially that of a similar case in the Empire late in the century, which was an important reminder that the circumstances of 1135 in England were by no means unique.[30]

The extent to which views of the reign had changed by the turn of the millennium was shown in major works by David Crouch, Donald Matthew and Edmund King. All three rejected the label 'anarchy': Crouch resolutely, Matthew angrily and King by not mentioning it (possibly because his introduction to the 1994 volume had endorsed the term). Crouch and King gave welcome attention to Stephen's religious life, neglected in a later twentieth century disinclined to take the Christian culture of the time seriously. Thereafter, the similarities end. Crouch and Matthew are both sympathetic to Stephen, but at times it scarcely seems that they are writing about the same king. For Crouch, a major cause of civil war, which led to localised violence and disorder but not the total collapse anarchy would entail, was the loss of confidence in Stephen's rule. Matthew, on the other hand, argues for a general acceptance of Stephen's kingship. Crouch sees that one of Stephen's core failures was his Anglocentrism and by failing to deal early and adequately with problems in Wales and Normandy, he allowed far greater trouble to develop there later. In the early years, Crouch dwells on the topic of bad advice and the 'aristocratic clique' around the king, which Matthew dismisses. Both take issue with Davis' harshness towards Stephen and look at some of the ideological considerations of the barons in the civil war. Crouch makes the crucial point that 'Stephen was not trying to preserve a constitution between 1135 and 1154, he was trying to rule a kingdom', and challenges 'the next generation of historians to start looking at Stephen and his reign more objectively'. His own opinion is fair and worth reflection: 'We find in Stephen's personal behaviour a more noble man than his royal predecessor and successor, and that perhaps is the fairest judgement that can be made upon him.'[31]

Matthew goes further, rather truculently taking issue with almost everyone who has ever written about the reign, habitually referring to previous studies and 'assumptions' without referencing or making clear which are meant. As a whole, Matthew's book provides an important challenge to some of the points about the reign which have been accepted too uncritically, and his examination of the nature of the relationship between king and barons is particularly valuable. On the other hand, the narrative is not easy to follow and his attempt to discredit the sources takes him rather too far in divorcing 'secular' and 'ecclesiastical' to an extent not plausible in the twelfth century. He makes much of the fact that the violence was localised and that the king clung on. Ultimately, Stephen's 'survival in these circumstances looks more like triumph over adversity' than failure. This seems to go too far. Stephen can be cleared of failure without being made an unrecognised success.[32] King's work is distinctly gentler, drawing on several decades of important contributions to the study of the reign. There is no question that Stephen was a failure, but while the portrait is critical, it is also fair and sympathetic. King has particular admiration for the role of Queen Matilda. Henry of Blois has a more ambiguous role, a slightly sinister presence in the background heavily influencing his royal brother. Quoting Henry of Huntingdon, whose account of Stephen before the Battle of Lincoln has him giving his lines to someone else as he 'lacked a commanding voice', King concludes his study by observing that this comment 'may stand as an image of Stephen's kingship' since he 'never made his voice heard'. It is an apt comment, too, on the biography, for Stephen's voice never emerges. He is a curious figure who is often absent or in the background, while others take centre stage in what is more a narrative of the reign than a straightforward life of the king.[33]

A decade into the twenty-first century, it seemed Stephen's fortunes might finally have changed. Historians still spoke of his 'mistakes', but even basically unsympathetic works now accepted that 'Stephen's failure was partly because of the formidable problems he inherited'.[34] His reputation was certainly on a sharply upward trajectory from its treatment at the hands of R.H.C. Davis, with historians recognising his abilities and the constraints he faced, and in one case coming close to arguing him a success. The odd populist history by a non-specialist might still speak in 2000 of 'chaos, carnage, famine, extortion; every jumped-up baron a kingling in his own shire', but this took no account of recent scholarship.[35] David I's biographer made the point that Stephen's 'Scottish campaign in February 1138 shows him to have been a skilled strategist and general who sought to inflict as much damage as possible on an elusive enemy', noting too that the Battle of the Standard could be portrayed in religious terms by the Archbishop of York because the king 'enjoyed a high reputation for personal piety'.[36] Elsewhere, it looked as though the view of the reign as a period of anarchy might at long last have been laid to rest. A 2008 book managed to include ten essays without a single mention of the word 'anarchy' in its titles; although one writer made a 'maximum case' for the level of violence, the introduction asserted firmly that 'it was not a time of anarchy'.[37] There was a greater appreciation of the regional variations and deeper analysis of Henry I's partial responsibility for the civil war. Stephen was at least receiving a fair hearing. Yet like the wheel of fortune which turned so often in Stephen's reign, the wheel of historians' interpretation turned again and this happy new consensus could not last.

Historians, unwilling to let a weary concept die and be decently buried, resuscitated the 'Anarchy'. The word 'anarchy' began to reappear in the titles and subtitles of books aimed at a popular audience, to whom the stark connotations of anarchy were likely to be far more gripping than the more accurate but hardly marketable label, 'period during which there were various times of disturbance of differing intensity in certain areas of the country'. Nevertheless, it was depressing that the terminology could continue to be used so uncritically despite half a century of challenges to its validity, especially in works which argued against a genuine 'anarchy' in the literal sense. On the other hand, there was a new biography of Matilda which addressed the question of gender in some detail and a volume of essays which looked properly at Henry of Blois in his ecclesiastical context, showing that historians were at last breaking free from the shackles of Victorian interpretations. Even Geoffrey de Mandeville, the Victorian villain incarnate, was offered redemption.[38]

The books by Carl Watkins and Matthew Lewis are admirable narratives of the reign which took full account of recent research. Watkins followed more in the tradition of R.H.C. Davis than Stephen's recent sympathisers, but by no means slavishly. Conditions are seen as anarchic in certain places at certain times, not uncritically as 'the Anarchy'. He portrays a count not up to the demands of kingship, ultimately a failure, although Watkins seeks to understand Stephen's decisions rather than dismiss them as 'mistakes'. The verdict is ambivalent, pointing towards Davis but lacking the harshness and willing to acknowledge the good: Stephen was 'gentle and mild, chivalrous and brave', but there were 'hints of darkness in his character that found expression in mistrustfulness and flashes of malevolence'.[39] Lewis' lengthier, very readable account of the reign is far more sympathetic, notable for its willingness to find the good in both Stephen and Matilda. While accepting 'the Anarchy' as 'a useful umbrella term', he views it more as 'a nineteenth-century interpretation of Stephen's reign'. Echoing Stringer, Lewis points out that Stephen faced simultaneous threats on multiple fronts, where 'many kings faced one of these threats in isolation and struggled' and many of his decisions were 'without a right answer, only a balancing of unsatisfactory choices'. Against those who criticise Stephen for his lack of ruthlessness, Lewis observes that 'a degree of mercy and certain adhesion to the rules of war were expected of any good king'. He points out that many remained loyal to Stephen and saw him as the rightful king regardless of the opposition he faced: 'Stephen was, all agreed, a likeable man, almost to a fault, lacking the killer instinct of a king.'[40]

So the wheel spins and spins. For all the daunting quantity of studies on Stephen, there is still no real consensus on anything apart from his personal bravery. Was it a period of anarchy and unusual violence or not? Was Stephen a weak king or not? Were his choices mistakes or sensible policy decisions? Were the barons rapacious local tyrants or agents of eventual peace? Did government collapse or continue? Entirely opposing answers to all those questions and many more (plus answers along the spectrum in between) can be found, all supported by the same evidence. Who was King Stephen and did he fail? One could read every history book about him and Matilda, and still it may well feel as though that question remains unanswered. That is why historians persist in what sometimes feels a distinctly quixotic venture. In passing, however, it may be observed that Stephen has possibly attracted no ardent defenders because, paradoxically, he comes across as too nice; there are no murdered nephews or malign lovers in his closet. He is not enough of a lost cause to prompt the inevitable revisionism of the historians of lost causes.

Stephen in Popular Culture

Stephen has never been a major figure in popular culture, but one of the best-known series of historical fiction is set in his reign. The Brother Cadfael novels by Edith Pargeter, published under her *nom de plume* Ellis Peters between 1977 and 1994, were an immense success for the author and Shrewsbury's tourist industry.[41] Thirteen were adapted for television by ITV in the 1990s, with varying degrees of fidelity to the original plot, Derek Jacobi starring as Cadfael. The protagonist is the Welsh crusader turned Benedictine monk, Cadfael, and while he and most of the main characters are fictional, the abbots and the prior are historical names and many real figures from these years parade through the narratives. The detective stories are set against the first ten years of Stephen's reign and what the series captures, in a way that no history book can, is the atmosphere of the times. It provides a snapshot of a decade of civil war from one particular local vantage point and although the necessary liberties of the novelist are taken, Pargeter's research and grasp of the underlying history is immensely impressive. At times, eloquent asides echo the chronicles closely:

> In the five years that King Stephen and his cousin, the Empress Maud, had fought for the throne of England, fortune had swung between them like a pendulum many times, presenting the cup of victory to each in erratic turn, only to snatch it away again untasted, and offer it tantalisingly to the other contender.

The national events of this decade form a backdrop to the action. There are moments when the violence erupts directly into the story. More frequently, the impact of disruption elsewhere makes itself visible through messengers, refugees and survivors appearing in Cadfael's abbey. Sometimes, Shropshire seems tranquil and the tussle between the royal cousins barely enters the narrative, but it is always there, an ominous shadow over everything. It is in these background allusions to fear of travel, the asides about instability, the mentions of lawlessness, that the uncertainty and worry of the period is laid bare. There is, though, also a recognition of the moments of peace, the different experiences of suffering: 'this shire had gone almost untouched by the war for more than four years now, and seemed to enjoy a degree of peace and order unmatched further south'. Cadfael's Shrewsbury is no place of endless suffering, at times it seems almost normal, but the threat and terror is omnipresent in varying degrees, albeit often at a distance. This surely represents the experience of many in these years.

In this context, reflections and asides about Stephen and his character crop up frequently. There are mentions of his short attention span ('Stephen never did have the patience for a siege') and decisions which seemed to lead to failure ('there had never been such a king as Stephen for conjuring defeat out of victory'), but acceptance that on occasion he could be resolute ('for once Stephen showed no sign of abandoning his purpose'). Above all, though, Stephen is presented as a generous, essentially attractive human being, even if this results in slightly baffling characteristics for a king.

> Had Stephen been the one to capture the implacable lady, with his mad, endearing chivalry he would probably have given her

a fresh horse and an escort, and sent her safely to Gloucester, to her own stronghold, but the queen was no such magnanimous idiot.

Although he is thus a spectre glimpsed throughout the whole Cadfael series, Stephen appears in person only in the second novel, *One Corpse Too Many*, and the last, *Brother Cadfael's Penance*. *One Corpse Too Many* is based around the real events of the siege of Shrewsbury in 1138 and the execution of those who had resisted the king after the castle fell to his forces. Stephen features only in a few scenes, but his uncharacteristic ruthlessness in ordering the slaughter of the garrison is central to the novel, where the fictional protagonists' acceptance of the king's right to do this echoes that of contemporary chroniclers. When Cadfael reflects on this several books later, it is considered very much out of character, as the monk recalls his encounter with the king and that he 'liked the man, even at his ill-advised worst, when he had slaughtered the garrison of Shrewsbury castle, to regret it as long as his ebullient memory kept nudging him with the outrage'. And the image of Stephen in *One Corpse Too Many* is a plausible description of a king who has eluded his many biographers.

> Energy and lethargy, generosity and spite, shrewd action and incomprehensible inaction, would always alternate and startle in King Stephen. But somewhere within that tall, comely, simple-minded person there was a grain of nobility hidden.

Lethargy is the driving vice of the king in this novel, his flashes of rage yielding quickly 'to his more natural easiness of temperament, not to say laziness', indicative of 'his natural indolence'. This is less apparent in *Brother Cadfael's Penance*, when a fictional peace conference at Coventry and its aftermath is a means of bringing the whole glittering array of characters on stage to end the series. Here, in what may be the best one-line summary of the man yet written, is 'King Stephen, soon roused, soon placated, brave, impetuous but inconstant, a good-natured and generous man who had yet spent all the years of his reign in destructive warfare.' He is tall, commanding, and contrary to Henry of Huntingdon this Stephen has a strong, bellowing voice which can silence crowds. He is a man of his word, brave and not given to cruelty. Against him, in her only personal appearance in the series, is his cousin Matilda, who in many ways embodies the imperious, arrogant woman of the chronicles, albeit with nuances.

There is something satisfying about the fictionalised Stephen of Cadfael's world, with his contradictions and elusiveness. For all his failures and puzzling habits, he presents as a king and as a fundamentally honourable man, perhaps more real than in any history book because he is presented as human, living in the confusion of the moment rather than judged as a theory against the tidiness of hindsight. Perhaps, too, Pargeter understood something too often overlooked, as in the final novel a young man expresses horror that Matilda might hang her nephew: 'It would be to shatter the one scruple that had kept this war from being a total bloodbath, a sanction that must not be broken. Kinsman may bully, cheat, deceive, outmanoeuvre kinsman, but not kill him.'

Amid the violence, destruction and suffering there undoubtedly was, there were none of the cycles of revenge killings or executions of noblemen which would plague future civil wars. Stephen was no blood-crazed or paranoid tyrant and as early modern writers appreciated as much as the fictional Cadfael, he did not rely on the executioner's axe or murder to cow his nobility. That fact should be remembered more often.

In the footsteps of Cadfael, mystery series set in Stephen's reign abound. One by Roberta Gellis makes Magdalene, the madam of a Southwark brothel, an unlikely detective, while Sarah Hawkswood's Bradecote and Catchpole series is set in Worcestershire. Acknowledging their debt are the six volumes of the Janna Mysteries (2005–11) by Felicity Pulman. Originally aimed at young adults and rebranded for the adult market as *The Janna Chronicles* in 2015, this continuous narrative is set between 1140 and 1143. The heroine is the eponymous Janna (Johanna), with strong echoes of a secular, female, teenaged Cadfael. Like Cadfael, her skills are with herbs and healing. Unlike Cadfael, she tends to be treated unfairly, as might be expected for an orphaned, landless teenaged girl in the 1140s. The main storyline involves her quest to bring her mother's murderer to justice and find her unknown father, and for the first two books the action all takes place in Wiltshire, the struggle for the kingdom only mentioned in passing. As the series progresses, Janna finds her quest ever more entangled with the contest between the royal cousins, finding herself at Winchester during the turbulent summer of 1141, at Oxford in December 1142 and at Wilton in summer 1143.

Matilda and Stephen only make brief personal appearances, in which something of the regality of both is captured. The historical background is well researched and clever use is made of plausible plot lines away from known events. What the Janna Mysteries capture particularly well, though, is the sense of a young woman trying to make her way in a difficult world and how the violence and competing loyalties of these years impacted ordinary people. The scenes in Winchester, as the city is set ablaze in the struggle between bishop and empress and the cathedral becomes a makeshift field hospital, are especially evocative. Suspicion and doubt dominate. 'Trust no one' is an oft-repeated motto amid uncertain loyalties and strained family relationships. Although it initially seems that Janna gives her allegiance to the empress' cause for rather shallow reasons, on reflection this is a salutary reminder that the people of the time lacked the luxury of historians to argue at length over all available sources; the decisions had to be made swiftly with imperfect knowledge and instinct. In the later chapters, there are hints of the anger and frustration at those who perpetuate the fighting, and of weariness that there is no discernible end. Yet it is possible to find admirable qualities in all of the major historical protagonists.

The Pillars of the Earth (1989) was an unlikely success for Ken Follett, previously known as a writer of thrillers. It is a story on an epic scale, more than a thousand pages, covering the period 1120–74, although mainly concentrating on Stephen's reign. At the foreground of the narrative is the construction of the fictional Kingsbridge Cathedral, but numerous other stories and characters are entwined around that tale, interweaved with real characters and events. There is trouble and violence in the background, as well as impinging more directly on the main story, but against all this Philip, Kingsbridge's prior, persists with his dream of a cathedral. Whether intentionally or not, this echoes a true picture of the reign as a time when ecclesiastical building flourished. The king himself makes occasional appearances throughout the novel, a man with the demeanour of a king, affable but capable of stern regality, brave but easily distracted. It is a balanced, justifiable interpretation. In 2010, a television adaption was released. A lavish production, it made major plot changes and unlike the novel, which despite some anachronisms was basically faithful to the historical narrative, the screen version took immense liberties. In particular, the character of Stephen (played by Tony Curran) is changed dramatically, both from history and the novel. In the television version, he is considerably more malevolent, the R.H.C. Davis portrait taken to extremes, which does both Stephen and a well-crafted novel a disservice.

Other historical novels have tried to fictionalise the reign itself. Sharon Penman's *When Christ and His Saints Slept* (1994), considerably longer than any history of these years, is easily the most satisfying novelisation of the reign. Penman is scrupulous about observing the historical chronology and the basic nature of the main characters. Equally, she echoes the religious language of the chroniclers, having people dwell on the language of God's favour and punishment in a way which reflects the twelfth century more authentically than the quasi-modern mindset other novelists tend to impose on their characters. While she makes full use of the novelist's right to fill in the gaps with plausible scenarios and fictional characters, bringing the protagonists to life, she avoids changing their personalities or deeds. Unlike elsewhere, Queen Matilda is developed as a character in her own right and given a main role. Very rare in novels, there is also criticism of the empress' father's failure to prepare her to rule: 'It was not enough merely to name her as his heir. She needed guidance as much as she did a husband, and she did not get it. In a sense, we are paying now for Henry's shortsightedness.' Stephen himself is an immensely affable man who inspires friendship by his nature. His good qualities, not least his bravery, chivalry and mercy, are brought out, to the extent that one can appreciate why people might like and follow such a man. However, he is also prone to accept bad advice, to take impulsive, poor decisions, and to lack the resolution necessary for a king. It is left to his wife to understand that 'the qualities she most loved in Stephen were the very ones that were crippling his kingship'. Perhaps the approach in this novel is summed up best by a character who feels a 'sudden, sharp pang of pity for Maude, who had right on her side but little of Stephen's generosity and none of his charm'. And above all, there are glimpses beyond the power struggle, beyond theoretical questions of succession and hereditary right, into how it was the ordinary people of the realm who suffered most. It is left to the abbess of Wilton to vocalise this in 1143, in an outburst aimed at the Earl of Gloucester:

> Look around you, Robert, at what you and Stephen have brought to Wilton. What did we do to deserve this misery? You think that [a] burned-out wainwright cares whether the crown goes to Stephen or Maude? I assure you his only worry is how he is going to feed his family now that his shop has been gutted. Ask the draper in Frog Lane, his shelves plucked bare and every scrap of cloth stolen. Ask my sisters in Christ, forced to take refuge in Amesbury while God's Acre is turned into a killing ground! […] Sympathy makes a poor gruel, Robert, fills no empty stomachs. Just tell me this, in all honesty. How much longer is this accursed war to continue?[42]

Other attempts to render the reign as fiction are less convincing. An early effort is Graham Shelby's *The Villains of the Piece* (1973, US: *The Oath and the Sword*). Most of the main figures of the reign appear, although if there is a protagonist it is Brian fitz Count. He recalls a one-night stand with Matilda in

1132, which she uses to hint (falsely) to him that Brian is Henry's father; the novel plays strongly and uncomfortably on the empress' use of her sexuality. In the end, Brian stays loyal to the cause but turns savagely on Matilda herself. The novel moves swiftly from episode to episode, brief snapshots which leave the reader struggling to follow any one character but perhaps give a sense of the confused reality of the times. Stephen appears rarely, but he comes across as a weak, easily-led, affable man, prone to nightmares and tantrums. The main weakness of the novel is that none of the characters are likeable; while most of the storylines can find support in at least one chronicle, the interpretation is always the worst, so the titular villains of the piece seem to be pretty much everyone who appears in the book.

Later works try to inject a fresh perspective by falling back on a familiar theme, the love affair turned sour, drawing (consciously or otherwise) on the thirteenth-century legend of an affair between Stephen and Matilda. Examples include Ellen Jones, *The Fatal Crown* (1991), Haley Elizabeth Garwood, *The Forgotten Queen* (1998, where Matilda is more like a modern soap opera character than a twelfth-century noblewoman) and Lise Arin, *Matilda Empress* (2017). *The Fatal Crown* is as good an example as any. While the broad picture is accurate, many of the finer details are changed to make the plot work. Beyond the historical inaccuracies and occasionally cringeworthy bedroom dialogues, Jones does give life to the characters. Henry I is an unpleasant, shifty character, his breaking of his own oath to the barons over Matilda's marriage setting a context for Stephen later going back on his oath to Henry. Robert of Gloucester is an honourable character, Henry of Blois a devious, self-aggrandising one. The double standards of an age where men could commit adultery with impunity, but women were shamed for doing so, is brought out well. At the heart of the novel, though, is the affair between Maud (Matilda) and Stephen, with this adulterous liaison resulting, unbeknown to anyone but the couple, in the conception of Henry II. This causes Stephen to accept Henry (in this world, while Eustace still lives) as his heir. It is the ongoing attraction between Stephen and Maud which underpins their interactions throughout, although even within this fictional world the scene where they have sex during Stephen's imprisonment is a little ridiculous. Stephen is chivalrous, brave, kind and honourable, if easily-swayed, while Maud's complexity emerges in a world where a woman in power is treated sceptically. The main problem is that turning this into a story of attraction and sex, a version of the love to hatred theme, rings false to what we know of the characters (especially the happily married Stephen) and ignores both the conventions of the time and some of the less obvious complexities in the various relationships.

Few of the other novels set in the reign cast much light on the king, most focusing on Matilda. Novelists seem unable to resist projecting debates over Stephen's claim to the throne back a decade or so, or else making it part of some dastardly long-term plan of Henry of Blois to secure the archbishopric. The need for conspiracy theories and illicit love affairs in an already confused and breathless plot perhaps says rather more about modern historical novelists and their readers than about the twelfth century. Ultimately, the novels which have Stephen's reign as a backdrop to another plot are more satisfying than those which simply try to fictionalise the reign. Perhaps that is because those nineteen years already make such a gripping narrative. To bring something fresh to the story, the irresistible temptation is to play with the chronology or the key characters, so inevitably it ends up ringing false. That is why Cadfael and the Janna Mysteries and *The Pillars of the Earth*, where fiction and historical background can coexist and interact, are so much more vibrant and successful, for they deliver both a good story and a sense of the period. And for all the privileges of the novelists with history, for all the leanings towards Matilda, Stephen emerges far better from their pages than from those of the historians, for he is allowed to be a human being, with all the contradictions and limitations that entails.

Verdict

The real problem is that Stephen is something of an enigma, never quite coming into sharp focus in the foreground. Novelists have been rather kinder to Stephen than historians, although several more recent biographies have moved in the direction of understanding and sympathy. Stephen's alleged failings were in undertaking his office, not human ones: indecision, lack of focus and staying power, paying too much heed to advice, lacking a ruthless streak, even indolence. These may be failings in the characteristics required by a successful medieval king, but hardly great moral flaws. Although there were occasional flashes of rage, notably at Shrewsbury in 1138, they were not considered excessive by contemporaries. Stephen was never guilty of the personal cruelty of Henry I.

Part of Stephen's problem was exactly that: he lacked a cruel streak. He is a distinctly more attractive character than the 'successful' king he followed, but medieval kings had to be respected rather than liked. As one chronicler observed early in the reign, Stephen was rarely a roaring lion inspiring fear. His bravery was in no doubt. What few glimpses we have of Stephen himself suggest he was a likeable man, even if there are hints of occasional duplicity in some dealings with his earls. There were flashes of great, sometimes baffling, generosity and enormous courage, but he had no killer instinct or ruthless determination. Those qualities which historians before the twentieth century all found worth mentioning, especially his amiability and his lack of cruelty, may have been undesirable in a twelfth-century king, but make him a considerably more appealing human being to modern eyes. That is why the Stephen of Brother Cadfael's world resonates more strongly with many today than the Stephen of the historians. The greatest disservice some twentieth-century historians did to Stephen was not to highlight his alleged failings as king, but rather to try to strip from him the basic humanity which was partly the cause of his problems.

Being a fundamentally decent person was scarcely sufficient qualification alone for the role of king in the twelfth century. He was, by most accounts, a good, amiable man and a brave warrior, but did he lack the skills necessary to be a successful monarch? He was not able to deal effectively with the challenges facing someone coming to the throne in the circumstances of 1135. The chroniclers exaggerated the scale of suffering, but they certainly did not invent it. That said, we need to remember the important point that our sources were written in the epicentres of trouble, with nothing from the more peaceful zones. England was no more 'anarchic', indeed arguably less so, than during later civil wars, and by its nature any civil war involves competing authority. Was the suffering and death really so much greater than that of the civil wars in, for instance, the seventeenth century that Stephen's reign deserves such a uniquely negative designation as 'the anarchy'?

That said, if it was not an anarchic period and disruption was certainly not endless or ubiquitous, these were undoubtedly disturbed years of conflict and uncertain authority, at least in parts of England. There may be arguments over the extent of the violence and disorder, but civil war in some form overshadowed most of his time on the throne and some places did suffer terribly. Whether this level of violence and disorder was 'unusual' is subjective, depending on the point of comparison. But for almost his entire reign, Stephen was engaged in struggles of some form. If a core duty of a king was to maintain peace and order, Stephen might well be judged a failure. On the other hand, he never lost his throne and died peacefully in his bed; this civil war had no loser in the conventional sense and Matilda's loss was surely greater than Stephen's. In a reign blighted by civil war, Stephen clung on to his crown with incredible tenacity. We must also bear in mind the responsibilities of Henry I. If he is to be praised as an administrative genius, he must be held to account for a failure to ensure a peaceful succession which avoided civil war.

Does the civil war justify the reputation of King Stephen as a weak king? The worst charge against him is incompetence. He was clearly no tyrant and no one could accuse him of being evil. Yet even incompetence is hard to sustain. Contemporaries and modern historians alike recognised kingly qualities in him. He was indefatigable in his quest to secure his kingdom and his throne; he was not guilty of idleness or lack of devotion to duty. True, his judgement is certainly open to question on occasion, especially in the manner he tackled Geoffrey de Mandeville and Ranulf of Chester. Maybe being more ruthless at times would have helped, although that is far from certain. Perhaps it can be argued that his most fundamental mistake was making a bid for the crown in the first place, although that is obvious only in retrospect with the civil war that followed; had his reign worked out differently, he would have been just like Henry I, a man seizing an opportunity. Beyond that, it is hard to see what he might have done to avoid disaster given that a powerful rival to his throne existed. Would he really have had more success had he been more ruthless at Exeter, turned a blind eye to the bishops at Oxford and ignored his chivalrous instincts at Arundel? That is debatable at best. It is arguable that for the most part, Stephen played the dreadful hand he was dealt as well as he could and better than anyone else might have done. Critical historians have been too quick to condemn him on the basis of perfect theoretical approaches which show little regard for the constraints under which he operated.

Those who question whether anyone coming to the throne in 1135 could have had a successful reign surely have a point. Matilda's sex was an insurmountable issue for many contemporaries, exacerbated by her father's failure to ease her path, and the fact that she could not even secure the crown in the circumstances of 1141 is telling. Robert of Gloucester's illegitimacy was a barrier, but even without that it is hard to see that he would have been any more successful than Stephen at holding the Anglo-Norman realm together; another decent man, he had the sense to eschew any claim on the crown. Theobald of Blois is more of an unknown quantity, but he made no decisive bid for the throne in 1135 and there is no evidence to suggest he would have succeeded where his younger brother failed. It is difficult to imagine who else would have been a realistic candidate. Thus while Stephen failed if a reign of civil war is deemed a failure, he did so in circumstances where there is no obvious person who would not have failed, even if they would have done so in different ways. Whoever became monarch in 1135 would probably have been a failure to some extent and may well have been judged with even greater severity by posterity. That was Henry I's legacy.

Chapter 2

John: An Awful King?

John, John, bad King John
Shamed the throne that he sat on;
Not a scruple, not a straw,
Cared this monarch for the law;
Promises he daily broke;
None could trust a word he spoke.[1]

Too late to be known as John the First
He's sure to be known as John the Worst
A pox on that phony king of England![2]

The Confessor, the Conqueror and the Lionheart aside, the English have never really taken to giving their kings descriptive names. Only Æthelred the Unready has had the misfortune to go down in history permanently linked with a negative epithet. This aversion is fortuitous for King John, who might otherwise have found himself in a rather exclusive club with William I of Sicily, known as 'the Bad' or 'the Wicked'.

The two snippets above, from a 1930s poem and a 1970s Disney film, show that in popular culture John is a very strong contender for the worst monarch ever to wear the crown of England. In the family-friendly version, he is a cruel, weak, spiteful, avaricious tyrant. The adult version additionally has him as a serial seducer and murderer. His connection with Magna Carta means most people have heard about him, and what they remember will not be positive. Here is a man who murdered his nephew, lost Normandy and governed so badly that he was forced to concede to his barons at Runnymede. In the popular canon of English monarchy, John is the epitome of the evil king.

This has not always been the case. Strangely, there have been periods during the eight centuries since his death when the very opposite has been true: John has been a model king. In modern times, he has found his champions, largely working on the 'no one can be that bad' principle. To his detractors, he is an evil tyrant. To his defenders, he is an able administrator and defender of English liberties. Only Richard III divides opinions more strongly than John. John's reputation is dominated by Magna Carta. This document has taken on a life of its own in the English-speaking world, which has led many to portray the king's reign as an inevitable journey to Runnymede. Magna Carta, though, came sixteen years into John's seventeen-year rule. There is plenty before 1215 in an action-packed, controversial reign which contributes to John's reputation and legacy.

John's Life and Reign

John was born in Oxford, the youngest son of Henry II and Eleanor of Aquitaine. His date of birth long appeared in history books as Christmas Eve 1167, but recently historians have favoured Christmas 1166. With three living elder brothers (Henry, Richard and Geoffrey), John's inheritance prospects were uncertain, even though he was later considered his father's favourite. Following French practice to guarantee the succession, Henry was crowned king during his father's lifetime in 1170 and thereafter ruled alongside him, known as the Young King, although there was no doubt that the father remained the real sovereign. Richard later received responsibility for Aquitaine. As a child, John spent five years in the care of Fontevraud Abbey. In 1173, he was betrothed to the daughter of the Count of Savoy. Unfortunately, this provoked a revolt from Henry's other three sons.

None of the four brothers ('the Devil's brood') ever got along especially well, but Henry, Richard and Geoffrey were now encouraged by their mother and the king of France. Several nobles and the king of Scotland joined in the greatest rebellion Henry had faced, but over the next eighteen months the king vanquished the rebels one by one, until by late 1174 he was victorious. However, John's intended bride had died, so in 1176 he was betrothed to Isabella, the youngest daughter of the Earl of Gloucester. In 1177, at a council in Oxford, Henry declared John the future king of Ireland. John had also been granted various revenues. Yet for all the glittering promise of future lands and the income he enjoyed from other estates, John was still landless in the early 1180s. It was his own father, with his cruel sense of humour, who gave him a nickname which stuck: Lackland.

After the Young King's death in 1183, Henry II unsuccessfully tried to make Richard hand over Aquitaine to John. In 1185, John was sent to prove his worth in Ireland. The story of his time there is told by the unremittingly hostile Gerald of Wales, a man bitter at his lack of ecclesiastical preferment

35

under the Angevin kings. Gerald recounts how members of John's entourage insulted the Irish by pulling their long beards and portrays the visit as an expensive failure. Some modern historians are more positive about John's time in Ireland and see a mission competently accomplished; he was the first to assume the title 'lord of Ireland'. However, there were also behavioural traits which boded ill for the future, not least signs of an obsession with hostage-taking.

Geoffrey died in 1186, leaving his wife to give birth to his posthumous son, Arthur. In 1189, Richard once more revolted against his father, joining with Philip II of France (Philip Augustus) against an exhausted, sick Henry. By the summer, Henry was in real trouble and worn out. One story tells of how the list of rebels was brought to the king to be read out. The first name was John's, after which a distraught Henry refused to hear any more and died soon afterwards, at Chinon on 6 July. In the short term, his father's death brought John considerable advantages. He now married Isabella of Gloucester, bringing him the extensive lands of the Gloucester earldom in the West Country and South Wales, along with the disapproval of the Archbishop of Canterbury who saw the couple as too closely related. The new king, Richard I, also gave his brother control of several English counties, castles and honours, and created him Count of Mortain. John was Lackland no longer.

Even more promisingly, Richard was unmarried and John was in a strong position to succeed to the crown in the event of his elder brother's demise. However, even though their nephew Arthur was only two at Richard's accession, throughout the next decade (and beyond) there would be considerable debate about whether he or John had a better claim to the throne. When Richard married Berengaria of Navarre in Cyprus in 1191, it raised the possibility of John being supplanted by another nephew who would have had an almost unassailable claim to the crown. The king was only in his early thirties, so it was perfectly possible that he would live long enough for an adult son to succeed to his throne.

Richard I was determined to go on crusade. Despite the considerable grants he had made to his brother, the king clearly distrusted (or had his mind poisoned against) John. Once he had raised his crusading funds, he summoned John to Normandy in February 1190 to extract a promise that John would stay out of England while Richard was in the Holy Land. In the end, persuaded by their mother, Richard relented and John became part of the regency council under William Longchamp, chancellor, justiciar and Bishop of Ely. Things did not go well. On route to the Holy Land, in Sicily, Richard recognised Arthur as his heir for diplomatic reasons. Longchamp was arrogant and unpopular, and relations with John were strained. By 1191, there were plenty who wanted rid of Longchamp. After a spat in which Longchamp besieged Lincoln Castle, John garrisoned his castles, but peace terms were negotiated. This peace was short-lived and with precious few friends and allies, Longchamp was deposed, exiled and replaced by the Archbishop of Rouen, Walter de Coutances.

After Philip Augustus had returned ignominiously from crusade at the end of 1191, John intrigued on various fronts during 1192 to stir up trouble in England and strengthen his position. When news reached England in early 1193 of Richard's capture while travelling home, John crossed to Normandy to collude with Philip. Back in England, the government was forced to appease John as he fortified castles and his forces ravaged parts of England, although the key officials remained loyal to the king. When ransom terms were agreed between Richard and the emperor, John connived with Philip to prevent Richard's release through bribery. In an agreement of January 1194 John promised the French king a huge slice of the Angevin lands in return for accepting his homage. As it was, the regency council had raised the ransom, albeit with great difficulty. In February, the English bishops excommunicated John and his castles were besieged. Richard returned in March and before that month was out had retaken Nottingham, John's last rebel castle, and confiscated his brother's lands.

John had behaved deceitfully and treasonably, laying the foundations for his later reputation as someone not to be trusted. In fairness, those who criticise John for conspiring with Philip against Richard tend to conveniently forget that Richard himself had conspired with Philip against Henry II, so was equally guilty of treason against his father. Yet by medieval standards there was something especially heinous about betrayal of a king who was on crusade. Eleanor sorted out her squabbling sons and negotiated John's forgiveness, with John kneeling before Richard in contrition. Richard having indulgently declared John (then in his late twenties) to be a mere child, John was left with only Ireland, but over the next two years he achieved partial rehabilitation and restoration. Arthur was now at the French court, which made John the favourite for the succession. John spent the period 1194–99 largely in Normandy, campaigning for the king, a politic move given his behaviour in the first half of the reign.

Richard died on 6 April 1199, succumbing to gangrene from a crossbow bolt wound obtained while besieging a castle in southern France. He was only forty-one and his marriage was childless. Even now, the rules of succession were not clear, not least because the Angevin empire was a patchwork of territories with different customs, some of which initially opted for Arthur of Brittany. John raced immediately to secure the Angevin treasury at Chinon. Key members of Richard's administration, including Earl William Marshal of Pembroke and (with some persuasion) Archbishop Hubert Walter of Canterbury, threw their support behind John, while Eleanor ensured he received Aquitaine. John was installed as Duke of Normandy in Rouen on 25 April and then crowned King of England in Westminster Abbey on 27 May. (As this was Ascension Day, a moveable feast forty days after Easter, John's regnal years were calculated from one Ascension Day to the next and were thus, uniquely, of variable length.) There were doubts about him from the start, for he already had a reputation for treachery, while the chroniclers complained about his reluctance to receive the sacrament at mass and his stinginess on post-coronation visits to the major pilgrimage centres at Bury St Edmunds and Canterbury. The reliability of these stories has been endlessly debated; other evidence suggests John conformed with at least the minimum conventional standards of piety for his day.

John recrossed the Channel and stayed on the Continent for much of the next four years. In this early phase of his reign, while he still ruled over extensive French territories, he was as much of an absentee king as Richard had been. There were initially various skirmishes, sieges and exchanges of insults with the French until a truce was agreed. France had been placed under interdict in January 1200, caused by King Philip's repudiation of his wife, and Philip and John agreed a treaty in May. Heavily criticised subsequently, this agreement was a reasonable one at the time and secured John's position, although it did create future problems and entail a payment that the depleted royal treasury could ill afford. Fragile peace allowed John to attend to his own marital affairs. His childless union with Isabella of Gloucester, which had caused problems at the time as it took place without the dispensation necessary on account of their kinship, was annulled. Sparing himself the effort of learning a new name, he married Isabella of Angoulême in that city in August 1200 and returned to England for her coronation and a royal progress. At the working funeral of Bishop Hugh of Lincoln in his cathedral city in November, John received the homage of William the Lion, King of Scotland. John's first eighteen months as king had gone relatively well.

Yet for all the strategic advantages, his second marriage had disastrous consequences. Isabella's age is disputed, but she was possibly under 12, the lowest permitted age to marry under canon law, and maybe even as young as nine.[3] Moreover, she had already been betrothed to Hugh de Lusignan. Hugh appealed to Philip, which led to conflict between the two kings. Philip, looking to secure Normandy, declared John a 'contumacious vassal' before joining forces with Arthur of Brittany. The two made war against John on different fronts. In summer 1202, Arthur trapped his grandmother, Eleanor of Aquitaine, at Mirebeau.

At this point, John showed himself his father's son. Louis VII had been so amazed at the speed with which Henry II moved around his dominions that he speculated Henry could fly. John covered the distance to rescue his mother at a spectacular rate. He captured Arthur and his whole army, sending his nephew to imprisonment in Falaise and then Rouen. Over the following months, things went badly but not disastrously for the king as he raced around his French territories trying to quell rebellion, although his harshness to prisoners and refusal to win over certain rebels meant he ultimately squandered the advantage won at Mirebeau. There is an entire catalogue of evil deeds attributed to King John, but what probably happened at this point is the darkest of all. By the spring of 1203, Arthur had vanished and ugly rumours accounted for his disappearance. It was generally believed that John had murdered his teenaged nephew. Whether, as the most explicit accounts say, John himself killed Arthur in a drunken rage and tossed his body into the Seine, or whether he had someone do the deed for him, the outcome was the same. Arthur had been taken while engaged in military action against John, but he was only 15 and this was clandestine, cold-blooded murder, not the result of due process. It wrecked John's credibility with the families of those he held hostage and has stained his reputation ever since.

Worse still for the king, Philip declared that John had forfeited his French lands. The French king made steady inroads into Normandy and Aquitaine as John faced increasing defections. Towards the end of the year, he scurried back across to England, a bewildering decision given the grave threat to Normandy. His perceived cowardice was summed up in a new nickname he acquired in the opening years of his reign, 'Softsword'. In March 1204, the imposing Château Gaillard was captured. On 1 April, John's mother, the redoubtable Eleanor of Aquitaine, died. By the summer, Normandy had fallen to Philip's forces, with the old Angevin heartland of Maine and Anjou also conquered. Only Gascony, along with Angoulême and La Rochelle, stayed loyal. Modern apologists have sought to shift the burden of blame onto treacherous barons and vassals, but this cannot obscure the fact that John was the ruler and he was absent from the struggle. Not only had John suffered the humiliation of losing the majority of his father's continental lands, he had not been present at the final fight to save them. There was some benefit to John, for by confiscating the English estates of those who stayed loyal to Philip in France, he greatly enriched himself and his supporters.

Yet the damage to his reputation and kingship from his timid loss of all the northern French possessions was incalculable.

For all his seeming lethargy as they were conquered, John's overwhelming purpose over the next decade was regaining the continental territories, even as his barons increasingly came to doubt John's ability to do so. Those who had profited from the English redistribution had no desire for him to succeed. The French and their allies continued to nibble away at John's remaining possessions. Yet the financial demands were heavy. How far John's financial position relative to Philip II's disadvantaged the English king in the struggle up to 1204 is hotly debated, but thereafter John sought to build up a substantial war chest. Both Henry II and Richard I had made heavy financial demands, but John hyperactively toured England in pursuit of his aims, unwelcome to those unused to a king permanently resident in England and continually hassling them in person.

John made particular use of scutage ('shield tax'), which was paid in place of sending knights for the royal army; John would levy eleven scutages in a seventeen-year reign, an unprecedentedly high frequency which is reflected in the limitations placed on it in Magna Carta. Five were demanded in the years 1199–1204, with only abject military failure to show for the expenditure. Further scutages were raised for John's aborted campaign of 1205 and his 1206 continental venture which yielded precious little result. Taxation was meant to be raised only in times of necessity, but John was raising huge sums with no consent and little obvious return. Such hefty demands with so few tangible results were deeply unpopular, although taxation is never popular and there is an unresolved modern debate about how inflation affected the king's income in real terms. Other types of taxation were levied at various points in the reign, with additional exactions, fines, 'gifts', and sales of offices. The king also loaned money to his barons and many became indebted to John, which he would use to his advantage. As security, he often took sons or family members as hostages. Sir James Holt famously wrote that the revolt against John leading to Magna Carta was 'a rebellion of the King's debtors'.[4]

Amid all this came a major breach with the Church. In Innocent III, John faced one of the most formidable popes of the Middle Ages and their turbulent relations would dominate ecclesiastical affairs in England for the next decade. The archbishop John had inherited, Hubert Walter, died in 1205 and Innocent blocked John's effort to fill the vacancy at Canterbury. Instead, after a convoluted tussle involving John, Innocent, the monks of Canterbury and various others, in 1207 the Pope consecrated Stephen Langton, Lincolnshire born but long resident in Paris. Both the method of his appointment and the fact that John saw him as the creature of his enemy, Philip, led to Langton being refused the king's permission to enter England. Other kings would likely have reacted with similar rage to the papal attack on royal prerogatives, but few would have let matters escalate to the same extent. John confiscated the Canterbury estates and Innocent retaliated in March 1208 with an interdict on the country, a weapon he had previously used against Norway and France. Today, in a secular age, it is hard to imagine the trauma of Church bells silenced and masses unsaid for the general population. There is some debate about the true impact of these measures, for some Church business demonstrably continued, but the bishops went into exile. There are terrible stories about desperate measures for dealing with the dead, and tales of oppression and cruelty against the clergy, although as they were all told by clergymen it is hard to disentangle truth from elaboration.

John seems to have rather enjoyed the interdict. He was personally excommunicated in 1209, but the overuse of this sentence by Innocent's aggressive regime had rather blunted its effect. John certainly profited from appropriating Church revenues, which in general the baronial laity supported as it reduced demands on them. Alongside the income from his lands and taxation, he was now a wealthy man with access to considerable quantities of cash. At his accession, his annual income had been around £22,000. By 1211, it was somewhere very close to £100,000.[5] If (clerical) contemporaries were horrified by his impiety and treatment of the Church, John seemed far more interested in earthly treasure than his immortal soul. Interdicts were a good source of income and this gave John little incentive to come to terms. Innocent had badly miscalculated how long John would hold out. He had also failed to realise that the English in general had little time for his pretensions and were not going to rebel against the king on behalf of Rome's ideas of papal authority.

John was simultaneously busy alienating his barons. He was a suspicious, almost paranoid man who saw treason all around. While capable of promoting talented men and instilling loyalty in a chosen few, one of John's most egregious failures was his inability to manage or earn the trust of his barons. Doubts about the reliability of his nobility had been a factor in the loss of Normandy. More than once, John compelled the barons to renew their oaths of loyalty to him in elaborate ceremonies emphasising his majesty. His conduct was hardly conducive to inspire that loyalty. William Marshal, the fundamentally loyalist Earl of Pembroke, found himself suspect and accused of treason, taking refuge in Ireland. The two were estranged for some years.

John had a reputation for seduction; with some eight bastards, he was second only to Henry I in this respect. John's five legitimate children by Isabella, including two sons, Henry III (born 1207) and Richard of Cornwall (1209), meant John avoided the succession questions which plagued his great-grandfather. However, he certainly had plenty of mistresses; highly irregularly, he also continued to pay for the household of his first wife and even have her at court on occasion. Where Henry had avoided entanglements with political consequences and was notably generous to the mothers of his illegitimate children, John was less astute in his sex life. Some of his alleged liaisons would have been politically risky, while there are stories of the seduction, coercion and possibly even rape of noble wives and daughters, which has given him the reputation of a sexual predator. Whatever the truth, John was viewed in unsavoury terms by his contemporaries.

Threats or accusations of disloyalty were commonplace against his lords. The king continued to exact fines and hostages while trusting increasingly in mercenaries and foreigners, never a popular move. In 1209, John demanded security for loyalty even from King William of Scotland. Threatened with an invasion, William yielded to the Treaty of Norham, giving John hostages and a large sum of money, and surrendering his daughters into John's custody. Shortly afterwards, John secured the renewed homage of Llywelyn of Wales, the husband of his (illegitimate) daughter Joan. Despite this rule by suspicion and fear, at the end of 1209 John apparently reigned supreme, his military achievements in Britain in stark contrast to his continental failures.

In the summer of 1210, the king crossed to Ireland. The visit was a powerful demonstration of strength and largely successful, but had some dark consequences. His latest insistence on hostages angered the Irish. John pursued two dissident barons whom he had hounded in recent years: Walter de Lacy and William de Briouze (or Braose), but both managed to escape to Scotland. Briouze had been a loyal adherent of the king and John had given him extensive holdings in South Wales, but then with characteristic suspicion turned against him and forced him to flee to Ireland. However, while he escaped, Briouze's wife Matilda and their family were captured. By now, William Marshal was the last English baron holding firm in Ireland, so hostages were demanded for his loyalty. Back in England, the Briouze saga had a grim end. Although John subsequently issued a justification of his conduct, it reflects very badly on him; if the chronicles can be believed, Matilda and her adult son were starved to death in the dungeon of either Windsor or Corfe Castle. William died in exile in Paris. Few saw due process or justice in the king's treatment of the family.

In 1211, John twice led an army into North Wales to bring Llywelyn back to heel. His submission obtained, John's mind turned to another campaign in Poitou. In 1212, the king of England sent an army to aid the king of Scotland, in return for significant concessions. John's (legitimate) daughter Joan was betrothed to William's heir, the future Alexander II. John's authority across Britain appeared absolute, his excommunicate status notwithstanding. One chronicler noted that across the British Isles, 'there was no one who did not bow to the nod of the king of England'.[6]

Yet there were undercurrents of dissatisfaction. In northern England in the summer of 1212, a man called Peter of Pontefract (or Wakefield) was predicting that John would cease to be king by the following Ascension Day. He was sent to imprisonment in Corfe Castle, but his words circulated throughout the realm. Llywelyn rebelled again and twenty-eight Welsh hostages from the 1211 campaign were executed. At Nottingham in August 1212, on his way to a muster at Chester to deal with Llywelyn's latest challenge, John received news of an alleged plot against his life. He abandoned the planned campaign, heading to York and Durham to secure the North before returning to London. Some plotters fled into exile. New hostages were demanded from those of suspect loyalty. It is a measure of how feared the king was that many of those targeted complied, although John did also make some limited concessions.

More serious for John was the potential threat from abroad. In the spring of 1213, Philip Augustus was preparing to invade England. The extent of the Pope's involvement in this plan is unclear, but John responded zealously. Meanwhile, frantic negotiations between John and Innocent took place behind the scenes, as they had been doing on and off since the start of the interdict. Near Dover in mid-May, in front of Pandulf as papal legate, the king swore homage to the Pope, conceding that he held England as a vassal of the papacy, in return for a promise of the lifting of interdict and excommunication. It was an astonishing turnaround for the man who had been fighting so successfully against the papacy for six years. However, it was almost certainly a shrewd political move to bind the Pope to him, for John had shown himself utterly indifferent to the penalties of excommunication and interdict alike. It instantly discredited the barons supporting Philip's invasion and removed any justification from the French king, who had to abandon his plan. It would also serve John well in the remaining years of his reign, when Innocent became his stalwart supporter. Ascension Day 1213 passed with John still on the throne, after which the prophet Peter and his son were dragged from Corfe to Wareham and hanged.

Philip had turned his wrath on Flanders. While he was besieging Ghent on 30 May, the English fleet wreaked considerable damage on the unguarded French ships lying at anchor off the coast. John, seeing a chance to capitalise and try to regain his French lands, was frustrated by baronial delaying tactics. The king and Stephen Langton were reconciled at Winchester in July 1213, with John's excommunication lifted and restitution for the Church agreed. This left John free to launch another continental campaign, but he met further resistance and once more had to abandon it. Much of the rest of the year was occupied in the south with preparing for a campaign the following year. It was the closest John ever got to a charm offensive: reconciliation with barons and bishops, restitution to the Church, filling ecclesiastical vacancies and the formal process of ending the interdict (finally lifted on 2 July 1214).

John had never abandoned his intention of winning back the lost French lands, even though he had spent almost all his time since 1204 in the British Isles. Indeed, his preparations in the ensuing years were determined and often ruthless, not least the raising of considerable sums to finance a campaign. In parallel, he had built a coalition of Northern European rulers against Philip in readiness. In February 1214, John sailed for La Rochelle. Over the next few months, he made some progress and had notable successes, not least at Nantes, but he was unable to hold the ancestral seat of Angers and fears of treachery and unreliable followers dogged him endlessly. In June, he evaded battle with Louis, the son of King Philip. Meanwhile, in Flanders, the coalition which John had carefully constructed with the Holy Roman Emperor Otto and several counts met Philip's forces at Bouvines on 27 July. The French were victorious. John's diplomacy and expenditure had been for nothing. In October, he returned to England, his reconquest ambitions in tatters. In retrospect, the failure was even more catastrophic: 'The road from Bouvines to Runnymede was direct, short, and unavoidable.'[7]

Mutiny was in the air. For a decade John had been planning the reconquest and it had failed. The cost had been enormous in more than one sense. His ruthless pursuit of the necessary resources had alienated large numbers of his lords. He had never sought to win their support for what became his personal obsession, only repeatedly demanded their money and their hostages. Demands for overseas service and scutage met with refusal from northern lords in both 1213 and 1214. Many of the rebels were deeply in debt to the king. Gradually, the long-term grievances against the oppressions and injustices of sixty years of Angevin kingship, along with the shorter-term anger against John's behaviour, were coalescing into a coherent opposition.

How coherent it was and how it developed have long been debated. Throughout, the rebel barons had different expectations and demands, ranging from hard-line opponents of the king to lukewarm waverers. A document known as the Unknown Charter, preserved in the Paris archives, is typically dated to late 1214 or early 1215. The Unknown Charter is a copy of Henry I's coronation charter with additional notes, some of which are proposals included in Magna Carta and others which are more radical. The opposition were articulating their grievances. According to the chronicler Roger of Wendover, at Bury St Edmunds in November 1214 a confederacy of barons swore to force the king to accept their demands for the enforcement of law and confirmation of their liberties. Not all barons were active in revolt, although few sympathised with John and there was plenty of side-switching to complicate matters further. Opposition was most concentrated in, but not exclusive to, the North, the West and East Anglia. The early discontent manifested itself in the North and both contemporaries and historians use the shorthand 'Northerners' for the rebels. Part of the problem was that John had spent far more time north of the Trent than any of his predecessors, and familiarity did not endear him to his northern subjects.

The king spent Christmas 1214 at Worcester, but on his return to London for Epiphany 1215 he was confronted with the request of the barons to address their grievances. John played for time and secured an adjournment of the question until Easter. Tensions rose, meetings took place, rumours circulated. John won the sympathy of the Pope by taking the cross, although it is unlikely he seriously intended to go on crusade. In the week after Easter, a sizeable number of rebels assembled at Stamford. Negotiations at Brackley in Northamptonshire failed and on 5 May the rebel barons renounced their homage to John and appointed Robert fitz Walter as their leader. He rather pompously styled himself 'Marshal of the Army of God and the Holy Church in England'. With John now preparing for war, the rebels numbers grew quickly. John suggested arbitration, ordering the confiscation of the rebels' lands and goods when this was declined.

Things were looking desperate. Most seriously, London fell to the rebels. The king had few supporters left and needed to buy time. More earnest negotiations began in early June. A document known as the Articles of the Barons was the preliminary basis for the final agreement and was largely incorporated in Magna Carta. After a series of meetings, John accepted Magna Carta at Runnymede, a meadow on the Thames between Staines and Windsor. (It became known as the 'Great Charter' early in Henry III's reign to distinguish it from the smaller Charter of the Forest, and the name stuck.) In return, the barons renewed their homage and chose the twenty-five barons who would ensure John's compliance. The traditional date of Magna Carta is 15 June 1215, as found in the dating clause, but it was actually the result of a process which took up most of the month.

Magna Carta has taken on a life of its own, independent of the context of 1215. Indeed, although four copies of the 1215 text survive (two in the British Museum and one each in Lincoln and Salisbury), it was the 1225 version which became the definitive text for later use on the statute roll. While some of the grievances were long-standing and could have been levied against Henry II and Richard I, most are aimed specifically at John and his (mis)rule. To those who hold up the charter as the cornerstone of liberty in the English-speaking world, chapters 39 ('No free man is to be arrested, or imprisoned, or disseised, or outlawed, or exiled, or in any way destroyed [...] save by the lawful judgement of his peers or by the law of the land') and 40 ('To no one will we sell, to no one will we deny or delay, right or justice') are key. They tend to ignore the specific penalties against named individuals in chapter 50, or the provisions about fish weirs in the Thames and the Medway in chapter 33, on which it is rather harder to construct a case for immemorial liberties. It is also a conventional religious text of its time, the opening clause a concession of the liberties and privileges of the Church.

Magna Carta was a result of negotiations in a particular context, a compromise which at the time satisfied almost no one. That the barons distrusted the king is shown by the enforcement mechanisms included within the text. Neither barons nor king would have considered for a moment the idea that they were laying the foundations of a constitutional system. Amid the weight of history and ideology which has been loaded onto Magna Carta in the subsequent eight centuries, it is also easy to forget that it was an almost instant failure. It was meant to bring peace and reconciliation, but the result was civil war. Neither king nor barons were negotiating in good faith. The barons subsequently did their best to humiliate John and were secretly preparing for war. For the more radical, the charter did not go nearly far enough. John had one major advantage on his side. Having entrusted England to the Pope as his overlord, John appealed against Magna Carta to Innocent and in August an indignant Pope quashed it. The descent into war began.

The king was far more ready than the barons, who at this stage held only one major stronghold, London. John had spent the summer preparing royal castles. Troops and mercenaries had come from overseas to join the king's cause. Some barons remained loyal, including Earl William of Salisbury, a bastard son of Henry II and hence John's half-brother. Papal support bolstered the king and ensured the loyalty of most bishops; Langton was suspended for refusing to excommunicate the rebels. The rebel barons' main concern was to keep John from seizing London. In mid-October, John besieged Rochester Castle, which had been seized by rebels. He threw everything into the attack, including a herd of pigs with burning torches tied to them, sent to set fire to the siege tunnels. The garrison clung on heroically until St Andrew's Day, 30 November, then surrendered. Despite his inclination, John was talked out of hanging them all and settled on imprisonment for most. Meanwhile, he had energetically set about confiscating rebel lands.

The rebel barons had sought the aid of the French Prince Louis, the treasonous invitation to a foreign prince a gift to John's propaganda. The barons had also been excommunicated by the Pope, a sentence which John gleefully had read from every pulpit in the land. After Christmas at Nottingham, John headed north, asserting himself through the surrounding lands as he travelled. The previous autumn, Alexander II of Scotland had besieged Norham (unsuccessfully) and reached a deal with the northern barons. Now the English king wreaked his vengeance and asserted his sovereignty on a fearsome and rapid military progress. Alexander burned Newcastle upon Tyne, then withdrew to Melrose, so John raided northwards towards the Forth, as far as Dunbar. After torching Berwick-upon-Tweed, he then made his way back south more slowly. Although some castles held out and the war continued, John had given a creditable demonstration of power in the North.

In March, the king moved through East Anglia before his sights turned on London. The mood there had been buoyed by Louis' promise that he would be ready to cross to the city's aid by Easter. To justify an invasion and fend off papal intervention, the French king had constructed a detailed argument in which careful propaganda use was also made of the murder of Arthur. The papal legate forbade Louis from invading England, but the prince received his father's blessing and headed for Calais. John spent late April and early May charging around Kent, preparing defences and watching for Louis' arrival. He also tried to blockade Calais, but a storm scattered his ships. Louis landed on 21 May, witnessed by John from a distance. Few English lords were still with John, but William Marshal was an exception and he counselled caution. Not for the first time, John evaded a decisive battle and slipped away to ensure Dover was well-garrisoned before heading for Winchester. Louis quickly entered Canterbury unopposed and won Rochester Castle in under a week. The papal legate, Guala Bicchieri, had fled Canterbury to join John in Winchester, from where he excommunicated Louis.

Ignoring this, Louis was received happily into London at the start of June and took oaths from barons and citizens. He then made towards John, but the king had fled Winchester for the stronghold of Corfe Castle by the time Louis arrived. Louis took Winchester along with the allegiance of some defecting earls, including John's half-brother, William of Salisbury. He made further gains in Hampshire while a mixed baronial-French army sacked and plundered in the East. King Alexander ravaged the North. Yet although Louis' power was extensive in the southern and eastern parts of the country by late July, critical castles like Dover, Lincoln, Nottingham and Windsor were still held for John.

John stayed at Corfe for a month. Once Louis had begun sieges of Dover and Windsor, without which he had no hope of controlling England, and was therefore tied down further east, John emerged. The western heartlands of his great-grandmother's struggle against Stephen were still loyal to the Angevins and John toured the key centres and castles of the region. August took him into Wales and Shropshire before he turned back to Worcester, Gloucester and Bristol. Elsewhere, Carlisle fell to Alexander II on 8 August, after which he marched south to Canterbury to perform homage to Louis for his English lands. Louis continued with a gruelling and increasingly frustrating siege at Dover. John charged east with western troops and Welsh allies. Cambridgeshire, Lincolnshire and other parts of East Anglia found themselves burned and plundered by both sides in September and October. Louis was making no further progress and some of the earls, including Salisbury, returned to John.

By mid-October, though, the king was desperately ill with dysentery. Having lost part of his baggage train in an ill-advised shortcut across the mud of the Wash, he purportedly succumbed to rage and comfort eating at Swineshead Abbey. Fever set in, but he struggled on to Sleaford. Finally, in great pain, he made his way to Newark, having to be carried in a makeshift litter for most of the journey. In the Bishop of Lincoln's castle at Newark, the abbot of Croxden tended to the dying king's broken body and scarcely less broken soul. John made provision for the succession of his eldest son, Henry, and for the burial of his body at Worcester, before he died on the night of 18/19 October 1216. Like his father's, John's death was undignified. His followers fled, including the abbot once he had rapidly embalmed the king and taken his entrails for Croxden Abbey. It was mainly mercenaries who accompanied the king's body from Newark to Worcester. This was probably a second-choice burial site, since his own foundation of Beaulieu Abbey was in rebel-held Hampshire, although John had visited Worcester in most years of his reign and had a particular devotion to St Wulstan.

With John died the rebel cause, for without him there was little left to fight against. Gradually the royalists regained the initiative. Under the steady hand of the elderly, loyal William Marshal, John's young son was crowned

Henry III by Cardinal Guala in Gloucester Abbey. Although it took time, the rebellion was ended, Louis went home and the kingdom was won for Henry, who would go on to have what was then the longest reign in English history, albeit one with plenty of troubles of its own. However, John's death gave new life to Magna Carta, for what had been a futile attempt at peace in 1215 was reissued in modified form by Henry's government in 1216 and 1217 and became a fundamental text in the English legal tradition and mythology.

Ironically, given his tempestuous relationship with the Church during his lifetime, John's body was treated with particular honour and he is the earliest king of England whose mortal remains still lie peacefully in their grave. In death, he has been an object of dispute and curiosity. Afraid that they were going to lose their royal burial when the monks at Beaulieu staked a claim in 1228, the Worcester monks set about showing Henry III that their cathedral was a suitable resting place for his father. They succeeded. In 1232, Henry was present as John was reinterred in a place of honour at the heart of the quire, where he still resides, and the king became a notable patron of Worcester for the rest of his reign. The Purbeck marble effigy, which can still be seen today, dates from this time. This, the oldest surviving effigy of a king, was originally coloured and bedecked with precious stones. In 1532, the tomb was opened and the chest on which the effigy has rested ever since was constructed; the treatment of John was in stark contrast to that meted out to others among Henry VIII's predecessors. John was disturbed again in 1797, thanks to the efforts of local antiquary Valentine Green, when the body was measured (revealing John to have been 5ft 6½in) and it was discovered that John had been buried in his coronation cap, his attire mirrored by the effigy. According to Green, thousands came to view the skeleton before the tomb was resealed. The colouring was still discernible into the nineteenth century, although as part of a heavy-handed restoration of the cathedral in the 1870s the last remnants were cleaned away, the effigy controversially gilded and given a metal crown. These were removed in 1930 and the tomb took on its modern appearance. The king whose life was so tumultuous and who died amid such chaos now rests tranquilly beside the Severn, disturbed only by passing tourists and the sound of cricket matches across the river.

John through the Centuries

'Foul as hell is, it is defiled by John's presence.'[8] This verdict by Matthew Paris, writing in Henry III's reign, is the most damning moral judgement passed on an English king by any medieval chronicler. While the idea of

John making hell worse may seem extreme to us, most chroniclers implied that eternal fires were more fitting than heavenly bliss for this king. Few good words were written about him by contemporaries and even occasional comments from early in the reign which seem positive are often ambiguous or barbed. There are some more balanced approaches, such as that of the chronicle traditionally (if wrongly) attributed to Barnwell Abbey, but even this shows limited understanding rather than sympathy. John certainly had no supporters among these writers. The moral judgements of the chroniclers range from viewing John as bad, to seeing the devil incarnate.

All were churchmen and a king who managed to provoke a five-year interdict on his realm and more than one personal excommunication was never going to earn their approval. He is slammed for impiety and mistreatment of the Church and its clergy. John was unfortunate insofar as his reputation was left entirely in the hands of the monks; there was no English equivalent of the French royal historians based at Saint-Denis, who glorified Philip Augustus. The chroniclers revel in tales of John's barbarity. Undoubtedly some stories they tell are exaggerated or confused. The most famous is the story of how Geoffrey, archdeacon of Norwich, was starved to death in a cope of lead, a vivid story which on examination proves problematic and led one modern commentator to observe of the chronicler that 'since he has the wrong year, the wrong cause, and the wrong man, the odds are heavily against him being right about the leaden cope'.[9]

The stories grew over time and John evolved into a perfect monster. The strongest accusations of tyranny appeared after his death, although some came in his lifetime. The most devastating attacks were by two writers based at St Albans Abbey after John's reign, Roger of Wendover and Matthew Paris. From the mid-twentieth century it became fashionable to sneer at their immensely hostile views of John as being posthumous legend-making, but as has been observed in response to this approach, 'they said remarkably little which is not in embryo in the earlier chroniclers'.[10] Even those who wrote before John became king are not impressed, condemning his treachery. For all the biases and probable exaggerations, all chronicles, from throughout John's life and beyond, from all parts of England and beyond, paint a picture whose broad outlines are almost identical. It is of a man who was cruel, suspicious, irreligious, treacherous and vindictive.[11] It is hard to see how there is not at least some grain of truth in this, but the important point is that however much hyperbole there may be, from his lifetime through the rest of the Middle Ages John was seen as the embodiment of the evil king.

Amid the tumult of Henry VIII's reign, John's reputation suddenly enjoyed an abrupt reversal in fortune. As early as 1528, William Tyndale in *The Obedience of a Christian Man* and Simon Fish in *Supplication of the Beggars* portrayed John as a righteous man seeking justice, persecuted by Church and papacy for his pains. As Henry broke with Rome, Thomas Cromwell carefully managed a propaganda effort which presented John as a victim of unjust suffering inflicted by a malevolent papacy.[12] The anti-papal complaints of the Reformation were projected back 300 years, so John became a proto-Henry VIII anachronistically fighting the perceived abuses of the sixteenth century. John was a Reformation hero, a patriot who courageously opposed papal tyranny and was cruelly persecuted for doing so. Of course, there were those committed Catholics who drew the opposite conclusion from the parallel between John and Henry, seeing Henry as the antichrist and hoping he would meet the same end as John (who according to a popular but baseless medieval myth had been poisoned by a monk). Yet the official position miraculously converted John from anti-Christian tyrant into noble warrior for true Christian justice.

While positive approaches to John continued into the Elizabethan Age, notes of ambiguity began to creep in. John is presented with sympathy in Foxe's *Book of Martyrs* as a good king, but he sometimes comes across as weak. In his *Chronicles*, Raphael Holinshed is ambivalently negative, seeming to be not quite willing to accept the hostility of the medieval monastic writers but nevertheless repeating some of their main accusations before deciding on studied agnosticism. By the reign of Elizabeth I, John's reputation was already on a steady descent from its apogee. Under the Stuarts, it would plummet. There was one last Protestant defence by John Speed, who condemned the chroniclers and judged John 'a King of as great renown as misfortunes'.[13] Thereafter, Samuel Daniel's sketch of the reign shows how clearly 'Good King John' had been abandoned by the later years of James I. At the start, Daniel notes that John commenced on a reign of 'great injustice' which 'through his violence and oppression […] produced desperate effects'. At the end, noting John's conventionally pious death, Daniel sharply asserts that 'his death takes not away the reproach of his life, nor the infamy that follows him'.[14] The seventeenth century had returned to the evil king of the medieval chroniclers.

In 1628, Magna Carta was explicitly referenced in the struggle between Charles I and the House of Commons which led to the Petition of Right. It gave a new lease of life to the charter and drew attention to the king who had conceded it. There were obvious parallels for opponents of Charles between their situation and the barons of 1215 who had been compelled to force a statement of liberties from a tyrannous king. Charles I, like Henry VIII, was a new John, but this time the comparison was not intended as a positive one. Despite its different context and it having been repeatedly altered since 1215 (and half-forgotten for many years), Magna Carta suddenly became a cornerstone of English liberties. It was cited in foundation documents for English colonies in the New World and retained its totemic status when those colonies rebelled and formed the United States, with George III now cast as John. The evils of the king required to grant these basic liberties, so the thinking went, must have been great indeed. The seventeenth century turned John into a bad king for the transatlantic world. As the British Empire grew over subsequent centuries, so John became a paragon of depravity wherever English settlers took themselves. Anachronistic images of him signing Magna Carta would become a favourite for Victorian-era public buildings, not just in England.

By the end of the seventeenth century, James Tyrrell could write of an 'unhappy prince' who was a coward and lazy, who oppressed his people by subjecting them to endless arbitrary taxes and oppressions, who 'had very few good Qualities to recommend him to the Affections of his Subjects, or the Admiration of future times'. He does concede that John was unlucky in having Philip Augustus and Innocent III as foes, accepting that some of the monastic accounts may be 'too severe', but otherwise John is an indolent, lustful, cruel, disreputable character.[15] By the middle of the eighteenth century, John's return to absolute villain was complete. His death, wrote the acerbic David Hume, 'freed the nation from the dangers to which it was equally exposed by his success or by his misfortunes'. John's character was 'nothing but a complication of vices equally mean and odious, ruinous to himself and destructive to his people'. In case of doubt, Hume lists these vices: 'Cowardice, inactivity, folly, levity, licentiousness, treachery, tyranny, and cruelty'. John is castigated for losing the French lands, submitting England to a 'shameful vassalage', for allowing crown prerogatives to be diminished and even (bizarrely given Hume's religious views) appearing as an atheist to the monks. There are no redeeming features here.[16]

The Victorian constitutional historians took up this approach to John with glee. At the height of British imperialism, John's reputation was naturally to suffer for his loss of overseas lands. Victorian moralism and beliefs about work ethic had little time for John the seducer, John the murderer, or a John by now perceived to be idle and dissolute. There could be no greater contrast with the carefully-cultivated domestic rectitude of their own Queen-Empress. John's essential redeeming feature was being so bad that the barons forced Magna Carta on him, which for the historians of this era was the fundamental starting point on the relentless road to the governmental paradise that was Queen Victoria's parliamentary democracy. In a savage assessment, William Stubbs opined that 'John had neither grace nor splendour, strength nor patriotism' and was 'a mean reproduction of all the vices and of the few pettinesses of his family'. After a catalogue of failings and vice, 'even in the abject humiliation of his end we have no word of pity as we have had none of sympathy'. Crushingly, he 'deserved none'.[17]

Yet the most damning judgement, which came to epitomise the Victorian view of John far more than Stubbs, was that of John Richard Green. Green drew back from the absolute villain, noting that 'John possessed all the quickness, the vivacity, the cleverness, the good-humour, the social charm which distinguished his house.' He dismissed the myth of laziness, conceding that 'he toiled steadily and closely at the work of administration' and that 'the closer study of John's history clears away the charges of sloth and incapacity'. But the overall verdict was brutal:

> In his inner soul John was the worst outcome of the Angevins. He united into one mass of wickedness their insolence, their selfishness, their unbridled lust, their cruelty and tyranny, their shamelessness, their superstition, their cynical indifference to honour or truth. […] His punishments were refinements of cruelty […] His court was a brothel where no woman was safe from the royal lust.

Worse was the fact that Green saw John had 'an inborn genius for war', that in many ways 'he far surpassed the statesmen of his time'. This was the horror of the reign: 'The awful lesson of his life rests on the fact that the king who lost Normandy, became the vassal of the Pope, and perished in a struggle of despair against English freedom was no weak and indolent voluptuary but the ablest and most ruthless of the Angevins'.[18]

This evil mass of contradictions is found in Kate Norgate's *John Lackland* (1902). Norgate is no admirer of John: she quotes William of Newburgh in calling him '"Nature's enemy," a monster' and has no qualms about referring to the king as a tyrant. He is portrayed as shifty, a breaker of promises, one 'absolutely indifferent' to 'outward personal humiliation of any kind' if he could profit by it. His brutality is brought out in full and while the failures of his predecessors are noted, he is held to account for his character defects, cruelty and misrule. For all the work done subsequently, *John Lackland* remains a readable, sensible study of the reign. It is the starting point for modern views of the reign, not just because of its longevity, but because Norgate's final sentence perhaps encapsulates the Victorian belief about John:

> John had indeed earned for himself in a new sense the nickname which his father had given him at birth; and he had earned it not by blunders in statecraft or errors in strategy, not by weakness or cowardice or sloth, but by the almost superhuman wickedness of a life which, twenty years before its end, a historian of deeper insight than Matthew [Paris] had characterised in one memorable phrase – 'Nature's enemy, John'.[19]

Having started the twentieth century heavily demonised, 'a selfish cruel tyrant of the worst type',[20] John ended it with his reputation at least partially enhanced. It was perhaps inevitable that some would seek to redeem so dark and hopeless a cause by presenting John as misunderstood, underappreciated and unfairly demonised. In general, this school of thought distrusted the chronicles and had an almost reverential faith in the record sources. The careful deconstruction of the most obviously inaccurate or exaggerated episodes is used to devalue the entirety of the chronicles. John's impiety is questioned through reference to his conventional piety (such as almsgiving and founding abbeys). There is an emphasis on the structural weaknesses of the Angevin 'empire', stressing the heterogenous nature of the territories and the deep-rooted problems, not least the financial ones, which gave John an impossible inheritance. Sympathetic historians highlighted John's misfortune in facing one of the most able kings of France in Philip Augustus, at the same time as one of the most able popes in Innocent III. Much is made of the difficult situation John inherited from Richard I, whose perceived achievements are downplayed and who comes in for heavy criticism for bleeding England dry of money, for never being in his kingdom and for showing no interest in or talent for administration. Magna Carta is seen as a response to all three Angevin kings and their system of government. John's acts of cruelty are relativized within the demands and rights of medieval kingship. Some credit him with founding the navy. Even his love of books is cited in his defence.

This approach can be traced through the twentieth century. In 1934, Edmund B. D'Auvergne painted a sympathetic, eccentric picture of a man 'born out of his time' who would have been a much better Tudor king.[21] However, the real turning point came with the work of V.H. Galbraith in the 1940s. Galbraith talked of John's 'great abilities' and his 'great services to his country', dismissing the chronicle and Victorian accounts alike in favour of the 'hard facts' found in government records.[22] He had no time whatsoever for the portraits of the two St Albans monks which had so influenced the Victorians. Thereafter, a far more positive picture of John which stressed his administrative brilliance became academic orthodoxy. In the 1970s, Maurice Ashley and Alan Lloyd published sympathetic, even admiring, popular biographies, with more guarded sympathy found in the works by John T. Appleby and J.A.P. Jones.[23] The major creed of this school, echoing Galbraith, came in its most concise form from the pen of Doris Mary Stenton: 'Nor should any chronicler be believed who is not strictly contemporary, and is not supported by record evidence when he makes extravagant statements about the king's evil deeds.'[24] Lady Stenton was not uncritical of John, but his administrative achievements definitely outweighed his defects in her judgement.

The problem with the record evidence so beloved of this line of thinking is that it can be ambivalent or even bewildering. One entry for 1204–5 is often quoted: 'The wife of Hugh de Neville gives the lord King 200 chickens that she may lie with her husband for one night. Thomas de Sanford stands surety for 100 chickens and her husband, Hugh, for 100.'

The quantity of ink poured forth in trying to explain this has been incredible. These must be by far the most written about chickens of the Middle Ages, the theories about their purpose are almost as crazy as the entry. The idea that the clerks writing it were drunk (which has been proposed) is distinctly appealing. The point is that record evidence is not neutral, that it recorded particular things for a particular purpose. The weakness of Lady Stenton's creed is that a man of John's intelligence was hardly going to leave a paper trail of murders in the national accounts. Moreover, there is a considerable arrogance in assuming that modern historians have access to the truth through their balancing of government records in a way not possible for religiously-obsessed, biased chroniclers; too often these historians were blind to their own biases and preconceptions. As J.C. Holt perceptively observed, with great ease 'a legend of King John was created in the thirteenth century and preserved in the nineteenth', which should alert historians to the danger that it 'is just as easy to create one now'.[25]

The fullest case for the defence was laid out in 2012 by Graham E. Seel, whose thesis is nearly summed up in the title, *King John: An Underrated King*. This is a comprehensive reassessment of John which looks at all aspects of his reign. However, Seel's argument early on that 'the king that emerges is associated more with greatness and less with tyranny' rather reveals the approach taken. The attempts to justify or explain away the acts of cruelty and to remove from John any blame for the loss of Normandy fail to convince. That there was 'no equivalent to the Pilgrimage of Grace' of 1536–37, here noted to suggest that John did not offend popular religiosity, is a case of comparing chalk with cheese; unlike Henry VIII, John was not overthrowing the entire Roman Catholic system, nor would it have occurred to him to do so. In the end, John is seen as unlucky, Seel arguing that if certain events had gone John's way, 'John may even have become Good King John'. It is a spirited defence, but this is surely to travel too far along the path towards John's canonisation.[26]

If not everyone was willing to go as far as these admirers of John, most twentieth-century studies slanted in a direction more positive than negative, recognising his faults while highlighting his achievements and positive qualities. Even Sir Winston Churchill was moved to infuse his quasi-Victorian portrait with some recognition of John the able governor.[27] In a summary which largely echoed the increasingly sympathetic new orthodoxy, A.L. Poole highlighted the essential problem faced by any student of John:

> Almost any epithet might appropriately be applied to him in one or other of his many and versatile moods. He was cruel and ruthless, violent and passionate, greedy and self-indulgent, genial and repellent, arbitrary and judicious, clever and capable, original and inquisitive. He is made up of inconsistencies.[28]

Most historians were remarkably consistent in their deployment of the positives as a counterweight to the negatives. A good sense of the ambivalence can be found in Warren Hollister's article summarising scholarship as it stood in 1961, which could argue that 'most historians now recognise that he was a highly talented man, perhaps in certain respects even a genius', but also that 'John remains a curiously twisted and enigmatic figure'. 'It will not do […] to conclude that John was a good king but a bad man, for the deficiencies in his personality could not but affect his success as a monarch.'[29]

A similar sense of ambivalence can be found in the work of the most influential historian of the reign working in the second half of the twentieth century, J.C. Holt. In the 1960s, Holt published a trio of highly significant works: a pamphlet on King John, a monograph called *The Northerners*, and what became a classic work on Magna Carta. On John, he steered a middle course, arguing that one of John's problems was that his rule 'had been far too effective', yet 'he lacked what most helps a man in a crisis – a level head'. Holt examines in detail the northern barons who became rebels and those who stayed loyal, leading him to conclude that John's treatment of his lords meant that 'in 1215 too many people had not enough to lose' and that few 'have ensured so effectively that those who were not for him would be against him'. For all John's abilities, he brought Magna Carta on himself.[30]

Three biographies, by Sidney Painter (1949), Lewis Warren (1961) and Ralph Turner (1994), chart a similarly ambiguous course. In a twentieth century rather saturated with biographies of John, some of distinctly dubious merit, these stand along with Kate Norgate as the best and most significant. In varying degrees, all are understanding, if not overtly sympathetic, and have moments of admiration which stand in sharp contrast to Norgate, yet all stop well short of an overall positive verdict. Painter is the most critical of John's 'complete lack of military renown' and possession of 'none of the chivalric values'. Yet he praises John's 'active, ingenious and inventive mind' and believes it strongly possible that the administrative innovations of the reign were the king's. Despite acknowledging his 'all-pervading suspicion' and viewing 'the central features of John's character' as 'his pride, ambition, and jealousy' and the loss of Normandy as something which 'warped his character beyond repair', and accepting many of the charges of cruelty against John, it is nevertheless Painter who comes closest to the 'good king, bad man' approach criticised by Hollister as he notes 'a failure to distinguish between the man and the monarch'.[31]

Warren, in a well-written, lively biography, gives due weight to John's abilities and the problems he faced, but never quite resolves the ambiguities of John and ultimately judges that 'he was inadequate for the tasks confronting him as king'. Warren's conclusion is both memorable and damning: 'He had the mental abilities of a great king, but the inclinations of a petty tyrant.'[32] Turner concludes that it is 'impossible to avoid a negative attitude towards King John'. He compares John to US Presidents Lyndon Johnson and Richard Nixon, with 'some great achievements, but whose psychological make-up cost them popular support and limited their successes'. John's administration is placed in the context of his military plans, and Turner is adamant that contemporary views 'cannot be ignored when seeking an accurate view of him'. On the other hand, he does point out that John's flaws seem rather less terrible in the aftermath of the twentieth-century dictators.[33]

Predictably, the increasingly sympathetic treatment of John invited a backlash from those perplexed by how he had become so divorced from the man of the contemporary chronicles. As Jim Bradbury sensibly pointed out, if the picture from the records 'diverges from the narrative-source picture, then perhaps something has gone wrong'. In an article comparing his reputation with that of Philip Augustus, Bradbury (a biographer of Philip) concluded that 'on the whole, modern historians have been kinder to John than he deserves, and less kind to Philip than *he* deserves'.[34]

Some voices, few but passionate, were not remotely kind to John. One French historian rather fancifully diagnosed the king as 'subject to mental disease well known to-day [...] as the periodical psychosis' and declared that 'Philip Augustus had a madman as his rival'.[35] Sellar and Yeatman, rather tame by comparison in a section titled 'John, An Awful King', deemed John 'a Bad King' who had 'begun badly as a Bad Prince'.[36] Although a work of satire, this verdict was quoted approvingly at the end of the century by John's most vehement modern scholarly detractor, John Gillingham, who went on to assert for good measure that John was indeed 'one of the worst kings to rule England'. In the late 1970s, the same author had already stated that 'John is the most overrated king in English history'.[37] As Richard I's biographer and author of a series of important studies about the Lionheart, Gillingham's sympathies lie unashamedly with Richard. This leads him to play down some of the manifest problems John inherited from his brother, but he is not alone in his challenge to the belief in John's military competence. It is hard to avoid the point that 'Softsword' was a contemporary label and that John's reputation as warrior was badly dented in contemporary eyes by the events of 1203–4. In terms of results, losing half an empire is not a good way to prove generalship or military ability. Even many of those who rated John as a military leader held him culpable for 1204.

John also fell victim to the short attention span of the twenty-first century. People had no interest in reading complex arguments but wanted heroes and villains presented to them in concise caricatures with no subtlety or shading. Even a lengthy and curiously old-fashioned book like that of Frank McLynn, with its savage demonisation of John, cannot resist the temptation of heaping on the obloquy.[38] In its way, our own era is as moralistic as the medieval, with its clamour for straightforward 'good' or 'bad' and its eagerness to condemn historical characters by modern values which would have made no sense at the time. 'Best' and 'worst' polls became ubiquitous on television, with historical leaders deemed as fair a subject as Eurovision entries. In both the United Kingdom and the United States, John became a standard feature on 'most evil in history' television programmes. In print, he featured in Simon Sebag Montefiore's *Monsters*.[39] The problem with this sensationalist nonsense is not only that the basic history is typically bad and the use of 'facts' extremely partisan. It is also that it is patently ridiculous to consider John alongside the likes of Hitler, Stalin and Pol Pot and other modern architects of genocide and mass murder. Even if the category of 'most evil people in history' has any validity, which is highly questionable, John is simply not in it. Such judgemental hysteria is utterly unhelpful in assessing John in his thirteenth-century and historical contexts.

Nevertheless, serious scholarship has trended back towards 'Bad King John', albeit in much more nuanced, sober form. In part, this is a result of historians no longer idolising the government records and demonising the chroniclers. Historians avoid assuming that a record-based approach automatically gets us closer to the truth. This was not just a cyclical reassessment; there was also detailed research into key issues affecting our view of John. Much of these were to do with technical financial questions. A detailed study of his income concluded that 'John's attempts to maintain his financial position' were 'the greatest level of exploitation seen in England since the Conquest'.[40] On the other hand, a volume of essays which looked at key themes in John's reign devoted several chapters to economic questions, demonstrating how divided historians remain on the topic. There were also in-depth studies of John's household knights and his religion.[41]

The edging back towards John as bad king and failure is evident in the three twenty-first-century biographies that have been published. Interestingly, none of them have much hesitation in using the language of tyranny in relation to John. Stephen Church is perhaps the most ambivalent, at least in his overall study if not in his conclusions. He argues that 'John was not a villain capable of the worst venality we can imagine; he was a man placed, by accident of birth, the vagaries of life and his own ambition, into a position of power for which he proved himself to be ill suited.' However, as the subtitle of the book makes clear, 'how John came to be seen as a tyrant is at the heart of this account'. Church concludes that the king was 'without any doubt, a catastrophic failure' and that no king 'can leave a legacy like John's and expect to be remembered kindly by posterity'.[42]

Nicholas Vincent is less ambivalent, stating from the outset that 'John was a bad king' who 'died as he had reigned, a failure'. For Vincent, John's reign was poisoned by his character defects and his human failings. Even though he 'was perhaps not an evil king' and 'lacked neither brains nor guile', in the end 'his political intelligence, like his personality, was warped by cruelty, dishonesty and mistrust'.[43] Marc Morris is entirely unambivalent. His verdict tends towards that of John's severest critics, seeing the king as a failure and a cruel tyrant.[44] Indeed, amid this swing among English historians back to a more critical portrait, John's most sympathetic recent biographer is French, seeing part of the problem as being that 'despite everything, John did not succeed in projecting a favourable image' and that he 'misused the tools at his disposal to impose his point of view'.[45] Even here John cannot escape criticism and is judged, on balance, a failure.

The eight-hundredth anniversary of Magna Carta in 2015 unsurprisingly saw a deluge of commemorative literature. It was a subject which had never ceased to fascinate. *King John and Magna Carta* (1969) was arguably the most memorable of the books in the Ladybird history series, shaping children's views for a generation and republished for the anniversary. Throughout the nineteenth and twentieth centuries, memorabilia ranged from the tacky to the bizarre, such as the Worcester porcelain company which produced a china inkstand in the form of John's tomb in the 1840s. There were games and jigsaw puzzles depicting the signing of the charter, commemorative postcards, pageants and all manner of other commemorations.[46] In 2015, while looking at the global legacy of Magna Carta, attention was also focused back on the king compelled to concede its terms. Above all, this showed that the general academic view of John was once more a negative one, albeit with none of the rabid Victorian excesses: 'Without the intense hostility to him as a person, there would have been no revolt and no Magna Carta.'[47]

For centuries, the historians' John has been a shapeshifter, taking the form of each generation's preoccupations. In the sixteenth century he was the virtuous anti-papal hero, only to morph into the tyrannous opponent of liberties of the seventeenth and eighteenth centuries, changing once more in the nineteenth century into the clever but morally depraved villain, which vesture he shed in the twentieth century to reflect the misunderstood administrative genius. Yet by the twenty-first century there were two Johns, for as historians battled over the true form of their king, popular culture had its own immutable villain, which no amount of historical revisionism appears likely to dislodge.

John in Popular Culture

Those raised on Robin Hood and wicked King John rarely realise that John's early appearances in fiction were extremely favourable, occurring as they did in the polarised, anti-papal hysteria of the sixteenth century. A testament to John's reinvention as Reformation hero is that he became the subject of the oldest extant historical verse drama in English, John Bale's *Kynge Johan*. Written in the late 1530s and revised in the early 1560s, Bale's work is essentially a morality play which has John in dialogue with allegorical figures representing the nobility, the clergy and the likes of Sedition and

Usurped Power. A flavour of the approving treatment afforded John is found in a summary of his struggle with the Church.

> Upon a good zeal he attempted very far
> For wealth of this realm to provide reformation
> In the church thereof, but they did him debar
> Of that good purpose; for by excommunication
> The space of vii years they interdict thy nation.
> These bloodsuppers thus of cruelty and spite
> Subdued this good king for executing right.

'Good King John' might raise eyebrows today, but in this play John is an exemplar of the virtuous king. Disregarding history entirely, John here suffers excommunication for his attempts at reforming the Church, portrayed as a proto-Henry VIII. If there is any doubt about the link between John's efforts and those of Henry, it is quickly dispelled.

> This noble King John, as a faithful Moses,
> Withstood proud Pharaoh for his poor Israel,
> Minding to bring it out of the land of darkness,
> But the Egyptians did against him so rebel,
> That his poor people did still in the desert dwell,
> Till that duke Joshua, which was our late King Henry,
> Clearly brought us in to the land of milk and honey.

John is the new Moses whose faithful struggle prepares Henry's liberation of England from the wilderness of papal subjugation; in the Bible, Joshua is Moses' heir who finally brings the Israelites into the Promised Land. In Tudor England, John had become the embodiment of the greatest Old Testament prophet.

In 1591, *The Troublesome Reign of King John* was published anonymously (it was possibly the work of George Peele). This has a complicated textual history because seventeenth-century sources attribute it to Shakespeare. Although longer, it is very similar to the Bard's *King John* (c.1596) and there is clearly a relationship between the two. Shakespeare's John is a distinctly more ambiguous character than Bale's, the reported and then actual death of Arthur (either in an escape attempt or suicide) given a central place. John is poisoned by a monk and has a very long death scene in which the poison burns him from within, which some have seen as an intentional echo of the burning of martyrs as described by Foxe. The essentially patriotic nature of the play and its implicit criticism of the barons is summed up in a famous line from the closing speech:

> This England never did, nor never shall,
> Lie at the proud foot of a conqueror,
> But when it first did help to wound itself.

Although a relatively popular play in the eighteenth and nineteenth centuries, King John fell out of favour and was rarely performed in the twentieth century. Possibly the most interesting modern performance took place on the 800th anniversary of John's death around his tomb in Worcester Cathedral, the king's effigy a mute witness to his fictionalised life.

The transformation of John from hero to villain happened at a slower pace in plays than in works of history. Robert Davenport's *King John and Matilda* (published 1655) has a considerably less flattering portrait of John, but it is far from wholly negative. Yet at the same time as Shakespeare was writing, Robin Hood was entering into John's posthumous story, a time bomb which would destroy his reputation in later centuries. In 1521, the Scottish historian John Mair (or Major) had been the first to place the legend of the notorious outlaw in the late twelfth century, medieval versions of the story normally being under a King Edward. Two linked plays by Anthony Munday, *The Downfall of Robert Earl of Huntingdon* and *The Death of Robert Earl of Huntingdon*, were published in 1601. While John's resistance to papal pretensions is still viewed positively, there is also space for his negative characteristics and most significantly, the king is presented as Robin Hood's enemy.

For all these early precursors, various editions and retellings of the medieval Robin Hood ballads, the work which firmly cemented the link between John and Robin Hood in popular imagination, simultaneously securing John's negative reputation, was Walter Scott's romantic novel of 1819, *Ivanhoe*. Set during Richard I's captivity (although the Lionheart later appears in order to save the day), the usurping Prince John is 'light, profligate and perfidious', 'at least as licentious in his pleasures as profligate in his ambition', 'of all the sons of Henry the Second […] most distinguished for rebellion and ingratitude to his father'. Ambitious traitor to his brother, cruel villain and opponent of the noble cause of Robin Hood became the three strands of John's character which have endured in popular imagination for more than two centuries since the appearance of Ivanhoe. The modern image of King John descends from this portrayal by Scott.

Tales of Robin Hood increased in popularity during the nineteenth century and most located the story during the later twelfth century. John was often the background villain, the supporting act for the sheriff of Nottingham and Guy of Gisbourne, yet he was definitely a villain. Part of the enduring appeal of the legend is its contrast of the 'good' outlaw with the 'bad' king, the moral that tyranny can be resisted. Through the twentieth century and beyond, the story was retold in books and comics, a story for children which fixed the idea of bad Prince/King John in infant minds from early days. For all the many books by historians and literary scholars debating the reality of Robin Hood and the development of the legends, King John and the outlaw of Sherwood Forest are now inseparable in the popular mind.[48]

This is demonstrated by the King John of the cinema and television age. John has probably been portrayed on screen more than any other English monarch. The first instance was remarkably early, in 1899, with four heavily edited scenes of Herbert Beerbohm Tree as John from Shakespeare's *King John*, released ahead of Tree's stage production of the whole play in London. Only the third of these silent clips, showing the exaggerated death scene of a white-robed John in his chair, survives, although still frames exist of the other three scenes. Thereafter, nearly all the many depictions of John appear in adaptions of Robin Hood or Ivanhoe, which made John the perfect villain for the silver screen.

The tone was set early for this Hollywood version of the evil king by the Canadian actor Sam de Grasse, with a suitably malevolent portrayal of John in the 1922 film *Douglas Fairbanks in Robin Hood*. Thereafter, as sound and colour came to film, John became typecast in a succession of Robin Hood/Ivanhoe films which repeatedly rehashed what was essentially the same plot, only the cast, budget and special effects changing. From Claude Rains in *The Adventures of Robin Hood* (1938), which starred Errol Flynn as Robin, John was a perennial tyrant. In various films and (mainly British) television series, the likes of Ian Holm (*Robin and Marian*, 1976 film) Ronald Pickup (*Ivanhoe*, 1982 TV film) Phil Davis (*Robin of Sherwood*, 1984–86 ITV series), Edward Fox (*Robin Hood*, 1991 film) and Toby Stephens (*Robin Hood*, 2006–09 BBC series) have starred as John opposite the green-clad outlaw. It was the perfect role for actors to prove their villainous credentials. There have been moments of light relief from the conventional version, such as that provided by Richard Lewis in the 1993 Mel Brooks parody, *Robin Hood: Men in Tights*. The odd portrayal has been rather different, such as that of Oscar Isaac in Ridley Scott's *Robin Hood* (2010). For the most part, however, the traditional interpretation has been remarkably durable and versions of Robin Hood, complete with Bad King John, continue to be made with remarkable regularity.

As the Robin Hood stories were reworked and marketed for children in print, so they proved lucrative for a similar audience on screen. John has the dubious distinction of being the only king of England to feature in a Disney animation (discounting his brother's cameo at the end), as a wicked, cowardly, sulky, thumb-sucking lion with a mother complex voiced by Peter Ustinov in *Robin Hood* (1973). Forbes Collins played a distinctly unpleasant John in Tony Robinson's offbeat BBC children's series *Maid Marian and her Merry Men* (1989–94). In 2012, John Michael Higgins voiced yet another cartoon John (albeit human this time) in *Tom and Jerry: Robin Hood and His Merry Mouse*. It was a bizarre path indeed from Shakespeare to Tom and Jerry.

Even without Robin Hood, John is an irresistible villain for novelists and scriptwriters. James Goldman's play *The Lion in Winter*, which premiered on Broadway in 1966 and has been performed several times since on both sides of the Atlantic, gives a distinctly unflattering portrait of a spoiled John amid the machinations of his elder brothers and the French king against Henry II. It was made into a film in 1968, with Nigel Terry taking the part of John. In 1978, a thirteen-episode BBC series, *The Devil's Crown*, dramatised the reigns of all three Angevin kings, the adult John of wildly-fluctuating moods played by John Duttine. Non-Robin Hood novels often present John as a mix of lustful playboy, cruel tyrant and murderous villain. Such is the John who emerges from Graham Shelby's *The Devil is Loose* (1973) and *Wolf at the Door* (1975), and Jean Plaidy's *Prince of Darkness* (1978). On the other hand, there are novels which show more sympathy towards John, although none which redeem him, for even less hostile writers allude to a darkness within the king. Sharon Penman's *Here Be Dragons* (1985) and more recent novels by Elizabeth Chadwick are the most notable in this category. Films featuring John without Robin Hood are a rarity, but one recent exception, *Ironclad* (2011), based around the siege of Rochester in 1215, shows that the image of tyrant king survives without Robin Hood.

So well-known is King John that he can also be adapted into distinctly more eccentric plots. Philip Lindsay's 1943 novel, *The Devil and King John*, has John introduced to the 'Old Religion' (witchcraft) by Isabella of Gloucester, which then explains his conflict with the Church. A two-part *Doctor Who* episode in 1983, *The King's Demons*, had John replaced by a shape-shifting robot as part of a plot to prevent Magna Carta. (When an episode about Robin Hood and also involving space robots, *Robot of Sherwood*, was broadcast in 2014, John was absent from the plot.)

With or without Robin Hood, King John is simply too fixed in the popular mind as a villain. Even the most sympathetic fictional portrayals stop well short of being positive. Whatever the historians say, there is no place in fiction (or at least fiction that anyone wants to read or watch) for a man redeemed by his record keeping. People know and want the pantomime villain set in the dramatic stories of good and bad, of evil deeds and heroic actions. Two centuries after *Ivanhoe*, there is still a market for endless retellings of the evils of John. In the world of popular fiction, John will remain Bad King John. He is just too good a baddy.

Verdict

If there is little chance of any reversal in John's popular reputation, how unfair is this? As the stereotypical wicked king of English history, there have been plenty from his own day onwards who have condemned him. When he has found champions, or at least apologists, it is often because he is a useful representative to appropriate for a later cause. In the sixteenth century, his reign was a gift to Reformation propaganda. In the twentieth century, his attempted redemption reflected a challenge to the certainties of the medieval world view, not least religion.

Much of the case for a positive reassessment of John rests on analysis of the inherent biases of the chroniclers and a rather arrogant assumption that historians know better. Yet the way this was done in the twentieth century itself reflected the inherent biases of the post-Christian era. How, after all, does a generation which no longer believes in the punishing fires of hell understand Matthew Paris' verdict on John, let alone engage with it on its author's terms? It is true that all the chroniclers of John's reign were churchmen and that John's tangles with the Church were never going to win him a sympathetic hearing. It is equally true that some of what they wrote was vituperative and exaggerated. Yet in the thirteenth century, a king was meant to embody Christian values and be a defender of the Church; such promises were contained within the coronation, which invested the king with a sacred duty. If they wrote with an agenda, the chroniclers nevertheless reflect a contemporary view. It may not be as universal a one as the chroniclers would have us believe, but it is too ubiquitous to dismiss out of hand.

In this regard, it is instructive to look at the contrasting fortunes of Richard I and John in modern times. Twentieth-century historians imposed their own values on the two brothers, in the light of two World Wars and (in Britain) the creation of a welfare state. An age horrified by warfare and religious conflict but awed by bureaucratic government and good administration looked with greater hostility on Richard the crusader and greater admiration on John the (perceived) administrator. This was not how contemporaries viewed things. Without approving of Richard's Crusade, we must accept that for many contemporaries this was an honourable Christian pursuit. Likewise, we may approve of the record-keeping of John's regime, but in contemporary eyes that was no substitute for his perceived failure as a warrior. We need to remember that the nicknames Lionheart and Softsword were contemporary and give an insight into how the brothers were viewed by the standards of kingship in their own time.

There can no longer be serious doubt that John was an energetic king with an interest in government. However, some caution must be exercised in using this fact to redeem John. The equating of energetic administration and detailed records with good kingship is dubious. Too often in modern times, the assumption has been that a king who presided over such an intricate bureaucracy cannot have been a bad king. Yet Nazi Germany and Stasi East Germany were incredibly bureaucratic; that is not to draw any parallels between those regimes and John's England, but to remind us that bureaucracy is not inherently good and can be used as a tool of evil regimes and good governments alike. In John's case, even if we accept the questionable fact that he was personally responsible for the proliferation of administrative records, a case can be made for this being part of his suspicious, avaricious nature. A king so determined to raise revenue, keep track of debts and demand surety for loyalty needed an efficient means of doing so. To accept John's energy and the competence of his administration is hardly a moral exoneration. Contemporaries did not judge a king on how well he kept detailed patent rolls.

Perhaps the crux of the matter is that most modern historians are far less comfortable with moral judgements than medieval chroniclers, at the same time as modern society leaps rapidly to extreme, inappropriate moral verdicts. Nevertheless, we can hold him to account by the standards of his own time. One of the most common defences is that other kings did the same things: take hostages, torture or execute prisoners, deal ruthlessly with treason. That is not in question, but with others these were isolated incidents, often tempered with acts of mercy. The picture which emerges from John's reign is one of a king who was unusually cruel, with some particularly shocking acts. Such deeds were as repulsive to the thirteenth-century mind as to ours. Even permitting for exaggeration, the accusations against John's character are hard to dismiss. Individual incidents might be challenged or explained, but there are simply too many incidents to claim the whole picture is a fabrication. For all the exaggerations and mitigations, there seems little reason to doubt that John was a pretty unpleasant man.

That does not automatically make him a bad king. Unpleasant men could nevertheless be successful kings. In John's case, however, his character directly caused the failure of his kingship. In modern idiom, he failed to even attempt to win over hearts and minds until far too late. His treachery against his father and his brother fatally damaged his credibility. His suspicious nature poisoned his relations with his barons. Focused on reconquering his lost continental lands, he ruthlessly exacted money and indebted lords for a cause to which others were much less committed, offering far too little in return. His behaviour and cruelty raised serious doubts about his commitment to justice. Whether, as many have alleged, his behaviour made him a tyrant is an open question, but it certainly impacted on his rule enough to make him a bad king.

It could be endlessly and pointlessly debated whether John was the worst king of England, but the inevitable verdict is that he must number among the worst. By any standard, including his own, he failed. He lost Normandy, Anjou, Maine and other continental territories in a fight from which he was absent, then devoted all his efforts for a decade to reconquering them at enormous cost and did not succeed. He behaved in such a way that he lost the support of the nobility, was compelled to concede Magna Carta, and died with his kingdom wracked by civil war. While there were longer-term factors which need to be acknowledged, John himself is culpable to a significant extent for bringing all this about. The failure of his kingship was his own fault, caused by the deep flaws in his character. He failed miserably in working with his political community. Magna Carta was not inevitable in 1199, but through sixteen years of misrule by suspicion, ruthlessness and brutality, John ended up at Runnymede, and his reign ended in conflict and with the succession of his son in peril. If there is any tragedy in his reign, it is that he had the potential and ability to be something other than the bad king posterity has rightly judged him to have been.

Chapter 3

Edward II: A Worthless King?

'Edward II (1307–27), the most hopeless king to sit on the English throne…'[1]

'Edward II was one of the most unsuccessful kings ever to rule England.'[2]

'In 1327, in the face of arguably the worst and ultimately the most dangerous king ever to rule England…'[3]

These three opinions show how bad the general perception of Edward II is, so dangerously hopeless that he became the first king since the Norman Conquest to be deposed. His incompetence is still proclaimed today, as fans at Hampden Park and Murrayfield lustily sing their unofficial national anthem about Edward's defeat at Bannockburn. Seven centuries have not lessened the impact of the most humiliating defeat of an English army by the Scots. His father became known as 'hammer of the Scots', while he is remembered for being hammered by the Scots. He spent more than half of his reign locked in conflict with his cousin, alienated his wife and ultimately lost his throne. Aside from his scandalous liaison with Piers Gaveston, the most infamous favourite in medieval English history, Edward's demise is one of the most memorable of any monarch, beloved of former generations of schoolboys. The reign of Edward II was certainly not dull.

Yet if there remains a broad consensus that Edward was a failure, why he failed has been hotly debated. The certainties of past generations have been challenged. The two 'facts' most people know about Edward, that he was gay and that his grizzly end involved a red-hot poker, are both questionable and have indeed been extensively questioned. Traditionally, he has been viewed as inept, lazy and unfit to wear the crown. For a brief period in the later twentieth century, he was seen as much more malevolent. By contrast, recent popular histories have tried to partially rehabilitate him, judging him unfortunate more than anything. Edward has also morphed into a king for modern times, becoming something of a gay icon and an almost heroic failure.

Edward's Life and Reign

Edward, the fourth son of Edward I and Eleanor of Castile, was born at Caernarfon Castle on 25 April 1284, hence was known as Edward of Caernarfon. A famous story has the king presenting the boy to the Welsh as a child born in Wales who could speak no English, but this legend apparently first appeared in the sixteenth century. The heir to the throne was Edward's only surviving brother, 10-year-old Alphonso, but he died in August 1284, leaving baby Edward as heir. After several alternative plans, a 1299 proposal that Edward should marry Isabella, daughter of Philip IV of France, resulted in their betrothal in 1303. The same agreement led to Edward I's remarriage, to Philip's sister Margaret, which soon gave Prince Edward two half-brothers: Thomas of Brotherton and Edmund of Woodstock, later Earls of Norfolk and Kent.

By now, Edward was a young man participating in Edward I's increasingly brutal campaigns to subjugate Scotland. He took part in several operations after 1300, performing considerably better militarily than he would as king. It seems that Edward II had had a standard education for the time. He was certainly conventionally pious, generally enjoying good relations with the Church and religious orders. In 1301, Edward of Caernarfon became the first heir to the English throne to be created Prince of Wales. In 1302, his father gifted him the Hertfordshire manor of (King's) Langley, where he had spent a lot of time as a child and which became a favourite manor when he was king. Much would later be made of his love of pastimes considered unsuitable for royalty, not least rowing, which nearly cost him his life when he almost drowned at Fen Ditton in Cambridgeshire in 1315.

Relations between father and son were strained. In June 1305 they had a major falling out after the prince clashed with his father's treasurer, Bishop Walter Langton of Coventry and Lichfield. The king banished his son from court and deprived him of most of his household. The quarrel was patched up in October and at Pentecost 1306 Edward I knighted his son and made him Duke of Aquitaine. Still, further troubles lay ahead. The main cause of these was a Gascon named Piers Gaveston, slightly older than Prince Edward, part of the prince's household since around 1300. The relationship between the two men has long fascinated people. There has been considerable debate about whether Edward was homosexual or bisexual, although it is worth noting that he fathered four legitimate children and at least one bastard. Contemporaries compared the relationship between Edward and Gaveston to that between David and Jonathan in the Bible, although that hardly helps; the friendship between David and Jonathan was similarly ambiguous and Biblical scholars are divided on its nature. The two men certainly became close and by the end of his life the king did not approve, although as late as May 1306 he knighted Gaveston alongside the prince. Some accounts record that in early 1307, when his son asked him to give Gaveston an earldom, he physically threw the prince out of the room. Gaveston was banished, crossing the Channel laden with gifts from Edward, but their separation was short. On 7 July that year, on his way to yet another campaign in Scotland, Edward I died at Burgh-on-Sands. As soon as he heard the news, the new King Edward II summoned his favourite back to England. The first charter of the reign created Gaveston Earl of Cornwall.

His relationship with Gaveston dominated the opening years of Edward's reign and proved catastrophic. Whether or not Edward's infatuation was sexual, it was widely condemned by chroniclers as immoderate and inappropriate. Edward's other immediate priority was revenge against Walter Langton, who was stripped of the treasurership and imprisoned. This move was popular, but the continued ascent of the favourite was not. Gaveston married the king's niece and possibly became his chamberlain, certainly controlling access to the king. Astounded contemporaries saw him as a second king. When Edward crossed to France in early 1308 for his marriage, it was Gaveston he appointed keeper of the realm. The favour bestowed by the king was both extraordinary and extraordinarily foolish.

In Boulogne on 25 January 1308, Edward married Isabella of France, who was around 12 years old. Back in England, the couple were crowned a week later than scheduled, on 25 February, with an additional clause in the king's oath (that he would abide by the laws and customs of England as agreed by the community of the realm). There has been a slightly ridiculous debate over the fact that the oath was administered in French rather than Latin, which some have tried to make evidence of Edward's illiteracy, but French was the language of the nobility and was again used for Edward III's coronation. The festivities were a scandal: Gaveston, robed in purple, played a prominent role, while the hangings at the coronation banquet were those of Edward and Gaveston rather than those of Edward and Isabella, with the king ignoring his queen to spend his time with Gaveston. The nobility, outraged at such flagrantly inappropriate behaviour, made the king fully aware of their displeasure when parliament met three days later.

Led by Henry de Lacy, Earl of Lincoln, most earls intensified their demands for Gaveston's dismissal. Parliament broke up in acrimony, with the king and Gaveston retiring to Windsor and civil war a distinct possibility. The opposition headed for Pontefract and drafted articles intended to restrain the king and get rid of Gaveston. These were presented to Edward when parliament met again in late April 1308. Once Philip IV added his voice from Paris to those demanding Gaveston's removal, the king's resistance collapsed. His favourite had to relinquish his earldom and was banished from England on pain of excommunication. Edward appointed Gaveston lieutenant of Ireland, escorting him to take ship from Bristol in late June.

Gaveston was in Ireland for a year, from June 1308 to June 1309. Edward never reconciled himself to his favourite's exile. Outwardly, he made efforts at conciliation and announced a Scottish campaign, which brought Lincoln and the others back from opposition. Behind the scenes, he worked for Gaveston's return. In April 1309, he asked parliament to permit Gaveston to come back to England but was rebuffed and presented with articles for reform. These had been composed by a group of earls during a tournament at Dunstable earlier in the year. The king refused an immediate response. At the start of June, a papal bull arrived from Clement V, like Gaveston a Gascon, who was favourably inclined towards Edward and absolved Gaveston from the threat of excommunication. Edward summoned Gaveston back and rushed to Chester to meet him. In his joy at the reunion, the king made several concessions at a parliament which met at Stamford the following month. In August Gaveston was restored to the earldom of Cornwall.

The year of enforced separation had made neither king nor Gaveston wiser or more cautious. Gaveston offended several earls by giving them derogatory nicknames: Warwick was 'the black dog of Arden', Pembroke 'Joseph the Jew' and Lincoln 'burst belly'. His behaviour undid all Edward's (limited) efforts at conciliation. The Earls of Lancaster, Hereford and Warwick were to be at the heart of the movement against Gaveston for the next three years. A planned parliament in October had to be abandoned when several earls refused to attend because Gaveston would be present. There were additional grievances which had been building since Edward I's later years, not least the issue of prises and purveyance, the deeply unpopular system where supplies were requisitioned for the royal household or the king's campaigns. King and favourite spent Christmas together at Langley amid an uneasy peace.

Another parliament was summoned to meet at Westminster in February 1310. Lancaster, Hereford and Warwick, now joined in opposition by the

Earl of Pembroke, came to London but for three weeks resolutely refused to make the short journey to Westminster to attend parliament until Gaveston was sent away. When the assembly finally met at the end of the month, Edward was threatened with deposition if he failed to agree to the establishment of a committee which would have the power to reform royal government. He had no choice but to accept the appointment of twenty-one bishops, earls and barons, known as the Ordainers. It was an abject humiliation for the king; although the Ordainers were a balanced mix of reformers and royalists, after less than three years on the throne Edward had effectively been forced to yield control of government.

As the Ordainers set to work, Edward headed north with Gaveston and made military preparations in southern Scotland, where Robert I (Robert Bruce) had been making significant headway. After an autumn tour of the English fortresses south of the Forth, from November 1310 until July 1311 Edward based himself at Berwick-upon-Tweed. Bruce avoided any military engagement and with few earls actively supporting the king, his attempted Scottish campaign was a miserable failure. Most preferred to stay in the south of England and work on government reform, viewing the king's venture north as distraction tactics. Lincoln died in February 1311. From this point onwards, the king's most resolute opponent was Thomas, Earl of Lancaster, who also held the earldoms of Derby and Leicester. Lancaster was the king's cousin, son of Edward I's younger brother Edmund. When Lincoln died, Lancaster also inherited his two earldoms (Lincoln and Salisbury), giving him a total of five and making him the king's mightiest subject. For all he would cloak his opposition over the next decade in the rhetoric of reform, Lancaster was as vindictive, stubborn and inflexible as the king, possibly more so; as one modern historian aptly puts it, he 'never located a burial ground for hatchets'.[4] When he went to swear homage for his new titles, Lancaster bluntly refused to enter Scotland and matters came perilously close to violence before Edward yielded and crossed the Tweed.

Lancaster was an irreconcilable opponent of Gaveston and a driving force among the Ordainers, along with Hereford, Warwick and Pembroke. By the summer of 1311, Edward had no choice but to head south to face his opponents. Despite resistance by the king, the result of the Ordainers' work, the Ordinances, were published in September 1311 and were to dominate the political agenda for a decade. Alongside various reforms to the royal household and the government, the king's ability to act was severely curtailed, with him being forbidden to leave the realm or go to war without the consent of the barons in parliament. Many of these problems had been an issue since Edward I's reign, but the removal of 'evil counsellors' was ordered and the primary target was obviously Gaveston, who was banished from all the king's lands. Yet by January 1312, Gaveston was back in England and Edward had revoked the Ordinances. Civil war was again a very real prospect. Archbishop Robert Winchelsey of Canterbury excommunicated Gaveston in March. By now, Edward and Gaveston were entirely isolated, even moderate earls joining in efforts to remove Gaveston. King, queen and favourite took refuge at Newcastle, but the arrival of Lancaster forced them to sail from Tynemouth to Scarborough, leaving jewels and supplies behind in their hasty flight. Edward and Isabella headed from Scarborough to Knaresborough and then York, in the hope of raising troops. This allowed Lancaster to place his forces between the two towns and Pembroke to besiege Gaveston in Scarborough Castle. After ten days, on 19 May, terms were agreed and Gaveston was taken to York under Pembroke's protection. Following inconclusive talks, Pembroke took Gaveston to Deddington in Oxfordshire, leaving him lightly guarded while he went to visit his wife. Seeing his chance, the Earl of Warwick sped to Deddington. On 10 June he seized Gaveston and dragged him to imprisonment in Warwick Castle. Pembroke objected strongly, but Lancaster, Hereford and others arrived at Warwick and were determined to see the end of the king's hated favourite. After some pretence of a trial, on the morning of 19 June Gaveston was led out of Warwick along the road to Kenilworth. Once he was on Lancaster's lands, at Blacklow Hill, he was summarily executed.

Gaveston's death solved nothing. It did bring Pembroke, deeply offended, back to the king's side, along with the Earls of Gloucester and Surrey. Yet it is a measure of Edward II's incompetence that such temperamentally loyal men had gone into opposition in the first place. For five years, the king's obsession for his favourite had dominated politics, poisoning political society and alienating even moderates. It is incredible that the king was unable to see this, or if he did see it, that he failed to act. It was the duty of a king to work with his nobility and Edward's stubborn refusal to curb his immoderate behaviour towards Gaveston was catastrophic. It was a disastrous opening to the reign which he had brought upon himself and from which he never truly recovered, not least as revenge was on his mind for the next decade.

For more than a year, Edward and his main opponents refused to reach a lasting settlement. Yet again, civil war threatened in the summer and autumn of 1312. There was a respite in November, when Queen Isabella gave birth to a son at Windsor, the future Edward III. In December, three months of agonised negotiations bore fruit with an agreement between the rival camps. In February 1313 the jewels left at Newcastle were returned to Edward, but the truce did not last. The level of mistrust was shown at the parliament of March 1313, from which the king absented himself through an illness widely believed to be feigned, while barons refused to attend on the grounds they had been improperly summoned. Thereafter, tensions began to ease. In May, Winchelsey died, allowing Edward to translate the loyal Bishop Walter Reynolds of Worcester to the archbishopric of Canterbury. Edward and Isabella crossed to Paris to spend time at the court of Philip IV, relations between the two kings warmer now Gaveston was dead. Finally, in October, a more stable peace was agreed between the king and his rebel earls.

With the English nobility all nominally back on the same side as their king, attention could turn to Scotland. Robert Bruce had continued to make significant advances and recapture key strongholds from English hands. By March 1314, with the likes of Edinburgh and Perth back under Scottish control, the English position in Scotland was in danger of collapse. The captain of besieged Stirling Castle agreed with Bruce that the castle would be surrendered if no relieving army had arrived by Midsummer's Day (24 June). Edward had already ordered the army to muster at Berwick. Pembroke, Gloucester and Hereford responded, although Lancaster and Warwick refused to come. The large English army came within sight of Stirling at the last possible moment, on 23 June. Hostilities began that afternoon, were suspended overnight, and resumed on the morning of the 24th.

The Battle of Bannockburn was the most catastrophic and humiliating English defeat of the Middle Ages. Gloucester was killed, Hereford captured and hundreds of Englishmen drowned in the boggy ground while trying to escape. Edward acquitted himself creditably before being dragged from the field by Pembroke and fleeing to Dunbar. From there, he sailed back to Berwick. Bruce took possession of Stirling and soon everywhere except Berwick was back in Scottish hands. Bannockburn did not end the war, but it was a disaster for Edward II. As the situation worsened for Edward in the following years and planned campaigns foundered in the face of his domestic problems, Bruce continued to make key gains and harass the northern counties, while his brother Edward Bruce launched an invasion of Ireland. Even the weather turned against the king of England. The middle years of the decade were plagued by atrocious meteorological conditions, endless rain causing harvest failure, famine and widespread starvation which killed as much as a tenth of the population in the years 1315–17. This would have been a challenge for any government, but was a particular problem for a divided administration like Edward's. It was impossible to launch military campaigns in such conditions, with shortage of money an additional complication.

Edward II: A Worthless King?

Unsurprisingly, the parliament which met at York in September 1314 was extremely uncomfortable for the king. He had to swear to uphold the Ordinances again, and in the following weeks several of his key officials were replaced. Following another lengthy parliament at Westminster beginning in January 1315, the court and royal household were purged. Foremost in the drive for reform were the Earls of Lancaster and Warwick. By contrast, after his release from Scottish captivity, the Earl of Hereford joined most of the other lords in returning to the king. When Gaveston was buried in the Dominican friary at Langley in January 1315, an occasion delayed because Gaveston had died excommunicate, several nobles even attended the ceremony. In August, Warwick died. Thomas of Lancaster moved from being a leader of the opposition to being the opposition. The quarrel between the two royal cousins overshadowed the reign's middle years. Despite reconciliations, truces, treaties and efforts by others to make them work together, Edward II and Thomas of Lancaster now hated each other and rarely made much effort to hide the fact. Their feud paralysed domestic government and prevented any meaningful effort to counter the growing Scottish threat.

Lancaster's political programme became a tediously repetitive demand for enforcement of the Ordinances of 1311. His tendency to resort to violence to get his way won him no friends. He showed little willingness to work hard or engage constructively, collecting positions of authority and titles while frequently turning up late for parliaments, often with an armed retinue. In his last years, he stopped turning up at all. While the king was hardly blameless, the earl did himself no favours by such behaviour, isolating himself and frustrating his more moderate colleagues. When parliament opened in Lincoln on 27 January 1316, for example, Lancaster was still eighty miles away in his castle at Kenilworth. Not for a fortnight did he deign to appear at Lincoln. He was then appointed head of the royal council, but Lancaster, in a very powerful position, was unable to work with the royalist-dominated commission for longer than two months. King and earl had a massive fight at York in the summer, after which Lancaster retired to his estates and spent most of the rest of his life there, sulking and causing trouble, protected by the large number of retainers in his service.

True, Lancaster's grievances had some legitimacy, especially the growing influence of a new band of favourites, including Hugh Audley the Younger, Roger Damory and William Montacute. Yet the earl's refusal to engage constructively seriously hindered domestic government and threatened English security. Edward needed Lancaster's cooperation to combat the continuing threat from Scotland, so their feud was a major obstacle to any

75

progress on this (or any other) front. The king had more success with the papacy. Although the new Pope, John XXII, was less pliable than Clement V and refused to release the king from upholding the Ordinances, he did order the Bruces to stop attacking England. Two cardinals were sent as legates in an effort to secure peace. In early 1317, northern England was largely spared as the Bruce brothers led a destructive but futile expedition to Ireland.

Returning from an embassy to the papal court at Avignon in 1317, Pembroke was kidnapped in France and had to be ransomed; Edward could not afford to be without his most valuable counsellor. Meanwhile, the new circle of intimates around Edward had conceived a violent hatred of Lancaster, which was mutual. In an act of startling foolishness in May 1317, the Earl of Surrey kidnapped Lancaster's wife, Alice. The Lancasters' marriage was unhappy and the countess was apparently not averse to being abducted, but it was a blow to the earl's pride which could not be endured. When Edward arrived at York in September to muster an army for a new Scottish campaign, Lancaster blocked bridges to prevent troops reaching the king. Near Darlington, the Bishop-elect of Durham, Louis de Beaumont, was kidnapped on the way to his consecration, along with the two papal legates; Lancaster was probably not party to this and swiftly secured the victims' release, but he was known to be hostile to Beaumont and his involvement was suspected.

The situation was getting out of hand rapidly and civil war loomed again. Encouraged by some of the hotheads in his entourage, Edward marched towards Pontefract and even prepared for battle, but the wise counsel of the cooler-headed Pembroke prevailed, the king drawing back and continuing south. In retaliation, Lancaster attacked the Yorkshire lands of Edward's favourites. The papal legates, sent to negotiate peace between England and Scotland, instead found themselves trying to broker an accord between two rival English parties. As they went back and forth between king and earl, the situation in the North deteriorated further. In April 1318, Berwick-upon-Tweed fell to the Scots. Scottish raiding into England resumed in earnest, reaching deep into Yorkshire, but the fact that Lancaster's lands remained untouched led many to believe he was in league with the Scottish king.

However, the catastrophic loss of Berwick was a spur to action. In April 1318, the Archbishop of Canterbury, Pembroke and others met Lancaster at Leicester and drafted a peace agreement. In the summer, negotiations continued, envoys shuttling between the king at Northampton and the Earl at Tutbury in Staffordshire. The discussions were often tortuous, sticking on Lancaster's demands for the punishment of the king's favourites and the obvious demands of the favourites that the king should not allow this. In the middle of these delicate proceedings, a man called John of Powderham was brought into the royal presence in July. John claimed to be the real king, Edward having been exchanged with him after an accident. While the king was inclined to treat this with amusement, others (including the queen) saw the potential damage and John was tried and hanged. One problem was Edward's reputation for enjoying 'common' pursuits like driving carts, rowing and thatching. While the tale was clearly a fabrication, the rumours of him being an imposter spread and were widely believed. This was not the only time in the reign frauds would appear to challenge the king.

Eventually, on 9 August 1318, the two royal cousins met at Leake in Nottinghamshire. The resulting Treaty of Leake confirmed the Ordinances, pardoning Lancaster and all his followers in return for Lancaster forgiving all the king's men except Surrey. A council was established to hold the king to account. However, though forgiven, Audley, Damory and Montacute were at court far less thereafter. From a point where civil war had looked almost inevitable earlier in the year, there was something approaching optimism by the end of 1318. Things finally seemed to be looking up for the king and his realm, as the weather brightened, people were no longer starving, and the Scottish situation improved. The Pope excommunicated Bruce and laid an interdict on Scotland. The Irish invasion was ended by Anglo-Irish forces who cheerfully sent Edward the head of Edward Bruce. Parliament met at York in October and Lancaster condescended to attend.

The optimism lasted into 1319, allowing plans to be made at last for tackling the Scottish problem. When the troops mustered at Newcastle in August, even Lancaster appeared with his men, the first time he had turned out for a campaign in twelve years. The army headed for Berwick and in September launched two failed assaults on the town. Meanwhile, a Scottish army slipped past the English and on 12 September defeated a hastily assembled defence force under the Archbishop of York at Myton-on-Swale in North Yorkshire. Edward had left Queen Isabella in York and she had a narrow escape. The bad news of the defeat at Myton reached an English camp at Berwick where the mood was already turning ugly. The king wanted to continue the siege, but Lancaster departed to protect his lands, leaving Edward no choice but to retreat to Newcastle. There was considerable suspicion about how Lancaster and the returning Scots had avoided each other, with renewed rumours of treasonous collusion by Lancaster.

The domestic peace resulting from the Treaty of Leake had always been fragile and it now shattered. Once more the major point of contention was royal favourites. The clique who had previously annoyed Lancaster and been dealt with at Leake had gradually been marginalised and a new set of favourites was emerging. One of these was Bartholomew de Badlesmere, who became steward of the king's household, to the fury of Lancaster, who was the hereditary Steward of England (something he never ceased to remind everyone at every opportunity). Far more insidious, though, was the man who over the next seven years would alienate the king from practically everybody and cost him his throne: Hugh Despenser the Younger. Hugh Despenser the Elder, his father, had been one of Edward's most loyal barons, backing him unwaveringly over Gaveston and the Ordinances. The younger Despenser was, in many ways, considerably more dangerous than Gaveston, especially for Edward's kingship. Where Gaveston was something of a playboy, Despenser was avaricious, calculating and ruthless. This was not a good combination with a king who was basically lazy and not especially interested in governance. Later stories would hint at a sexual relationship between Despenser and Edward, but there is as much evidence that Edward was attracted to Despenser's wife, Eleanor, who was also the king's niece. Indeed, it is possible Edward was afraid of his favourite as much as he was in love with him. Despenser had previously been relatively insignificant, overlooked by Lancaster at Leake, but in 1318 he became Edward's chamberlain, controlling access to the king's presence. It was a role to which he took with glee and which soon made him almost universally hated.

Growing resentment against Despenser simmered through the first half of 1320. In June, Edward crossed the Channel to do homage for Gascony to Philip V of France (1316–22) at Amiens. When he returned in August, the discontent with Despenser exploded into open conflict. Despenser had been accumulating enemies through his aggressive campaign to reunite all the lands of the earldom of Gloucester under his control. Now, in October 1320, Despenser persuaded the king to seize the lordship of Gower in South Wales rather than allow it to pass to the designated heir. This infuriated the Marcher lords, the barons who controlled the patchwork of lordships with special privileges across south and east Wales, uniting them against the favourite.

It was at this point that the king suddenly seemed to remember that he was king. The Anglo-Scottish truce agreed in December 1319 had reduced his financial and logistical pressures. A surprised but pleased Bishop of Worcester wrote to the Pope during the 1320 parliament about how Edward was now getting up early and attending to business industriously.[5] (The inference, of course, is that prior to this Edward had been lazy.) This new determination translated into a refusal even to pretend to accommodate Lancaster and quickly alienated many lords. Once Edward ordered his officials to take control of Gower in December 1320, the Marcher lords started preparing resistance. Foremost among them was the Earl of Hereford. As had been the case when Edward's infatuation with Gaveston had pushed even Gloucester and Pembroke into opposition, so now Edward demonstrated a staggering lack of political judgement in his deference to Despenser and his refusal to address the grievances of Hereford and others. Despenser was brazenly filling the royal household with his men and aggressively pursuing lands in South Wales, so that even some former favourites who had attracted Lancaster's ire before 1318 now moved into opposition. Whether through ineptitude or wilful obliviousness, Edward was allowing, even compelling, a powerful opposition to coalesce against him. He dubbed them 'Contrariants'. Lancaster declined to join them at this stage, although he was in contact with and sympathetic to the Contrariants. Although not in opposition, even Pembroke distanced himself from the court.

By the end of March 1321, Edward was at Gloucester antagonising the Marchers still further. Ignoring further requests from Hereford, by May the king found himself facing outright rebellion. Newport, Cardiff and Swansea castles, all Despenser holdings, fell in rapid succession. Others attacked the lands of Despenser's few allies. The Marchers soon gained control of the disputed lands and Edward and Despenser retreated to London. Lancaster, after years of sulking and isolated opposition, decided to join the party. He summoned two assemblies, called parliaments by some contemporaries (even though parliaments could only be summoned by the king). They both met near Lancaster's Yorkshire base, at Pontefract in May 1321 and Sherburn-in-Elmet the following month. Lancaster was now positioning himself at the head of the Contrariants, although a problem arose when Bartholomew de Badlesmere, sent by the king to the second meeting, defected to the opposition, leaving Edward incandescent. Unfortunately, Lancaster could bear a grudge like few others and he hated Badlesmere, resulting in serious division in the opposition ranks. Detestation of Despenser was the only unifying cause for a disparate coalition opposing the king. Edward summoned a proper parliament for Westminster in July. The opposition lords, minus Lancaster, arrived late. Efforts by the bishops to mediate proved fruitless. The still-loyal Earls of Arundel, Pembroke, Richmond and Surrey joined with the queen to exhort the king to yield, Pembroke cautioning Edward that failure to do so might cost him his crown.

In mid-August both Despensers were exiled. As had been the case with Gaveston, neither king nor favourite had the slightest intention of allowing the exile to be for any extended period. The younger Despenser did not even go abroad, basing himself in the English Channel and the North Sea, playing at being a pirate. Edward, meanwhile, had harboured a thirst for vengeance since Gaveston's execution nine years earlier. This time, he was determined he would not allow his royal dignity to be threatened and his favourite destroyed. With a zeal notably lacking for much of the previous fourteen years when it came to government, he now set himself to reverse his defeat and reassert control. He sent Queen Isabella to request entry into Leeds Castle in Kent. As this was held by Bartholomew de Badlesmere, the request was unsurprisingly refused. Edward duly besieged Leeds, which surrendered at the end of October after Lancaster, his hatred of Badlesmere undiminished, ordered the Contrariants not to intervene.

If hostilities had not yet been joined, this was civil war in all but name. At the end of November, Lancaster presided over another meeting at Doncaster, which sent a petition of justification to the king. The two sides were irreconcilable. In December, Edward persuaded a pliant council to agree that the exile of the Despensers had been illegal. Meanwhile, the Marchers had based themselves at Gloucester, determined to keep Edward out of Wales. The king headed to Cirencester, where he had ordered his troops to muster, to spend Christmas 1321. Two days later, the army marched out to encounter immediate problems. With the bridges over the Severn at Gloucester, Worcester and Bridgnorth in rebel hands, the king's army had to travel eighty miles north to Shrewsbury to enter Wales. Thereafter, however, the events of early 1322 went overwhelmingly in the king's favour.

By early February, Edward had crushed the rebellion in Wales and the marches, with several minor lords defecting back to him and others imprisoned. Even now, Lancaster refused to leave Pontefract and give any military support to the beleaguered Contrariants. Edward seized the earl's castle at Kenilworth and ordered the sheriff of Cumberland, Andrew Harclay, to prevent Lancaster reaching Scotland should he try to escape across the border. Lancaster's treasonous communications with the Scots were discovered by the Archbishop of York and made public by Edward in March, just before the king was reunited with the Despensers at Lichfield. After a failed stand at Burton-upon-Trent, most Contrariants now joined Lancaster at Pontefract, where the mood was desperate. It was agreed that the rebels would flee to Northumberland and wait for the king to calm down. They made it scarcely thirty miles north, to Boroughbridge, where they were intercepted by Harclay and his northern troops. Trying to force their way over the River Ure on 16 March, the Contrariants failed. Hereford suffered a particularly gruesome death, stabbed through the groin from underneath the bridge. The next day, Harclay's men surrounded the surviving Contrariants and Lancaster was captured trying to flee. He was taken to York, then to Pontefract, which Edward and the Despensers had reached in the meantime. On 22 March, in his own castle, Thomas of Lancaster was inevitably found guilty of treason and condemned to death. He was beheaded outside the castle walls the same day. Harclay was rewarded by elevation to the earldom of Carlisle.

Edward had his revenge for Gaveston's death. His cousin, who had been a thorn in his side for fourteen years, was gone, and with him died his precious, detested Ordinances. The king was firmly back in control of his realm. It was a moment which called for magnanimity, for Edward to show he had learned his lesson and reconstruct the political community. The problem was that Edward II was manifestly incapable of learning any political lesson, so rather than responding mercifully and rebuilding bridges, his regime embarked on an orgy of vengeance which ultimately turned almost everyone who mattered in the realm against him and cost him his throne. There were more than twenty executions in addition to Lancaster, including Badlesmere, and some of the bodies or body parts were left rotting on gallows and town walls for two years. Around a hundred men were gaoled, along with some wives and children of the rebels. Contrariant lands were forfeited to the king. Fines boosted the royal treasury. The elder Despenser was made Earl of Winchester while his son benefited from a constant stream of patronage. Even loyal Pembroke, who had so often saved the king from himself, was arrested for a short time in the summer. He was largely eclipsed thereafter, his death in 1324 robbing the realm of one of its last potentially moderating influences.

Parliament met at York in May 1322 to confirm the punishments, abolish the Ordinances and assert the king's freedom of action. The regime had every intention of crushing opposition and ruling by fear. 'The regime' was principally the Despensers, the younger Hugh being the realm's dominant figure. Yet there were a few other significant men who played a critical role and provoked sufficient hatred to meet unpleasant ends when Edward's rule collapsed. Robert Baldock, archdeacon of Middlesex, successively keeper of the privy seal and chancellor, was deeply unpopular and Edward's efforts to secure him a bishopric were repeatedly thwarted. Walter Stapeldon, Bishop of Exeter and treasurer, presided over a reform of the exchequer in the 1320s. Roger Belers, the chief baron of the exchequer, proved adept at appropriating rebel lands and increasing royal wealth. The regime's naked avarice caused enormous resentment over the next four years. Edward's stated intention was to become rich and these servants proved excellent at helping him achieve this aim. Despenser had a particular talent for forcing widows to disgorge their inheritances by cruel means. In September 1324, Edward even allowed Despenser to take some of the queen's lands and dismiss her French servants, which would have disastrous consequences. Financial reform, greed and taxation allowed wealth to pour into the royal coffers. Edward had begun the reign indebted by his father's wars and had struggled financially for fifteen years. Suddenly, his fortunes were transformed. The king did indeed become rich. In the process, he also became hated.

Moreover, Edward's abysmal military record continued. His only real success had come in civil war, against a disunited and weak opposition. Boroughbridge had been won on his behalf by a sheriff leading a makeshift army. Against the Scots, Edward's record was dismal. Before 1322, he could claim that Lancaster's opposition had thwarted him. Now, he had no excuse. While he had been occupied in Wales in January 1322, the Scots had ravaged the bishopric of Durham. In July, Bruce attacked North-West England. August saw Edward assemble a huge force at Newcastle. It reached Edinburgh before turning back in yet another failure. The Scots launched a retaliatory campaign in October. Edward and Despenser had to flee from breakfast at Rievaulx Abbey to safety inside the walls of York. Queen Isabella had to escape from Tynemouth by sea. The Earl of Richmond was captured near Byland Abbey and was ransomed for a sizeable sum almost two years later, parliament refusing to contribute to the miserly king's request to help with the ransom. 1322 saw Edward humiliated by the Scots yet again and some northerners had had enough. Andrew Harclay, who for a decade had been defending the border on Edward's behalf, now decided that the king was useless against the Scottish threat. He met Robert Bruce and agreed terms, but when Edward found out he denounced Harclay as a traitor and had him executed. Even the king now realised, however, that matters were serious if loyal lieutenants like Harclay had been driven to such measures. On 30 May 1323, a thirteen-year Anglo-Scottish truce was agreed at Bishopsthorpe, just outside York.

Discontent was growing. At Pontefract, by mid-1323 Lancaster's grave was rapidly becoming a shrine, with miracles reported and calls for the earl's canonisation. In August, Roger Mortimer of Wigmore, one of the Marcher lords captured at the start of 1322, escaped from the Tower of London by climbing a rope ladder down to the Thames before making for France. Having had good relations with the Church and papacy for much of his reign, the king was now starting to make enemies among the bishops, most prominently Adam Orleton of Hereford, who was accused of involvement in Mortimer's escape. As the bishops of Bath and Wells, Lincoln, and Winchester also incurred royal displeasure, Edward's relations with the papacy cooled markedly. So, much more ominously, did relations with France.

The French were getting through kings with unseemly haste; when Charles IV acceded to the throne in 1322, he was the fifth monarch in eight years. He demanded Edward renew his homage for Gascony and Edward prevaricated. In October 1323, a gang killed a French sergeant at Saint-Sardos in Gascony. The combination of a refusal of Gascon royal officials to travel to Paris for a trial and Edward's failure to do homage led Charles to send an invasion force into Gascony in August 1324, which resulted in significant English losses in what became known as the War of Saint-Sardos. A truce was agreed, but the events which followed unravelled Edward's kingship. Queen Isabella was Charles IV's sister, so she was sent to Paris to negotiate in March 1325, reaching a basis for agreement by the summer. The French made Edward's performance of homage a condition of any further progress, so in August he made his way towards Dover. He then had a change of heart and handed over the duchy to his 12-year-old son, Edward, sending him to France to perform homage in September 1325.

Unexpected drama ensued. Isabella, until this point a dutiful queen, declared that someone (obviously Despenser) had come between her husband and herself and that she was staying at her brother's court. Furthermore, she was keeping Prince Edward in Paris with her. Rumours quickly began that she and Roger Mortimer had embarked on an affair. These grew more persistent as the months passed. By 1326, Edward was alarmed by the group in Paris, which included his half-brother (the Earl of Kent), the Earl of Richmond and the Bishop of Norwich, along with other exiles from England. The king made increasingly desperate attempts to get his wife and son back to England, but the French saw no cause to help him. Edward knew the severity of the threat. His regime had made itself massively unpopular, as was proved by the assassination in Leicestershire of Roger Belers, chief baron of the exchequer, in January 1326.

In the summer, Isabella's party moved to the Low Countries. Prince Edward was betrothed to Philippa, daughter of the Count of Hainault, in return for mercenary troops and a dowry which financed the invasion of England. The invading force set sail from Dordrecht and landed at Orwell in Suffolk on 24 September 1326. Very quickly, key figures defected to her, among them the king's other half-brother (the Earl of Norfolk), Thomas of Lancaster's brother (Henry of Leicester) and several bishops. Edward received the news in the Tower of London three days later. Attempts to rally support among the hostile Londoners failed miserably. The king, the Despensers and Robert Baldock fled westwards as violence erupted in London. Bishop Walter Stapeldon was beheaded with a bread knife by a mob near St Paul's Cathedral. Treasure left behind by the king's party was looted and the prisoners in the Tower set free. Isabella progressed unimpeded to the West Country, acquiring large numbers of supporters on the way. Bristol, in the hands of Despenser the Elder, surrendered to her. Despenser was consciously subjected to the same treatment he had afforded Lancaster in 1322, tried and condemned with no right of reply on 27 October. His execution was gruesome.

Meanwhile, his son was with Edward and Baldock in Wales. They had set out for Ireland from Chepstow on 20 October but been forced into Cardiff by the weather. They made for Despenser's mighty castle of Caerphilly, although for some reason did not stay there. A vast sum of money travelled with them, but they could not buy their way out of desperate straits. In early November, they were at Neath Abbey, before turning east again. Near Llantrisant Castle on 16 November, they were cornered and captured by the Earl of Leicester, at a place which came to be known as Pant-y-Brad (Vale of Treachery). Baldock was entrusted to the Bishop of Hereford and sent to London, where he died in the Fleet Prison six months later. Despenser the Younger, reviled, could have no doubts about his fate. Taken to Hereford, where the Earl of Arundel had been butchered by a particularly incompetent executioner days before, Despenser tried to starve himself to death. Isabella refused to allow him to cheat her vengeance. He was brutally executed at Hereford on 24 November, his body divided and sent around the realm.

Edward was taken to Monmouth, compelled to surrender his great seal, then transferred to Kenilworth. At Isabella's Christmas court at Wallingford, intense discussions took place about the king's fate. Parliament met at Westminster in January 1327, faced with the awkward question of removing an anointed king. The solution was to have Edward abdicate, although as he surrendered his throne under compulsion, it is normally termed a deposition.[6] To reinforce the point, a series of articles was drawn up laying out Edward's misdeeds; the thrust of these was neglect of his duties and the words 'tyranny' and 'tyrant' were consciously avoided, as the 'elite drew back […] quickly from the more radical implications of its actions'.[7] The king was informed of this by a delegation which visited him at Kenilworth on 20 January. He reacted badly but had no choice except to acquiesce.[8]

The formal renunciation of homage took place the next day and, back at Westminster, the reign of King Edward III began on 25 January. The hostile Londoners had been a menacing presence in the background of proceedings and there was greater opposition than the surviving sources suggest, not least from certain of the bishops. The transition of power, however, was accomplished peacefully.

The decision had been taken back in December to keep Edward alive. Fears of a rescue attempt caused him to be transferred into the custody of Thomas of Berkeley and John Maltravers in early April. Edward was moved, via Gloucester, to Berkeley Castle. As plots to liberate the former king continued to be uncovered, in July he was moved around to various places including Corfe Castle, although was then returned to Berkeley. With news of another escape plan reaching Mortimer, the decision was taken to kill Edward. In 1330, Edward III would accuse Mortimer of being responsible for what happened to his father; it was two Mortimer followers – Thomas Gurney and William Ockley – who were convicted of committing the crime. On 21 September 1327, the former King Edward II died, probably murdered, at Berkeley Castle. Despite lurid later stories about the insertion of red-hot pokers, it is more likely that he was suffocated. That the chronicles give several different causes of death suggests that no one really knew, but foul play was widely suspected.

The funeral took place on 20 December in Gloucester Abbey, such a delay not being unusual for a royal burial. While the monks of Westminster Abbey expressed an interest in the former king's body, Edward had had a difficult relationship with them during his reign and his relationship with neighbouring London had been turbulent, so this option was ruled out. Although less prestigious than Westminster, Gloucester had royal associations and was close to Berkeley, so Edward was laid to rest there in a ceremony attended by his wife and son. A fine alabaster effigy was raised over the grave.[9] The tomb had elements of a shrine and attracted plenty of visitors, being a good source of income for the monks and financing the remodelling of the abbey. Edward III would later support Gloucester as a place of pilgrimage and showed considerable interest in both the soul and the resting place of his father.

Rumours about Edward's survival circulated, some given credence and others invented by modern historians, but these were commonplace in such circumstances and all evidence suggests Edward was dead and buried in Gloucester.[10] Mortimer and Isabella ruled, increasingly unpopular, in the name of Edward III until 1330, when the young king dramatically seized Mortimer at Nottingham. Consciously breaking with the cycle of violence and show trials which had so blighted the years since Gaveston's death, Edward had Mortimer tried and condemned in parliament in order to reassert the rule of law. The king then declared that his father had been murdered and had his murderers condemned. After Mortimer's execution, Isabella entered enforced retirement. From 1332 until her death in 1358, she lived comfortably at Castle Rising in Norfolk. In 1327, she had been sent Edward II's heart in a silver casket, which she kept with her until she died. At her own request, she was buried in her wedding dress from half a century earlier. Maybe this was guilt or atonement. But perhaps it was an indication that she had loved Edward despite everything, that things could have been very different had he not allowed Despenser to come between them. If so, there is no more poignant testament to the folly of Edward of Caernarfon.

Edward through the Centuries

The overall picture of Edward II in the chronicles is a negative one, but Edward is not demonised in the same way as King John. The manner of his death, the regime replacing him becoming unpopular very quickly, and the fact that Lancaster struck most as distinctly unlikable, softened the judgements of the chroniclers.[11] The best chronicle of the reign is the anonymous *Vita Edwardi Secundi* (*Life of Edward the Second*).[12] This stops after Isabella's defection, so unfortunately does not cover Edward's last year, although is not therefore coloured by his deposition and death. It was written by someone well-informed about events at court and national politics, who was critical of Edward without being hostile or unfair. The perceptive author wrote the sections of his work at several points throughout the reign, so it charts the shift in opinions, hopes and fears over the years. In 1313, the author lamented that 'King Edward has now reigned six full years and up until now he has achieved nothing praiseworthy or memorable'. Noting the military achievements of Richard I at the start of his reign, the author continued:

> If our King Edward had borne himself as well at the outset of
> his reign, and not accepted the counsel of wicked men, not one
> of his predecessors would have been more notable than he.
> For God had endowed him with every gift, and had made him
> equal to or indeed more excellent than other kings.

Edward did not lack abilities, but squandered them. The 1318 update was more optimistic. Noting that the Biblical King Nebuchadnezzar had done 'nothing memorable' for his first eleven years, and that at the same point Edward II had likewise done nothing 'that ought to be preached in the marketplace or the rooftops', the author states that 'great hope has latterly grown in us'. By 1325, however, all is despair again, in one of the most famous sections of the chronicle:

> Thus parliaments, consultations, and councils decide nothing these days. For the nobles of the realm, terrified by threats and the penalties inflicted on others, let the king's will have free rein. Thus today will conquers reason. For whatever pleases the king, though lacking in reason, has the force of law.

This statement assumed particular significance for twentieth-century historians who accused Edward of tyranny, a word the author of the *Vita* notably avoids. His text is of immense value to historians because of its detail, accuracy and largely balanced approach.

Definitely unbalanced was the savage character assassination by Robert of Reading, a monk of Westminster writing under Isabella and Mortimer. His portrait depicts a monster and he is the only contemporary to accuse Edward of tyranny. By contrast, Geoffrey le Baker, of Swinbrook in Oxfordshire and writing in the 1340s, paints a much more sympathetic picture of the king, especially after his deposition.[13] Yet far the most influential character sketch, summarised repeatedly in later works, came from Ranulf Higden:

> King Edward was a man handsome in body and of outstanding strength, but, if common opinion is to be believed, most inconsistent in behaviour. For shunning the company of the nobles, he sought the society of jesters, singers, actors, carriage drivers, diggers, oarsmen, sailors, and the practitioners of other kinds of mechanical arts. He indulged in drink, betrayed confidences lightly, struck out at those standing near him for little reason and followed the counsel of others rather than his own. He was extravagant in his gifts, splendid in entertainment, ready in speech, but inconsistent in action. He was unlucky against his enemies, violent with members of his household, and ardently attached to one of his familiars, whom he sustained above all, enriched, preferred, and honoured.[14]

Contained therein were nearly all of the main elements found in opinions about the king for centuries afterwards.

Baker and Higden told a graphic story of Edward's murder, with gruesome details of a red hot poker being inserted into Edward's anus to avoid leaving a mark on the body. It is far more likely that he was suffocated, but this was a symbolic form of anal rape and after his death, stories about Edward circulated to discredit him. They may have originated with a sermon by Bishop Adam Orleton of Hereford, after Edward's capture but before his deposition.[15] Later in the century, a chronicler at Meaux Abbey in Yorkshire would write disapprovingly that Edward 'delighted too much in sodomitical vice'.[16] The idea that Edward enjoyed being the passive partner in gay sex was intended as a damning criticism of his morals, although accusations of sodomy were quite frequently hurled around at this time to denigrate opponents. In Edward's case, despite the fact that there is no clear evidence for his homosexuality, the story stuck and the ground was laid early for his development in later centuries into the 'gay king'.

On the other hand, some saw his death as martyrdom and tried to promote a cult of sainthood. Edward's great-grandson Richard II was keen to foster such a cult and set the canonisation process in motion. His nobles preferred to draw other lessons from Edward's reign. Faced with Richard's tantrums at the Wonderful Parliament of 1386, they explicitly reminded him of Edward's fate. Thirteen years later, when Richard was indeed deposed, the precedent of 1327 was a significant influence. With Richard disappeared any notions of 'Saint Edward II'. Yet Edward continued to be viewed as a tragic figure at the same time as being judged a useless king. Later medieval and Tudor authors followed the same script as their fourteenth-century predecessors. Under Elizabeth I, Raphael Holinshed observed that Edward's 'disordered manners brought himself and many others to destruction'. While observing that he showed promise at the start, his obsession with Gaveston caused him to give himself 'to wantonness, passing his time in voluptuous pleasure, and riotous excess'. There is, in the summing up at the end of the reign, a veiled reference that can be (and has been) taken as a belief in Edward's homosexuality, that he 'was induced unto more heinous vices'. Yet the verdict is mild: 'He was known to be of a good and courteous nature, though not of the most pregnant wit'. His 'indiscreet and wanton misgovernance' brought about his end, but Holinshed portrays a king whose repentance and cruel death purged him of his sins.

Holinshed was the main source used by Marlowe when he wrote his play about the reign. This, more than anything, set the tone for views of the king for centuries afterwards and continues to be a major influence on popular perceptions of Edward II. Marlowe's popularity and influence derives from the fact that his play expressed a concern with an issue which troubled writers of the reigns of Elizabeth I and James I: the royal favourite. Political pamphlets and chroniclers made use of the story of Edward II, his favourites and his deposition for didactic purposes, although not always drawing the same lesson. As the first post-Conquest example of the deposition of a reigning monarch, Edward's proved particularly important in discussions over precedents. In the opposition to Elizabeth I's favourites, especially the Earl of Leicester, Edward II's story was an obvious parallel. Faced with the novel situation of a queen regnant with male favourites, rumours also circulated about the sexual nature of these relationships.[17] Across the Channel, the parallels between Edward and Henry III were even more apparent, the French king's famous minions were widely believed to be involved sexually with him. A similar situation arose once James I succeeded Elizabeth in England, Edward II again serving as the exemplar for critics of the Jacobean favourites with whom the king was believed to be sexually entangled. In parliament in 1621, the former attorney general Sir Henry Yelverton foolishly drew a comparison between the Duke of Buckingham and Hugh Despenser; as neither James I nor Buckingham appreciated the comparison, Yelverton was promptly imprisoned.[18] In late Elizabethan and early Stuart England, the story of Edward II and his favourites was topical and used as a polemical weapon.

Towards the end of the Civil War in the 1640s and again during the Exclusion Crisis in the 1680s, the deposition of Edward II became a contentious subject, used both as justification for removing an unfit king and dire warning of the consequences of deposing an anointed sovereign. With Charles I in 1649, the deposers took a step from which their predecessors of 1327 and 1399 had shied away, executing the king. James II in 1688 is a better parallel, for a king judged unsuitable both abdicated and was deposed. That the example of Edward II was still cited and argued over, 350 years later, demonstrates how momentous the events of 1327 were in English history. Edward II had become a warning employed by Stuart royalists and opponents alike. This story of incompetence, tragedy, favourites and obsession, Marlowe historicised, was repeated unchallenged in its basic form for three centuries. The work of Elizabeth Cary, Viscountess Falkland, published in 1680 but written half a century earlier, encapsulates this seventeenth-century view of Edward II as a warning to the Stuart kings.[19] The idea of Gaveston as Edward's minion survived a long time, finding its way without comment into the account of David Hume in the following century. Much as the Elizabethan and early Stuart era shaped fictional portrayals of the king's reign, the obsession with favourites also exerted a major influence on historical writing about Edward II.

In the nineteenth century, William Stubbs gave a suitably damning verdict on Edward, whose 'reign is a tragedy, but one that lacks in its true form the element of pity; for there is nothing in Edward, miserable as his fate is, that invites or deserves sympathy'. His fate 'was the direct result of his own faults and follies'. While acknowledging Edward's courage, at the heart of Stubbs' criticism is the king's failure to conform to nineteenth-century constitutional expectations: 'He is the first king since the Conquest who was not a man of business, well acquainted with the routine of government.' The censorious eye of the Victorian bishop could conceive of no greater sin than this, that a king should not be an industrious bureaucrat.[20]

Stubbs was cited in two works published at either end of the First World War which were enormously influential during the middle part of the twentieth century, by T.F. Tout and James Conway Davies. Both qualify Stubbs and produce a less negative view of Edward's character. Tout summarises the chronicles as portraying a 'strong, handsome, weak-willed and frivolous king who cared neither for battles nor tournaments, neither politics nor business, and had no other wish than to amuse himself'. The problem was 'not so much the king's vices as his idleness and incompetence'. Yet he softens the picture, arguing that if Edward 'did not like work, he was not very vicious; he stuck loyally to his friends and was fairly harmless'. The sustainability of this belief that Edward was 'not very vicious' is dubious in light of the bloodletting of 1322, but in an evocatively anachronistic moment, Tout reflects that the king would have made a perfect Edwardian gentleman at the University of Oxford, where he could have distinguished himself 'by his knowledge of motor cars and perhaps even rowed in the University eight'.[21] Davies, similarly exercised by Edward's un-kingly pursuits, notes that 'Edward II's character was feeble rather in comparison with his immediate predecessor than judged by an absolute standard', while misfortune 'must be numbered among the king's faults.'[22] Both see him as a hopeless king, but not an evil one nor without redeeming features as a man.

Tout was particularly influential,[23] but with differing emphases Stubbs, Tout and Davies all saw the reign as a time of constitutional advancement. As constitutional historians saw the awfulness of John as leading to the good of Magna Carta, so they viewed the weakness of Edward II as important for preventing England succumbing to royal tyranny. The administrative reforms of these years were especially admired, while in the Ordinances and the baronial opposition were seen a form of principled ('constitutional') opposition to royal excess, resulting in a limited monarchy. All three also wrote about a 'Middle Party' which existed between 1312 and 1321, seeking an ideological middle way between Edward and Lancaster. More surprisingly, Tout saw Despenser the younger as a reformer who made positive administrative changes.

The idea of 'baronial constitutionalism' and the 'Middle Party' held sway for some fifty years. In the mid-twentieth century these views were largely accepted and little detailed work was done on the reign. The most significant contribution was a study by Hilda Johnstone of Edward's youth and education, followed by an edition of his letters.[24] General histories concentrated on Edward's incompetence, his taste for common pursuits and the tragic circumstances of his end. In a notably sympathetic portrait, making much of the king's personal interests while skipping most of the reign's problems, John Harvey concluded that Edward was 'a pathetic and courageous man, a royal martyr even if he were no saint'.[25] Winston Churchill's cutting verdict, as Victorian as ever half a century late, was that Edward was 'a perverted weakling, of whom some amiable traits are recorded'.[26] Rather more ambivalent, if still negative, was May McKisack. Acknowledging the desire to 'pity the weak-willed prince, successor to a famous father' and inheritor of several intractable problems, she nevertheless concludes that he 'lacked altogether the dignity and high seriousness of a king' and never 'tried to rise to his responsibilities or to learn from his misfortunes and mistakes'. He was a 'lazy and indifferent king' who 'lived a life devoid of noble purpose or of laudable ambition', whose 'own folly delivered him into the hands of his cruel foes'.[27] Edward II was a hopeless if somewhat tragic figure whose reign was an unfortunate interlude between two great kings. As the editor of the *Vita Edwardi Secundi* observed, 'Edward II sat down to the game of kingship with a remarkably poor hand, and he played it very badly.'[28]

From 1970, these orthodoxies began to collapse. Critical to the rethinking of the reign were biographies of Thomas of Lancaster by J.R. Maddicott and of the Earl of Pembroke by Seymour Phillips.[29] Examining the lives and retinues of these two earls, key men so closely implicated in the events of Edward's reign, showed how personalities and patronage were far more significant than previously acknowledged. The earls looked first and foremost to their own interests and power, not abstract constitutional doctrines. Theories about 'baronial constitutionalism' and a 'Middle Party' were shown to be untenable. This opened the way to a more sympathetic appraisal of Edward himself, now that he was no longer portrayed as some kind of proto-absolutist fighting principled constitutionalists.

At the same time, lives of Edward II began to appear, aimed at a popular readership. Harold F. Hutchison's 1971 book was sympathetic and (remarkably) the first complete biography of modern times. Hutchison's Edward was 'a likeable failure'. He noted that Edward was 'a prince with several odd traits of character, but most of those which earned him the disapproval of his contemporaries would in no way disconcert a modern generation'.[30] This was the essence of much writing on the king which followed. The man of gentle pursuits like rowing and acting was far more in tune with the 1960s and 1970s liberal ideals of disarmament and peace movements than his warrior father and son, as a (supposedly) gay king was something to be celebrated in a twenty-first century of widely accepted fluid and divergent sexualities. Unwittingly, Hutchison revealed the anachronism which lies behind most popular views of Edward II since 1970: he has received a sympathetic hearing because he is seen as a man out of his time, judged by modern rather than contemporary standards. There were plenty who still wrote about the incompetent king, but where he attracted sympathy, it was often for this reason.

Nowhere was this more evident than in those perceptions of Edward's sexuality. Among the reforms of Roy Jenkins' time as Home Secretary was the decriminalisation of homosexuality in 1967 and taboos around discussion of the subject were relaxing accordingly. Victorian and later writers clearly entertained the possibility that Edward II was gay, but were unable or unwilling to discuss it explicitly, with the partial exception of a 1910 article which today appears as bizarre as it is offensive.[31] From 1970, this changed. Maddicott stated bluntly that it is 'very difficult to doubt' that Edward and Gaveston's relationship was homosexual.[32] It was Hutchison, however, who first discussed the matter frankly by exposing the circumlocutions of previous generations, concluding that it 'is more than likely that Edward of Caernarvon was a homosexual', but this did not mean 'he could not also lead a normal heterosexual life'.[33] What he was essentially suggesting was that Edward was bisexual, a term not in common currency in 1971. The idea of homosexuality as abnormal reflects the prejudices of Hutchison's time, but otherwise his consideration of the question was moderate and fair. Two years later, Caroline Bingham was more cautious still in an equally sympathetic biography, but she was something of an exception.[34] Since Hutchison, it has been generally accepted in popular thought that Edward II was gay. Most academics have been far less convinced, agreeing with Michael Prestwich that this reflects 'a change in modern attitudes rather than the discovery of fresh evidence',[35] and noting that even if Edward did have sex with men, it did not make him gay in a recognisably modern sense, but their caution is widely ignored. The ambiguities of the evidence which concern them are easily dismissed as the inherent caution of an intolerant, repressed age. A gay king in his doomed relationship with Gaveston makes a far better story for modern times.

While this sympathetic view of Edward as gay king beset by misfortune has held the popular imagination ever since, during the 1980s academic judgements diverged wildly. Over the years, the thesaurus had been deployed to exhaustion in using every synonym of 'hopeless' to describe Edward II's kingship, but he had never really been accused of being especially malign. Suddenly, historians briefly turned him into a tyrant. The seminal work, by Natalie Fryde in 1979, demolished any lingering notions about the constitutional advancements of the reign.[36] Such developments as did happen had one simple motive: greed. Fryde showed how Edward and the Despensers had stored up roughly an entire year's income by the end of the reign, at the same time laying bare the brutal nature of the regime and its unsavoury methods. While much of Fryde's thesis gained acceptance, many historians were nervous about designating Edward himself a tyrant. The articles of deposition had accused him of incompetence and showing too little interest in governing, the language of tyranny consciously avoided there and by most contemporaries: 'the implications of using accusations of tyranny to remove a legitimate and anointed king were too contentious and divisive to be of any practical use'.[37] Five years later, Nigel Saul developed Fryde's work to show how the Despensers 'ruled by instilling fear' and utterly failed to root themselves in the political or local societies of the country, which is why they were so rapidly overthrown in 1326.[38] Saul is clear that this was a Despenser regime and that any tyranny was theirs. To deem the king a tyrant seemed an anachronistic modern label with numerous problems. While more willing to entertain the idea of a tyrannous Despenser regime, historians quickly backtracked from the idea of Edward the tyrant.

These debates had little impact on popular consciousness, where Edward himself remained something of a puzzling figure. A short biography in 1997 tried to explain the king in amateur psychological terms, 'the evils of his reign' stemming from his 'unstable personality'. Many of the conclusions here are speculative and curiously old-fashioned, although it is stated bluntly that Edward 'chose to flaunt his homosexuality at a time when society was becoming increasingly homophobic'.[39] Popular historians no longer saw any need to debate the matter of Edward's sexuality; it was simply accepted (following John Boswell) that he was gay and that one of his problems was being so in an increasingly homophobic fourteenth-century society.[40] This is obvious in Simon Schama's pacy, rather eccentric treatment of the reign, where he refers matter-of-factly to Edward's 'boyfriends' and opposition to his homosexuality. In fairness, Schama makes a valid point when he notes that it was 'not Edward's rustic pastimes, his fancy clothes, his racehorses, his creepy boyfriends or even his extreme fondness for amateur theatricals that got him into big trouble', but the failure of his leadership, something defenders of Edward have tended to overlook.[41] Michael Prestwich reasserted the more sceptical academic view that Edward's relationship with Gaveston was most likely 'not homosexual in character', but by now Edward was too deeply ingrained in popular imagination as the gay king for the evidence (or lack thereof) to matter. Where there was still common ground was in Prestwich's assertion that Edward 'proved to be incorrigibly incompetent'.[42]

There was a strong biographical focus in the later twentieth and early twenty-first centuries. Key churchmen received particular attention in the late 1970s and early 1980s.[43] Gaveston was the subject of biographies by J.S. Hamilton and Pierre Chaplais, their conclusions about Gaveston's relationship with Edward were very different. For Hamilton, that 'the two men were lovers is beyond dispute', whereas Chaplais makes it clear from the outset that he views the two as adoptive brothers.[44] Surprisingly, Edward II was not the subject of a full-scale, scholarly biography until as late as 2003. Roy Martin Haines' volume is a slightly uneven treatment of the reign, strongest on the Church. Yet it is a sober study which recognises some limited success in Edward's rule rather than viewing him as an abject failure. Ultimately, though, Edward was a failure. Recognising his tricky inheritance, Haines nevertheless argues that it needed 'a man far more able and politically astute than Edward II' to successfully deal with the problems he was bequeathed. 'His style of kingship was not calculated to attract a following', while he responded to problems 'inadequately, sporadically and with vacillation'. His inadequacies and reliance on favourites brought about his downfall.[45]

Biographies of Queen Isabella and Roger Mortimer were published in 2003.[46] These served to reopen an old controversy, the question of Edward II's alleged survival after 1327. Paul Doherty resurrected the Fieschi Letter, a document widely discussed but largely dismissed by historians in the nineteenth and twentieth centuries.[47] Manuel Fieschi was an Italian priest, who, in about 1340, wrote a letter suggesting Edward II had escaped from captivity at Berkeley, fleeing to the papal court at Avignon, then to Cologne and eventually becoming a hermit in northern Italy. Doherty believes that even if Edward did not end up as an Italian hermit, he escaped and lived out his days in secret, peaceful exile. The body in the tomb in Gloucester is thus not Edward II, but that of an imposter used by Isabella and Mortimer to conceal Edward's escape. Ian Mortimer's version is even more dramatic. According to him, Isabella and Roger Mortimer deliberately kept Edward II alive while staging his death and funeral. When the Earl of Kent found out in 1330 that his half-brother was still alive and tried to free him, Edward III had to agree to his execution to stop the secret leaking out. Edward II was then sent to captivity in Ireland, until he found himself free and went, disguised as a pilgrim, to the papal court. He died, an obscure hermit, sometime around 1339–41, and was then clandestinely buried in the tomb everyone else believed he had occupied since 1327. Mortimer thus argues that Edward survived 1327 but is nevertheless buried at Gloucester. These are obviously simplified views of the two arguments, but although some historians have echoed them, few have been convinced. It is entirely unclear why Isabella and Mortimer would have kept Edward alive and orchestrated such an elaborate deception, but Ian Mortimer has argued his point stubbornly and repeatedly since 2003. This has kept the controversy going, despite several sober, well-considered works demonstrating it is most likely that Edward II died in 1327 and is buried at Gloucester.[48]

A 2006 volume of essays examined significant and hitherto neglected questions about the king's reign and reputation, including Edward's court and household, parliament, and the law. Especially important, given the uncritical popular acceptance of Edward as the 'gay king', was Mark Ormrod's article on 'The Sexualities of Edward II'. Ormrod pointed out that modern efforts to label the king 'heterosexual, homosexual, bisexual, whatever' were:

> both anachronistic and futile: anachronistic because medieval attitudes to sexuality were so different from our own, and futile because the nature of the evidence makes it impossible to tell what Edward actually did – let alone what he thought himself to be doing – whether and when he engaged in emotional and physical contact with women or men.

He sought to show how 'hostile commentators "queered" the king' by 'setting him at variance to the contemporary ideologies of kingship, politics, courtliness and gender'.[49] The idea of a gay Edward II is now too deeply entrenched for such work to dislodge them, but there is no clear, contemporary evidence to determine what the king was, even if we ignore the anachronistic approach to sexuality which allows the term 'gay' to be used with reference to the fourteenth century.

The final essay in that volume, by Seymour Phillips, briefly summarises the more extended treatment in a full biography published four years later. The result of almost forty years' work on the reign since his seminal study of the Earl of Pembroke, it is a comprehensive, balanced and largely sympathetic portrait. Phillips is clear about his intention to strike a balance between 'the extremes of the calamitous and incompetent Edward II on the one hand and the holy man on the other'. He makes the point that on his accession, he was reasonably well-prepared for the throne, that in military terms there was no evidence of 'special abilities' but equally nothing 'to suggest ineptitude', and that 'Edwards's readiness for the throne in 1307 should not be judged in the knowledge of the disasters which lay ahead of him'. Phillips notes that the king had some political abilities, as in the context of 1317: 'Edward II's attraction of such a wide degree of support and cooperation also suggests that he had a much greater level of political skill than he is usually credited with.' That said, he was always at his best 'and most active when faced with a challenge to his personal dignity and that of his crown'. He always had 'a very strong sense of his royal status and of his rights and duties as king'. There is no shying away from the fact that the post-1322 regime was 'arbitrary and brutal' and that 'Edward II was implicated in everything that was done in his name and with his acquiescence'. His actions in his last years show 'the world of fantasy in which he was living as his kingdom began to collapse around him'. In the end, as 'a king he was too able to be ignored but had too many weaknesses of character and behaviour to be a success'. He was a failure, but Phillips' careful sifting of the evidence shows a qualified failure rather than a hopeless one.[50]

Christopher Given-Wilson's shorter, pithier biography is much more critical of Edward than Phillips. At 'the heart of Edward II's failure' lay an inability to establish a modus operandi with his lords. He had an 'almost Olympian view of kingship', which did not help a man who was 'enormously stubborn' as well as 'devious and untrustworthy, continually making promises he had no intention of keeping'. 'Tactical inflexibility, internal dissension and a formidable opponent' led to defeat in the Scottish wars, but in addition what 'was needed was application and adaptability – qualities Edward lacked'. In the end, his failure was personal, caused by 'his inability to fulfil the two overriding obligations of a medieval king – to administer the law without partiality, and to defend his realm'. Ultimately, Given-Wilson's verdict is damning but fair: 'Edward faced challenges that would have tested the ability of any king; his singular ability was the talent he possessed for alienating those who could have helped him to overcome them.'[51]

Two popular biographies, by Kathryn Warner and Stephen Spinks, tried to present Edward as an 'unconventional' king, picking up the theme of a man out of his time whose interests make much more sense to the modern age. Neither succeeds in the declared intention to reveal Edward the man, something of an impossible quest when writing about medieval kings whose personal words and thoughts appear only in very occasional, distorted fragments. Both rightly stress Edward's complexity, although Warner's more critical (if understanding) portrait is the more convincing of the two. That said, her argument that 'it was his misfortune and his kingdom's that he was born into a hereditary monarchy and had no other choice than to succeed his father' is an anachronistically modern view, for Edward's jealous defence of his kingship showed that he was perfectly happy with his crown.[52]

Of Edward's five twenty-first-century biographers, only Spinks believes unequivocally that the king engaged in same-sex relationships. The others all entertain doubts, strongest in the case of Haines and Phillips. However, a useful contribution to the debate was published by Kit Heyam in 2020. They looked in detail at the development of Edward's reputation from his own lifetime until the end of the seventeenth century, above all his reputation for homosexuality and the difficulties of some of the terminology involved. Following Mark Ormrod, Heyam sees little use in trying to determine whether or not Edward did actually have sex with other men, instead focusing on the process by which he acquired the reputation for doing so until it became accepted 'fact'. Tracing that process, they argue that 'the majority of significant changes in the historiography of Edward and his favourites can be summed up as part of an overall increasing emphasis on features of the text that enhance reading pleasure'.[53] By the seventeenth century Edward had become akin to a literary character, his accepted story reflecting the elements of scandal and tragedy which most appealed to readers. In a study of the fictional portrayals of Edward in a more restricted timeframe, Michael G. Cornelius goes further, arguing that 'Edward II left the realm of history long ago', that he 'exists, today, because he was gay' and that he 'engenders more than memorisation: he inspires creation'. Cornelius identifies as a gay man and believes that Edward's 'gay existence' is what makes him 'so significant in the history, the fiction, and the lives of all gay men'.[54]

Therein is the problem faced by historians: Edward II has become a legend and an icon, whose 'reality' matters less than what he has come to represent. Nowhere is that clearer than in the extraordinary influence his life and reign have had over writers, poets and playwrights for more than four centuries.

Edward in Popular Culture

Christopher Marlowe's *Edward II* (c.1592) has had an enormous influence on later perceptions of the king. It is far from Marlowe's best work and shows scant regard for historical accuracy, with the timeline compressed and folded in on itself. Yet Marlowe conveyed the core themes of the reign: the king's obsession with Gaveston and the political offence he caused, and Edward's obsession with his royal dignity. Like Shakespeare's Richard II, Marlowe's Edward II wrestles with giving up his crown and accepting his fate as moments of resignation alternate with a desire to cling to the trappings of majesty. Modern interest has fixed predominantly on the homoerotic undertones in the text. One commentator argues that 'until the twentieth century, no other literary character will be as resolutely "gay" – and as identifiably so – as Marlowe's Edward II'.[55] That may be to go too far; the homosexual elements are coded, in classical allusions, most notably the references to Ganymede, which would have suggested a sexual relationship. Likewise, talk of minions was an obvious reference to King Henry III of France and his famous *mignons*, favourites with whom he was believed to have sexual relationships, drawing out the xenophobia and homophobia of Elizabethan society. If the language seems veiled today, at the time it would have been obvious that Marlowe was depicting Edward and Gaveston as lovers, subsequent analysis of which could fill entire libraries. The love story of king and favourite is at the heart of Marlowe's play.

Edward II stood the test of time and was a relatively popular play to perform in the twentieth century. The role of Edward has been taken by prominent gay actors such as Derek Jacobi (University of Cambridge, 1958), Ian McKellen (Prospect Theatre Company, 1969) and Simon Russell Beard (RSC, Stratford-upon-Avon, 1990). At Leicester in 1995, the genderfluid actor and comedian Eddie Izzard took the title role. Since the decriminalisation of homosexuality, the homoerotic elements have typically been given a central place in performances. When the Prospect Theatre Company version was shown by the BBC in 1970, it controversially featured the first gay kiss on British television, between McKellen and James Laurenson as Gaveston. The 1990 RSC adaption carried a warning about its unsuitability for children. Most famously, Derek Jarman's explicit 1991 film version with Stephen Waddington as Edward was released with an 18 certificate in the UK (subsequently revised down to 15 in less censorious times). In the shadow of the homophobic legislation of the Thatcher government, this adaption is avowedly political and intentionally anachronistic, in modern dress and making use of clips of gay pride marches. This was Marlowe for the Section 28 world, securing the reputation of Edward II as *the* gay king in the popular mind.

The influence of Marlowe on the Edward II story is such that his play has been adapted more than once in modern times. Bertolt Brecht's adaption, *Leben Eduards des Zweiten von England* (*Life of Edward II of England*) opened in Munich in 1924 and was revived in New York in 1982. A ballet by John McCabe was commissioned by the Stuttgart Ballet; *Edward II* largely drew on Marlowe's plot and premiered in the German city in 1995, with a first performance in the UK by the Birmingham Royal Ballet in 1997. In 2018, George Benjamin and Martin Crimp's *Lessons in Love and Violence* premiered at the Royal Opera House in London. A ROH co-production with a US and five European opera companies, this too was largely a reworking of Marlowe's script into operatic form. Most recently, the Spanish author Alfredo Cernudo's play *Eduardo II: Ojos de Niebla* (*Edward II: Misty Eyes*) premiered in Madrid in 2020, tracing the final years of the reign on a minimalist stage.

Edward II is unique among English kings in being the subject of Elizabethan, German and Spanish plays, an Anglo-German ballet and a Covent Garden opera, but his cultural reach is still wider and more bizarre. The 1967 song by The Corries, *Flower of Scotland*, showcases Edward's disaster at Bannockburn for the entire sporting world. Meanwhile, Edward must surely be alone among English monarchs in giving his name to a folk/rock/reggae band. Formed in Cheltenham in 1980, *Edward II and the Red Hot Polkas* took as their name a punning reference to the king's supposed murder at nearby Berkeley, and went through various breakups and re-formations and a variety of name changes, to *Edward II*, then *EII*, then finally *e2k*. Whether Edward II would have approved of his name being attached to their music is an unanswerable question, but it shows his extraordinary appeal to parts of modern culture.

Edward has been portrayed only rarely on screen. Three instances are versions of Marlowe (McKellen in 1970, Waddington in 1991 and a 1982 French version), with two additional appearances in French TV adaptions of a series of novels by Maurice Dubon. Otherwise, Edward features in films which essentially glorify Robert Bruce, including the parts acted by Richard Brimblecombe in *The Bruce* (1996) and Billy Howle in *Outlaw King* (2018). By far the most famous is Peter Hanly's Edward in the historical travesty that was *Braveheart* (1995). Hanly depicted a weak, cowardly, effeminate Edward, a tired, outdated, homophobic stereotype far from the historical reality of a king who inherited his father's legendary temper. Besides a gratuitously invented boyfriend thrown out of the window by Edward I, the utter disregard for history is shown by William Wallace cuckolding Edward to be the real father of Edward III, which is impossible on so many points that it is scarcely believable it was included. Whatever the truth of his sexuality and character, Edward II deserves much better than this and no one has ever portrayed him convincingly on film.

In literature, from Marlowe onwards the relationship between Edward and Gaveston has been the dominant theme. It was the subject of two poems written in the 1590s, by Michael Drayton and Sir Francis Hubert, although Hubert's fell foul of Elizabeth I's censors and was not published for thirty years. Writers have never lost their fascination with the Gaveston story, which has become a medieval gay romance imbued with tragedy, endlessly retold: 'Edward II survives as a literary figure not because of his spectacular failure as a medieval monarch but rather for his remarkable success at being a "gay" man.'[56] Many storywriters make much of accusations of Gaveston being the son of a witch and bewitching Edward, in case the story were not lurid enough. While there is often an assumption in fiction that Edward shifted his romantic attentions onto the younger Despenser soon after Gaveston's death, this is not typically portrayed as a love story in the same way, nor does it attract the same interest. One exception to the starkly negative treatment of Despenser is Susan Higginbotham's *The Traitor's Wife* (2009), which tells the story through the eyes of his wife, Eleanor de Clare. Elsewhere, though, Despenser the bully is seen as a less complex, far less likeable character than Gaveston, and it is the Gaveston story which attracts the novelists.

The most notable modern retelling is Chris Hunt's *Gaveston*, published by the Gay Men's Press in 1992, a sexually explicit work which gives Edward an essentially modern gay identity against the backcloth of the medieval world. Edward, the narrator, is the prime mover in the relationship, the one who pursues and needs Gaveston. While informed by a fairly detailed knowledge of history, there are definite liberties taken in the book, not least making sexual jealousy the motivation for Lancaster's destruction of Gaveston and enmity with the king. Less explicit, but also less readable, is Brandy Purdy's self-published *The Confessions of Piers Gaveston* (2007). As the title suggests, this takes the rather grating form of Gaveston's memoirs while he is besieged in Scarborough Castle in 1312. Gaveston here is more a petulant and less rounded character in a tempestuous affair with the king. Tellingly, both Hunt and Purdy make the brotherhood ceremony between the two men akin to a wedding, an unmistakably anachronistic approach to a fourteenth-century tale. It is a story retold for a modern audience.

Another popular way of fictionalising the reign is to tell the tale from Queen Isabella's perspective. Too often, she emerges as the 'she-wolf' of legend, albeit wronged by an equally blameworthy Edward who is too obsessed by the male lovers who share his bed. An early effort in this regard was *Harlot Queen* (1970) by Hilda Lewis. Intriguingly, in this version Isabella and Gaveston make peace with one another before his death, but Edward's turn to Despenser ultimately drives her to become Mortimer's lover and openly flaunt their increasingly scandalous liaison. The queen is driven by rage, hatred and resentment and manipulates an unsuspecting Prince Edward, although Mortimer is a still greater villain. In the end, however, while Edward is an irascible, often cruel king, both he and his wife are redeemed and make their peace, albeit in distinctly unhistorical fashion; there is that nagging need for a novelist to account for why, after everything, Isabella was buried in her wedding dress. More recent efforts include Edith Felber's *Queen of Shadows* (2006) and Marcia Maxwell's *Rogue Queen* (2015), which treat Isabella more sympathetically but lapse into anachronism.

A different approach is found in the series by the French novelist Maurice Druon, *The Accursed Kings*. These tell the story of the final years of the Capetian monarchy, capturing the intrigue and scandal surrounding the court during the 1310s and 1320s. Isabella naturally enters the story as a relative of the five kings who sat on the French throne in a turbulent decade. She has a particularly prominent role in the first novel, *The Iron King*, where she is the driving force behind the murky Tour de Nesle scandal which saw her three sisters-in-law accused of adultery. Edward is a background figure here, with a reputation for chasing after handsome young men. The fifth book, *The She-Wolf of France*, and the sixth, *The Lily and the Lion*, interweave the stories of England and France to tell of Isabella's refusal to return to England, her invasion, Edward's deposition and its aftermath. Druon brings a European dimension to the tale which is often overlooked by English writers.

The most extensive fictional treatment of the reign comes in two series of novels, one by Michael Jecks, the other by Paul Doherty. Jecks' *Knights Templar* series, set in the West Country, features Simon Puttock and former Templar Sir Baldwin Furnshill as the solvers of mysteries and crimes against the backdrop of the reign's stormy politics. As the story moves into the mid-1320s, the action comes to centre on the royal court and the collapse of Edward II's regime. Portrayed as lovers, the king and

Despenser are not likeable characters, with Edward 'happier to risk the life and livelihood of his own son than he was to risk the neck of his lover'. Yet it is a tempestuous relationship; Edward is irrational and prone to ferocious rages, and Despenser silently resentful because he has 'better things to be doing than listening to the regular complaints of the King' who, without the favourite, 'would lose his crown, realm and probably head in an instant'.[57]

A prolific author of historical fiction across multiple periods, Doherty earned a doctorate for his thesis on Queen Isabella, partially published in 2003. His fiction is thus imbued with an extensive knowledge of the history of this period and as might be expected, he offers a more nuanced picture of leading characters, Isabella especially, than most novelists. The Matilda of Westminster trilogy tells the story of the Gaveston years through the eyes of one of Queen Isabella's ladies. Here, an original gloss is placed on some of the incidents usually cited as evidence of Edward's foolishness. The wedding presents are given to Gaveston with Isabella's full knowledge, as part of a plan to provoke Philip of France. In the end, Edward allows Gaveston to be trapped at Scarborough, because however much he loves him, he realises the favourite has become too dangerous to his crown. There is a refreshing subtlety to the relationship between Edward, Isabella and Gaveston, not least because it draws out an affectionate connection between king and queen. Edward clearly loves Gaveston, but the question of whether this love is sexual is left deliberately unanswered.

Although it begins in the 1280s, the most recent books in Doherty's Hugh Corbett series are also set in the early years of Edward II's reign.[58] *Dark Serpent* (2016) takes place against the attack on the Templars and Edward's problematic relationship with King Philip in Paris. *Devil's Wolf* (2017) brings out the lawlessness and conflict on the Scottish border, while *Death's Dark Valley* (2019) draws on the John of Powderham saga to look at the issue of royal imposters and pretenders. Although he appears only rarely in person, there are penetrating insights in the series into the character of Edward II:

> He did not fully trust the king. Edward II was over six feet tall, broad-shouldered, with the long legs of a born horse rider and the wiry arms of a swordsman. He was handsome-faced, slightly olive-skinned, a striking contrast to his golden hair and nearly clipped beard and moustache. He had heavy-lidded blue eyes, the right one slightly drooping, which made him look as if he mistrusted the whole world, an impression heightened by the wry twist to his mouth. A strong man, a warrior and, in

Family Tree of King Stephen

Simplified – Only those mentioned in the text are shown
Dotted line denotes illegitimacy

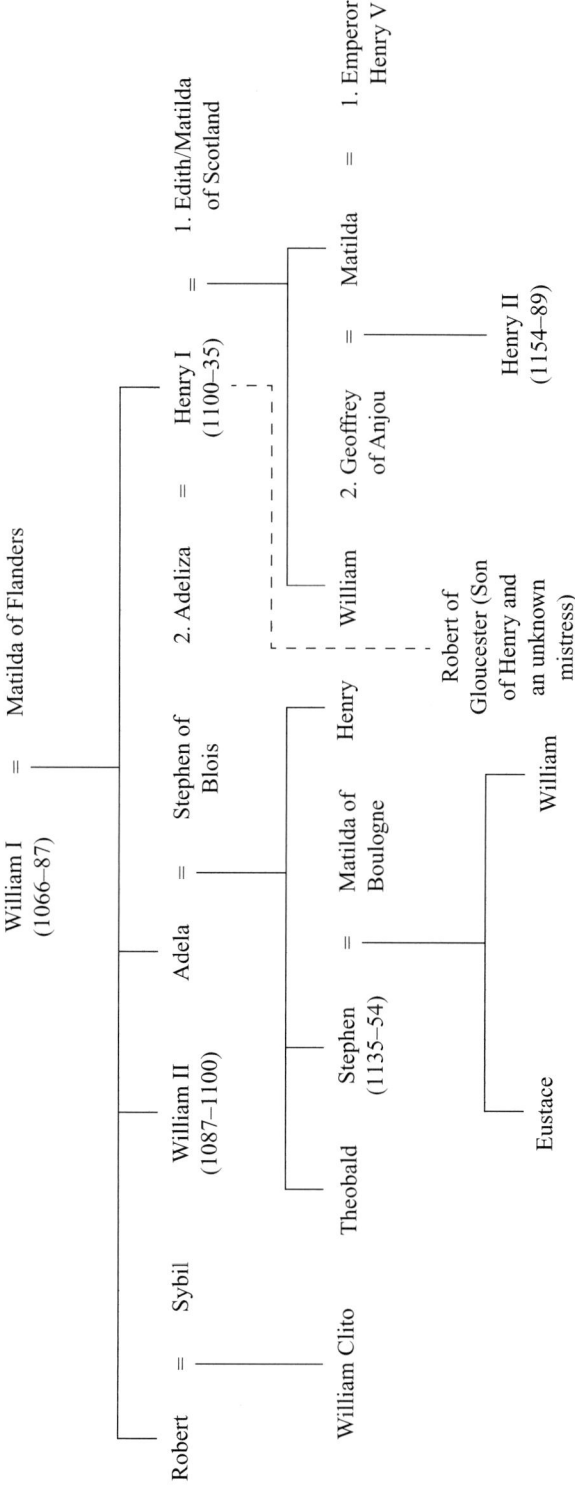

Family Tree of King John

Simplified – Only those mentioned in the text are shown

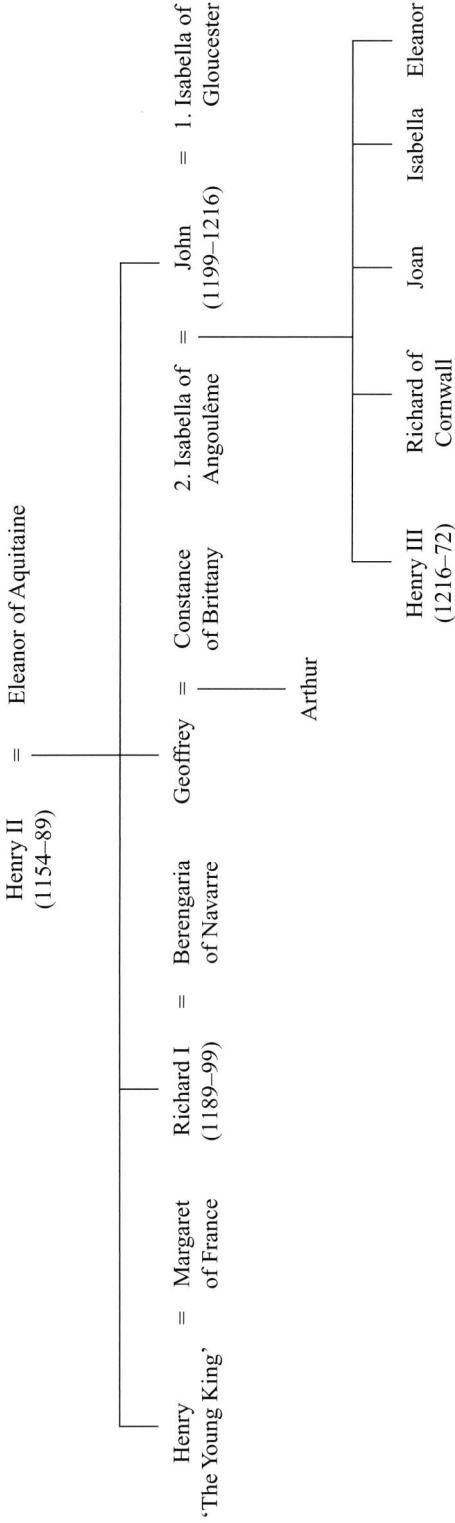

Henry 'The Young King'	Richard I (1189–99)	Henry II (1154–89)	Geoffrey	John (1199–1216)
= Margaret of France	= Berengaria of Navarre	= Eleanor of Aquitaine	= Constance of Brittany	= 2. Isabella of Angoulême
				= 1. Isabella of Gloucester

Arthur

Henry III (1216–72)   Richard of Cornwall   Joan   Isabella   Eleanor

Family Tree of Edward II

Simplified – Only those mentioned in the text are shown

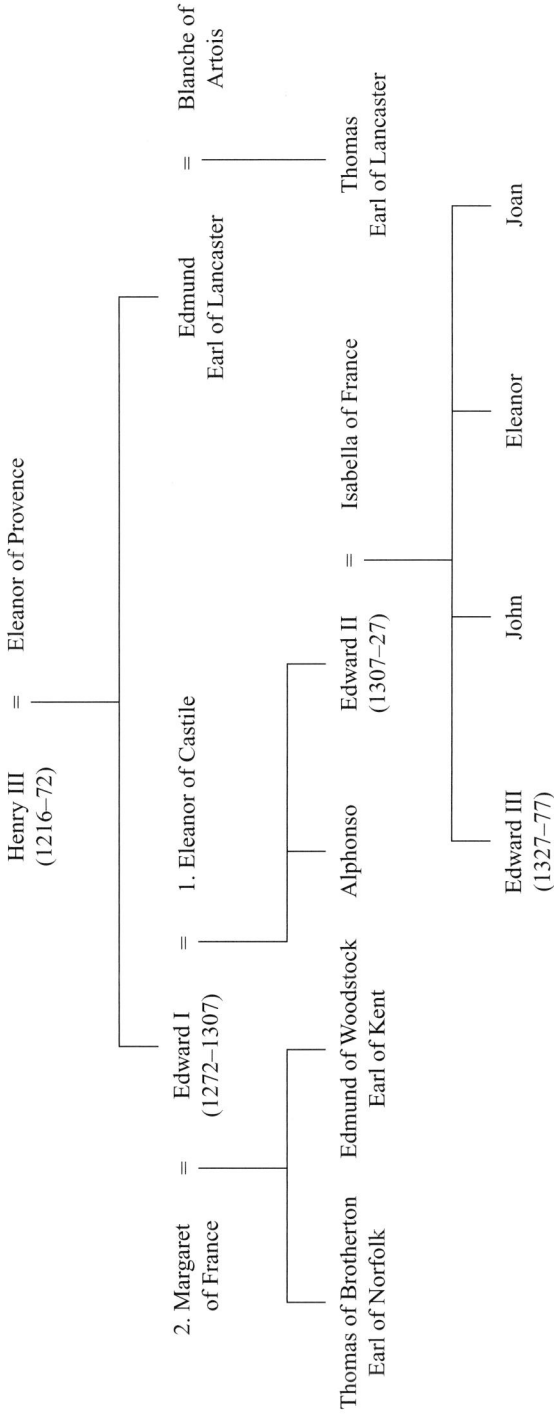

Family Tree of Richard II

Simplified – Only those mentioned in the text are shown

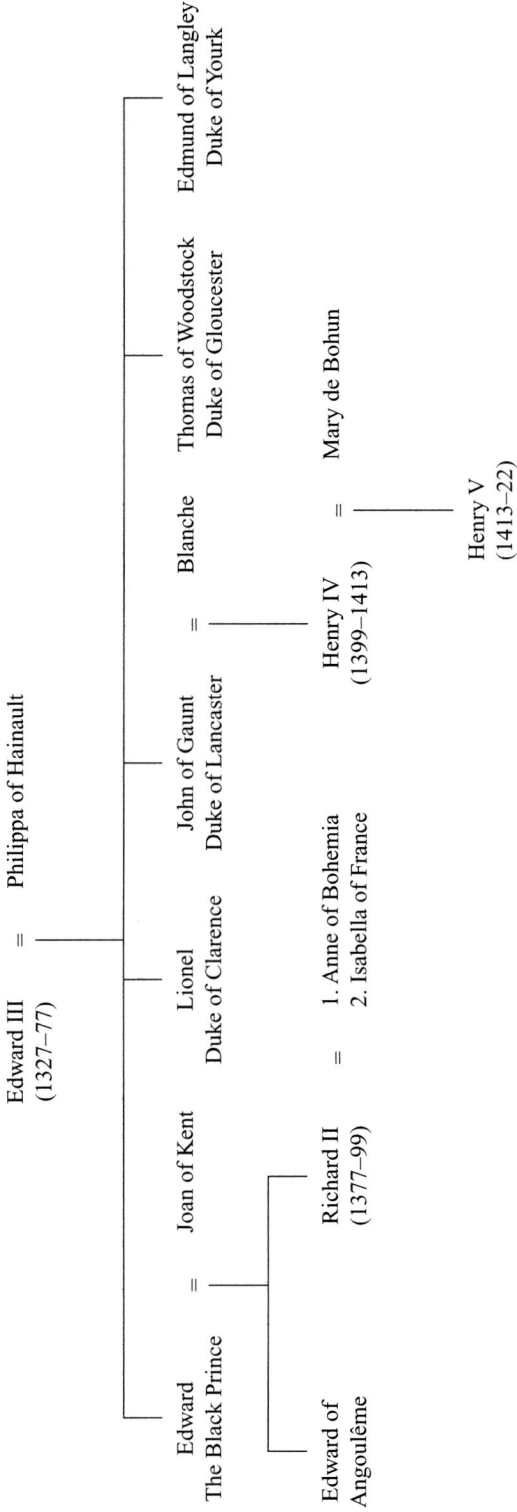

Edward III (1327–77) = Philippa of Hainault

Children of Edward III and Philippa of Hainault:
- Edward The Black Prince = Joan of Kent
- Lionel, Duke of Clarence
- John of Gaunt, Duke of Lancaster = Blanche
- Thomas of Woodstock, Duke of Gloucester
- Edmund of Langley, Duke of Yourk

Children of Edward The Black Prince and Joan of Kent:
- Edward of Angoulême
- Richard II (1377–99) = 1. Anne of Bohemia / 2. Isabella of France

Children of John of Gaunt and Blanche:
- Henry IV (1399–1413) = Mary de Bohun

Children of Henry IV and Mary de Bohun:
- Henry V (1413–22)

Family Tree of Richard III

Simplified – Only those mentioned in the text are shown

Edward III (1327–77)

Edward The Black Prince

Lionel Duke of Clarence

John of Gaunt Duke of Lancaster

Edmund of Langley Duke of York

Richard II (1377–99)

Philippa = Edmund Mortimer Earl of March

Henry IV (1399–1413)

Richard Earl of Cambridge = Anne

Roger Earl of March

Henry V (1413–22)

Richard Duke of York

Richard Earl of Cambridge = Anne

Richard Duke of York = Cecily Neville

Cecily Neville = (see * left)

Henry VI (1422–61, 1470–71)

Edward Prince of Wales

Edward IV (1461–70, 1471–83) = Elizabeth Woodville

George Duke of Clarence

Richard III (1483–85) = Anne Neville

Edward V (1483) and Richard Duke of York

Edward of Middleham

*

Left: King Stephen from a thirteenth-century manuscript. (British Library, MS Royal 14 C VII f.8*v*, via Wikimedia Commons)

Below: Lincoln Cathedral. On the morning of 2 February 1141, ill omens accompanied King Stephen's attendance at Mass in the cathedral. That afternoon, he was defeated and captured at the Battle of Lincoln. (author's photo)

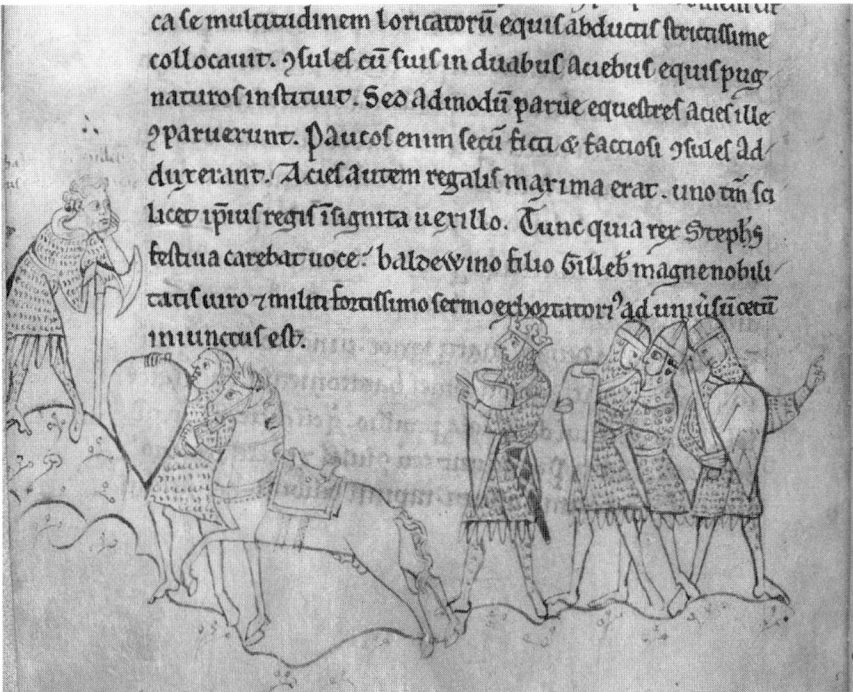

The Battle of Lincoln, 1141, illustrated in a thirteenth-century copy of Henry of Huntingdon. (British Library, MS Arundel 48 f.168*v*, via Wikimedia Commons)

Corfe Castle. This imposing fortress played a major role throughout much of the Middle Ages. King John undertook major building work and possibly made grisly use of the castle. (author's photo)

Left: King John hunting, from a fourteenth-century manuscript. (British Library, Cotton MS Claudius D II f.116, via Wikimedia Commons)

Below: Angoulême Cathedral. It was here that King John married his second wife, Isabella, in 1200. The marriage was to have serious diplomatic consequences. (author's photo)

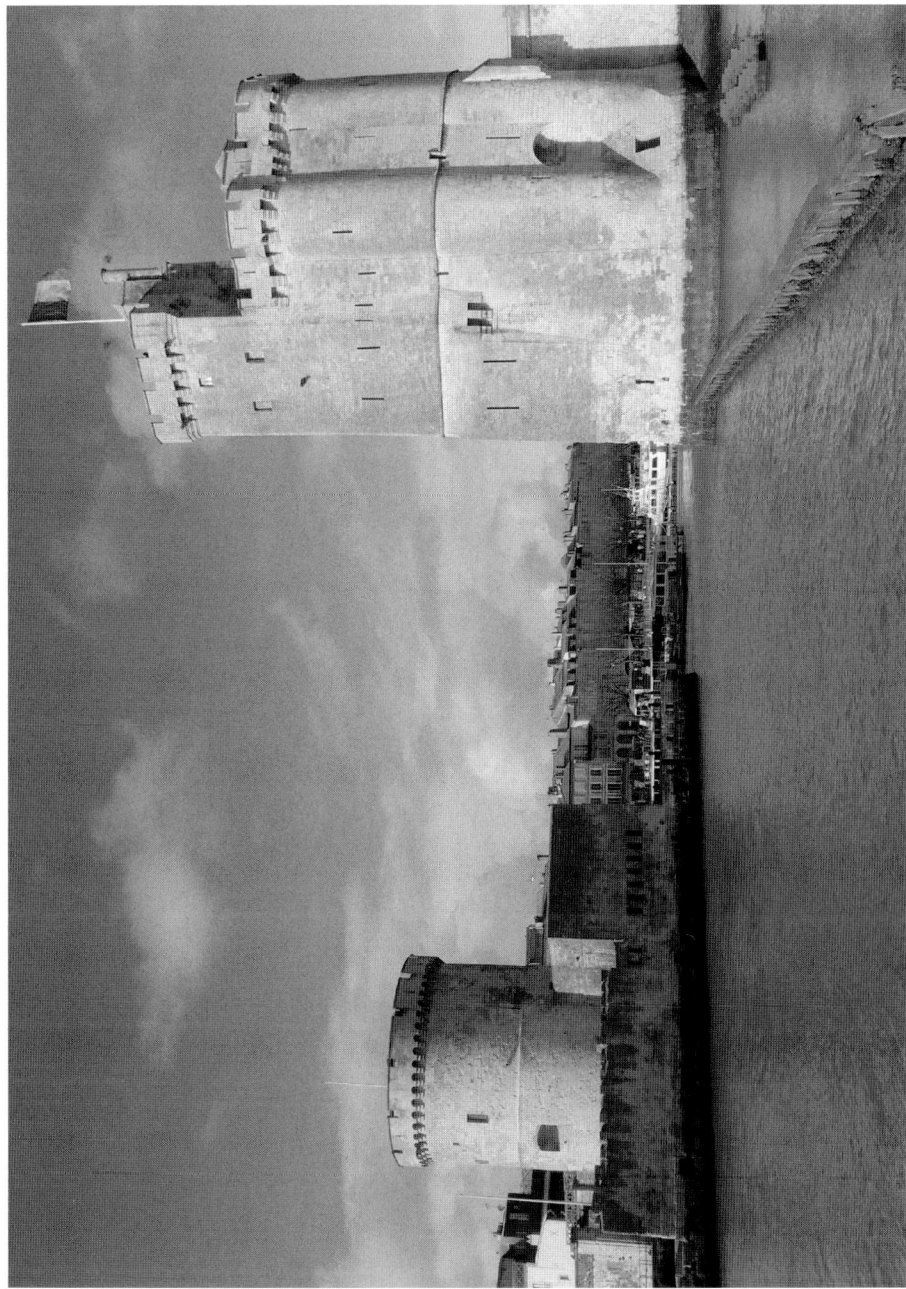

La Rochelle. After losing all his northern French lands, this Atlantic port became an important centre for John's futile plans for reconquest. (author's photo)

Magna Carta. Four versions survive from 1215, with this one of the two found in the British Library. (British Library, via Wikimedia Commons)

Above and below: King John's effigy in Worcester Cathedral was installed in the reign of his son, Henry III, and now rests on a sixteenth-century chest. (courtesy of Doug Chaplin)

Left: Edward II, from a contemporary manuscript. (British Library, MS Royal 20 A ii f.10, via Wikimedia Commons)

Below: Stirling Castle. It was the desire to avoid this major fortress being handed over to the Scots that brought Edward II to Scotland in June 1314. He lost the Battle of Bannockburn to Robert Bruce, whose statue now stands outside the castle. (author's photo)

Pontefract Castle. The surviving ruins hint at how impressive this Yorkshire fortress once was. Several significant violent deaths occurred here, including the beheading of Thomas of Lancaster in 1322, the murder of Richard II in 1400, and the execution of Lord Rivers in 1483. (courtesy of Mtaylor848, via Wikimedia Commons)

Berkeley Castle. Much altered in subsequent centuries, it was here that Edward II was imprisoned and murdered in 1327, and that the Duke of York defected to Henry Bolingbroke in 1399. (author's photo)

Detail from Edward II's alabaster effigy in Gloucester Cathedral. (author's photo)

The death of Wat Tyler, in Richard II's presence, during the Peasants' Revolt of 1381, from a fifteenth-century manuscript. (British Library, MS Royal 18 E. I, f. 175, via Wikimedia Commons)

Richard II dines with his uncles, the Dukes of Gloucester and York, and Duke Robert de Vere of Ireland in this fifteenth-century chronicle illustration. (British Library, MS Royal 14 E. IV f.265*v*, via Wikimedia Commons)

Flint Castle. Richard II and Henry Bolingbroke (soon to be Henry IV) met here after Richard's capture in August 1399. (author's photo)

York Minster. Richard III had a strong affinity with York; he possibly intended the recently completed cathedral to be his mausoleum. (author's photo)

truth, very dangerous. Corbett recognised this and was highly wary of this weathercock prince, whose mood could change at the twirl of a coin. If obstructed, Edward could give vent to the most violent tantrums, lashing out and kicking whoever opposed him.

Far from being weak, Doherty's Edward can be fearsome: 'despite his physical beauty, he nursed a nasty temper':

> Edward, too, seethed with rage, hence his treatment of the groom, a mixture of savagery and mercy that made the king so unpredictable: on one breath cruel ruthlessness, on the next unexpected generosity.

He is his father's son, something which is often downplayed elsewhere in fiction. Due recognition is given to the problematic relationship between the two men, which is far more balanced than elsewhere. The poisonous legacy passed from father to son in Scotland is recognised: 'Edward I had truly sown a tempest, and his son and heir […] was reaping the most savage whirlwind.' There are also, most unusually, comparisons between the two which favour the son:

> The King had proved to be a most loving and loyal husband to his young French queen Isabella, but that was Edward! If he was your friend, he would stand by you. In this he was quite different from his redoubtable father, a great and terrible king who would sacrifice anyone, kith or kin, on the altar of expediency.

As with Cadfael in Stephen's reign, the strength of Doherty's novels is that the protagonists and the storylines are largely fictional, but set against a plausible historical backdrop. Edward emerges as a complicated, three-dimensional character rather than the two-dimensional stereotype into which too many fictional portraits descend.

Both Doherty and Jecks deal, perhaps inevitably, with Edward's fate. In his biography of Isabella, Doherty states his belief that Edward II was not murdered but escaped. He takes up this same theme in two of his novels, *Death of a King* (1982) and *The Great Revolt* (2016). The latter is part of the Brother Athelstan series, set in Richard II's reign, so provides an interesting fictional retrospective from a period when

Richard was trying to promote the cult of his great-grandfather. Jecks likewise alters history in his novel *King's Gold* (2011), to have Edward rescued from Berkeley and disappear. There are other novels which also speculate about Edward's survival beyond 1327, including Ken Follett's *World Without End* (2007, sequel to *The Pillars of the Earth*) and Robert Goddard's *Name to a Face* (2007). As with many other cases of kings dying in mysterious circumstances, fashioning legends of Edward's survival is too tempting for novelists to resist, yet the wildly differing fates they afford him are a reminder that these are nothing more than good stories and fantasy. Edward is, after all, immortal in one sense: the drama and fascination of his reign make his a tale which writers endlessly wish to retell and make their own.

Verdict

It is hard to view Edward II as anything other than a failure. With our knowledge of subsequent depositions, that of Edward II seems less exceptional. Yet in 1327, the deposition of a reigning monarch was an unprecedented, radical step. That it had reached this point is a damning indictment of Edward's kingship, for key subjects and his own queen considered they had no option but to remove a manifestly unsuitable sovereign. It was a 'palace coup' rather than a revolution, but very few in the wider country had any interest in the survival of a man whose regime was widely viewed as avaricious, unjust and brutal. Core members of political society devised and then employed a mechanism to strip him of his crown and met little opposition.

Edward inherited substantial problems. Edward I had spent a considerable proportion of his thirty-five years on the throne at war, leaving the crown heavily in debt. He had faced stiff opposition from his earls and the Church in the late 1290s. The English position in Scotland was strong but far from secure. Tensions with France over Gascony were unresolved. Edward I bequeathed plenty of difficulties to his son and these need to be acknowledged as factors in what followed. However, Edward II's deposition was not a consequence of these. His reign was a failure because of his own character and errors of judgement, because he was ultimately not capable of meeting contemporary expectations of kingship.

It was the duty of a medieval king to work with his lords and take their counsel. Successful kingship depended upon constructive cooperation with the nobility and being seen to act justly. Edward's failure in this regard was spectacular, and his inability to learn from his mistakes breathtaking. Few kings have possessed so great a talent for alienating those who were basically loyal and would have proved sympathetic supporters had Edward shown even a modicum of flexibility and common sense. He was a tremendously loyal man to his friends, but he showed that loyalty to excess and only to a chosen few, at the same time never forgetting a betrayal. Edward was active and zealous solely in defending his own regality and his favourites, merciless in pursuing those he felt had wronged him or his inner circle. A wiser king would never have allowed himself to reach a point where the likes of Gloucester and Pembroke found themselves forced into opposition over Gaveston, nor alienated Hereford over Despenser. A king of sounder judgement would surely have questioned how he managed to turn former favourites, his own half-brothers and even his wife against him. Edward's obsession with Gaveston and his dependence on Despenser, at the expense of all others, poisoned the political community and made his reign twenty years of crisis punctuated by occasional truces.

In modern times, there has been an effort to portray Edward as a man out of his time. Yet fourteenth-century society did not understand another system and Edward did not reject it; all the evidence is that he guarded his royal status and rights jealously. In similar vein, modern writers have made much of the question of sexuality, seeing Edward as rejected for transgressing the norms of his age. So accepted has the notion of Edward's homosexuality become in popular thought that no examination of the king can overlook it. Edward may or may not have had sex with other men. We can never be sure, although on the balance of probabilities it seems unlikely. In a very important sense, the question is immaterial to Edward's performance as king, however important it became to his later reputation. He was not persecuted as part of some anti-gay crusade by a homophobic society. People objected because he showed immoderate favour to particular individuals, to the exclusion of those who considered it their right to be the king's counsellors and to receive his patronage. It was this unrestrained favouritism, the upsetting of the accepted sharing of responsibilities and rewards among the earls and barons, which provoked opposition, not any concerns about what the king was doing (or not doing) with his favourites in bed. It was symptomatic of Edward's inability to conform to the expectations of a medieval king.

The extent of the breakdown in the political community is shown by the way Edward's reign and its aftermath became a bloodbath. Prior to Gaveston's execution, no earl had been executed in England since 1076. Yet in the period 1312–30, six earls were put to death after the flimsiest legal processes, another died in battle in a civil war, while the first English bishop was murdered since 1170. Plenty below this top rank also suffered. Not only was the king failing to uphold the law and administer justice, but there was scarcely even a pretence of due process in his realm. The show trials and judicial murders of the Mortimer and Isabella years were a continuation of the dangerously vindictive system set in place under Edward II. It took his son to reassert the rule of law.

If he failed to do his duty as the kingdom's fount of justice, Edward II scarcely did better in his other core responsibility as defender of the realm. His victories were against his own subjects. His military record against external enemies was disastrous. Expensive campaigns in Scotland achieved nothing and normally ended in recrimination. His subjects in the North of England suffered terribly from border raids. The fate of Andrew Harclay shows how low morale had sunk in northern England and how little anyone trusted the king to improve things. In mitigation, Edward failed as military leader rather than warrior; the evidence from before 1307 and at Bannockburn suggests he was no coward on the battlefield. Part of the problem was his rival kings, as he faced a particularly skilful opponent in Robert Bruce and a determined foe in Charles IV. The favourites were a major obstacle, preventing Edward achieving the kind of domestic unity required for a successful military campaign. Bruce was able to make considerable advances while the English king was squabbling with his lords over Gaveston, then again while Edward and Lancaster fought each other. The problem was especially acute with France in the mid-1320s, when Edward knew Despenser was too unpopular to risk leaving the country, allowing Charles an enormous advantage in both war and legal propaganda. His ill-judged, immoderate defence of his favourites was a significant factor in his military and diplomatic failures against both Scotland and France.

It is also why his reign ended in such ignominy with almost no one willing to help him save his crown. His regime after 1322 was greedy, vindictive and often cruel. Was the king or Despenser culpable? That is a question much debated and never resolved. There is certainly evidence of the king's desire to become wealthy and of a personal vindictive streak, but plenty of evidence too for Despenser as the bullying power behind the throne. In a sense, the question is immaterial. Whether he personally directed such a regime or allowed another to do so, Edward was ultimately responsible as king for the failure to take counsel, uphold justice and defend the realm. The essential thrust of the charges of 1327 was that he failed to behave as king and do his duty. For that, he paid a heavy price indeed.

Since almost immediately after his murder, Edward's death has been seen as tragic, a redemption for his life. His final months and end were indeed pitiable, but for some this was retribution for the bloodthirstiness of his own regime. He suffered, but he had shown no mercy to others. Edward's reign was a tragedy full of paradox. He was not incompetent or hopeless, but he repeatedly brought disaster on himself. Our age may sympathise with what today would be called his 'common touch', but it baffled his contemporaries. He may now be seen as a gay hero, his loyalty to his favourites commendable and his passion for Gaveston a great love story, but in the fourteenth century his obsession with his favourites tore his kingdom apart and flouted all contemporary expectations of kingship. That was Edward's problem, his inability to play the game according to the accepted rules. He was an able man and a competent warrior who contrived to have himself remembered as one of the worst kings and generals in English history. That is a fair judgement.

Chapter 4

Richard II: An Unbalanced King?

The reign of Richard II could be portrayed as a golden age. English literature flourished in the era of Chaucer, with an artistic and architectural high point in the Middle Ages. Politically, however, these were febrile years, which saw the Peasants' Revolt, contentious parliaments, and a level of noble strife and bloodshed unknown since the reign of Edward II. As 1399 dawned, Richard seemed to reign supreme, his enemies vanquished and his majestic position assured. By the end of the year, he had been deposed, just seven decades after the same fate befell his great-grandfather.

The king at the centre of this drama is a curiously enigmatic figure. His rapid fall has long fascinated people, as has the personality which brought it about. *Richard II* is one of Shakespeare's most penetrating plays, for this is a story which makes for good theatre. Historians have been less successful. The ghost of Richard II has been repeatedly lain on the couch of historians posing as amateur psychoanalysts. There has been a desire to explain Richard in terms of childhood traumas and fashionable psychological theories. The results have been unsatisfactory and Richard remains a puzzle. Despite his end, he has never quite been viewed as a 'bad king' in the same way as Edward II or John. Yet he was an undoubted failure, for he lost his throne and was accused of considerable misrule in the process. In a way, the charges against the king in 1399 were even more damning than those of 1327. A reign which began with high hopes had ended in disaster.

Richard's Life and Reign

Richard was born in Bordeaux on 6 January 1367, the second son of Edward the Black Prince and Joan of Kent. The Black Prince was the English hero of the first stage of the Hundred Years' War (1337–1453) against France. A renowned soldier and chivalric hero, he was to pass little of this warrior instinct onto his unmilitary second son. Edward of Angoulême, his older son, had been born in 1365, but his death in 1370 left Richard second in line to the throne. By this stage, English progress in the war had stalled and after years of military campaigning, the Black Prince was in fragile health. In 1371 he returned to England with his family.

Richard seems to have lived with parents, mainly at Berkhamsted or Kennington, but the Black Prince's condition steadily declined until he died in June 1376. Aged 9, Richard was now heir to the English crown, receiving his father's titles in November, including that of Prince of Wales, along with his own official household. His grandfather turned 64 that month and was in delicate health, making it a virtual certainty that Richard would ascend the throne as a minor. After a long period of success, Edward III's final years as king were ones of decay and recrimination. The court was seen as corrupt and the influence of Edward's mistress, Alice Perrers, was especially resented. A long session of parliament, from April to July 1376, tackled this corruption and became known as the Good Parliament. Much of its work was undone early the following year by the Bad Parliament, under the influence of John of Gaunt, Edward III's third (and eldest surviving) son. One of its innovations was the first poll tax.

Edward III died on 21 June 1377 and his young grandson became King Richard II. The old king was buried in Westminster Abbey on 5 July, the new king's coronation staged in the same Church eleven days later. Richard was the first child to become king since Henry III in 1216, but whereas a regency government had been created for the 9-year-old Henry, in 1377 everyone pretended Richard was of age. The main problem was that John of Gaunt, the obvious regent, was too controversial and unpopular, while no one else had his standing or authority. England was officially under the rule of a 10-year-old, although until 1380 government was actually in the hands of a series of three 'continual councils'.[1] The first lasted just three months, replaced at the first parliament of the reign in October 1377. In October 1378, another parliament meeting at Gloucester changed the membership again. More sweeping changes of personnel were made on the second occasion, although it is notable that none of the king's three surviving uncles was given a named place on any of the three councils. From the start, the councillors faced considerable challenges.

Richard came to the throne four decades into the Hundred Years' War, at a point when English fortunes were at a low ebb with Charles V (1364–80) taking advantage of English domestic disharmony. Richard's uncles John of Gaunt and Thomas of Woodstock (Edward III's fifth and youngest son, then Earl of Buckingham and later Duke of Gloucester) led retaliatory raids against the French, but in uncoordinated fashion and with limited results. Gaunt remained unpopular and was embroiled in several messy disputes. The king was unable to act as a unifying focus by personally leading military

109

campaigns, nor did he yet have the authority to bring the squabbling lords to order. Moreover, the overseas campaigns were increasingly costly, with traditional revenues inadequate to meet the expense. This was the context in which poll taxes were introduced, with three levied in quick succession in 1377, 1379 and 1380.

After tricky negotiations, the third was granted in December 1380 by parliament at Northampton. It was the heaviest imposition so far at three groats (a shilling), triple the 1377 rate. Unlike the 1379 version, which had been graduated according to the status and means of each taxpayer, in 1380 a flat rate was imposed. Manifestly unfair, this was predictably unpopular and evasion was commonplace, with the best part of half a million taxpayers mysteriously vanishing from the tax records between 1377 and 1381. The government was compelled to act to improve the yield. Commissioners were appointed to deal with non-payment in March 1381. This move was even more unpopular and Margaret Thatcher might have benefited from study of what happened next, for the poll tax riots which played their part in bringing her down in 1990 had a precedent six centuries earlier. At the end of May, the inhabitants of Brentwood attacked the particularly zealous Essex commissioners. Soon South-East England was in rebellion.

The Peasants' Revolt had begun. Although it has frequently been noted that the name is misleading, since it was not led by peasants,[2] the label is deeply embedded in popular consciousness. It was the most serious popular rebellion in medieval England. Although the poll tax was the primary and immediate cause, the Peasants' Revolt also brought into the open longstanding grievances against landlords, the oppression of labourers and high prices. John of Gaunt, a target of popular ire, was fortunate to be in the North at the time the unrest erupted and was able to flee to safety in Scotland. Savoy Palace, one of his residences, was less fortunate, and would be burned down by the mob.

The trouble in Essex spread rapidly into Kent. The Kentish rebel leader, Wat Tyler, was instrumental in coordinating groups from the two counties, who by 10 June were ready to march on London. The king and a group of lords moved behind the solid walls of the Tower of London. The force of several thousand rebels arrived on the outskirts of the city and on the 13th, Richard was taken along the Thames to meet the rebels at Rotherhithe. Staying in his barge for safety, he and his advisors naturally dismissed the calls for the execution of Gaunt and others the rebels deemed 'traitors'. The royal party retreated to the Tower, while the rebels embarked on a spree of destruction. They broke into the Marshalsea and Fleet prisons and released all the prisoners, looted the Archbishop of Canterbury's palace at Lambeth and the lawyers' offices at Temple, and generally pillaged and wrought terror. A concerned king and council held urgent meetings in the Tower as they watched this perilous situation unfold. Councillors were divided between those wanting to end things by force and those favouring negotiation. Realistically, they lacked the means to crush the rebellion and it could have provoked a bloodbath, so on the morning of 14 June Richard rode to Mile End to meet several hundred rebels. The exchange was courteous, the king calm in the face of a genuine threat to his person. While allowing that only those judged traitors by due legal process could be punished, he promised that he would grant the demand for freedom from servitude.

These promises were understood differently by different rebel groups. One faction took Richard's words as licence to deal with 'traitors' and started to hunt them down; Archbishop Simon Sudbury of Canterbury was located in the Tower and suffered a gruesome beheading. Violence and bloodshed continued in London. With events spiralling dangerously out of control, the government hastily arranged another meeting. On the afternoon of Saturday 15 June, having prayed at the shrine of Edward the Confessor in Westminster Abbey, Richard rode out to Smithfield. After initially calm discussions between the king and Tyler, a scuffle broke out and Tyler was killed. Richard famously rode forward into the rebels, telling them that he would be their leader and urging them to meet him at Clerkenwell, part of a strategy to get them away from central London. There, Richard promised to uphold the Mile End promises from the day before. Shaken by the loss of their leader, the rebels began to disperse. The immediate danger had passed. Rebellions had also begun elsewhere in England, but news from London disheartened these and by July order had been restored across the realm.

The 14-year-old king had demonstrated considerable courage and nerve in the face of danger. The government was jolted into action by events, with a definite conservative shift in both social and religious policy. Commissioners were appointed to deal with the rebels in various counties. Essex alone required more effort, including the personal presence of the king, to fully pacify. When parliament met in November, a general amnesty was granted at Richard's behest, despite the desire of the Commons to exclude certain towns which had rioted in the summer. Yet Commons and Lords drew very different lessons from the Peasants' Revolt. The Commons pressed for reform in this parliament and those which followed. The Lords wanted to put off reform until the importance of obedience had been reasserted.

Meanwhile, on the cusp of manhood, Richard was a desirable figure on the marriage market. Negotiations had been taking place for some time with various European houses, complicated by a papal schism which divided sovereigns in their allegiance to two rival popes. England and the Holy Roman Emperor both backed Urban VI in Rome (as opposed to the antipope Clement VII in Avignon, whose supporters included France and Scotland). It was eventually agreed that Richard would marry Anne of Bohemia, who was a few months older than him and the eldest daughter of Emperor Charles IV (1355–78). Their wedding took place in Westminster Abbey on 20 January 1382, Anne's coronation following on the 22nd. Diplomatically, the marriage failed to bring any of the anticipated benefits. Personally, it was a conspicuous success. There is no evidence that either ever had other lovers, while Richard was so heartbroken when Anne died in 1394 that he had Sheen Manor, the place of her death, razed to the ground.

Still short of money, the government returned to the question of the French war. There were two views on the best way forward: attack from the south-west via Spain or from the north-east via Flanders. In pursuit of the first course, Edmund of Langley (Edward III's fourth son, then Earl of Cambridge and later Duke of York), led expeditions to Portugal in 1381 and 1382. They ended ignominiously. The alternative strategy was led by Henry Despenser, the Bishop of Norwich. A soldier in episcopal disguise, distinctly unreligious and spoiling for a fight, he led a crusade against the Count of Flanders (on the grounds that he supported the antipope) in May 1383. By October, he was back in England, being impeached by parliament for the fiasco over which he had presided. The failure of both strategies gave the upper hand to those who favoured peace with France.

Domestically, the king had turned 15 in January 1383 and was starting to assert himself. Over the next four years, complaints steadily increased about Richard's favourites. The king lavished his attention on an ever-narrower circle of intimates. Four in particular received notable favour and attracted corresponding criticism. Ralph Stafford, heir to the earldom of Stafford, became a close friend of Richard and would likely have risen far had he not been killed in an argument on the way to Scotland in 1385. Simon Burley had been Richard's tutor and through dubious legal chicanery managed to build himself a landed base in Kent. Michael de la Pole became chancellor in 1383 and worked closely with the king, being awarded the earldom of Suffolk in 1385. Robert de Vere inherited the earldom of Oxford in 1381 and was especially resented for monopolising royal patronage. In addition to these, Richard found intimates among the gentry, as well as the clerks and chaplains of the court. Suspicions that Richard's circle favoured peace with France and the cost of the court occasioned grumbling.

Dissatisfaction first erupted publicly at the Salisbury parliament of April 1384. The Earl of Arundel launched a furious attack on the king and his court, and an uneasy truce with the enraged Richard had to be brokered by John of Gaunt. Gaunt himself was the subject of a false accusation at the parliament in which a Carmelite friar accused him of a plot to kill the king. The affair was murky and ended tragically for the friar when he died in prison after being tortured. The meeting had exposed the fractious mood and mistrust among the nobility. There were further clashes at a council meeting at Reading in August and the next parliament at Westminster in November. There were echoes of the reign of Richard's great-grandfather, Edward II. Another holder of the mighty Lancaster title was at loggerheads with a circle of favourites around the king. John of Gaunt was still the realm's pre-eminent figure after Richard, powerful and ambitious, which irritated the royal favourites. An assassination plot against him was foiled in early 1385.

Meanwhile, there was discontent about the king's response to the growing French threat. The king's uncles favoured a renewed military offensive. Another group, led by Chancellor de la Pole, preferred to seek peace, partly influenced by an awareness of how hard it would be to raise funds for any campaign. Truce negotiations with France made little headway and by 1385 the French were planning to invade England. The South was threatened, but Richard dodged the whole French question with a distinctly bizarre distraction tactic: invading Scotland. This brought new problems. The tax granted by the previous parliament had been for war with France, so Richard summoned the feudal army and levied scutage (the tax paid in place of sending soldiers for the royal army). This was an archaic and wildly unpopular approach. Scutage had not been demanded since Edward III's abortive effort in 1340 and now it was hastily abandoned in the face of opposition. However, the feudal summons, the last of the Middle Ages, produced a good response and an army of around 14,000 joined the king at Newcastle in July 1385.

The campaign was a fiasco. The Scots melted away and refused to be drawn into battle, leaving the English to vent their rage on a few unfortunate monasteries. By the time they reached a deserted Edinburgh, food was short and tempers flared. By 20 August, Richard was back at Newcastle. Amazingly, given that the southern coast of England had been left open for the French to attack while the king and his lords went on their jaunt north, no assault had been launched. In the autumn, parliament was not happy. There was no chance of them granting any taxes. The Commons presented Richard with several petitions demanding reform, not least a pause in the reckless flow of royal patronage. Richard responded angrily and defiantly. His elevation of Robert de Vere to become marquess of Dublin was a stubborn retort; the title of marquess was until this point unknown in the English peerage. During the 1386 parliament, de Vere would be raised even higher to yet another novel title: Duke of Ireland.

In July 1386, John of Gaunt set sail for Spain, to pursue a claim to the throne of Castile. It left a gaping hole in the centre of English domestic politics, depriving Richard of a crucial advisor and leaving him more exposed to his opponents. In August, he was forced to address rising panic at the threat of an imminent French invasion. The planned attack was called off in November, but in the grip of this invasion scare parliament assembled at Westminster on 1 October 1386. It was now that Richard faced the consequences of Gaunt being overseas, for the most obvious steadying influence was absent from what turned into one of the most dramatic assemblies of the century, the Wonderful Parliament (so named after the description of a chronicler).

Unhappiness at the worsening military situation and the inadequate royal response turned to fury when de la Pole, as chancellor, requested an unprecedentedly high grant of taxation. The Commons refused and instead demanded the chancellor's impeachment. The 19-year-old king retorted that 'he would not dismiss the humblest of his kitchen staff from his post at their behest',[3] had a tantrum and stormed off to Eltham. Ignoring his attempts to abort the meeting, parliament continued in session. Richard's uncle, the Duke of Gloucester, went to Eltham with Bishop Thomas Arundel of Ely. Making thinly-veiled references to the fate of Edward II, the pair frightened the sullen king enough to make him return. Objectionable ministers were replaced. De la Pole was stripped of his office, impeached, tried and deprived of his estates. Humiliating though this was for Richard, he had to endure even worse when a 'great and continual council' was appointed with a twelve-month term and a broad remit to investigate the state of the realm. As with the Ordainers under Edward II, the council was reasonably balanced, but Richard viewed this as an intolerable intrusion and reacted in exactly the same way as his great-grandfather had in 1311, removing himself from the scene. In February 1387, he embarked on a lengthy tour of the Midlands.

By the summer, Richard was preparing his counterstrike. In a novel move, he held two secret meetings with the realm's judges in August, at Shrewsbury and then Nottingham. The ten questions Richard asked the judges were intended to bolster his position and the judges compliantly backed him with every answer: the king had the right to dissolve parliament;

the continual council infringed the royal prerogative; royal officials could not be impeached without the king's agreement; and those who opposed the king in these matters were traitors. While some would later claim compulsion, it seems that the judges gave their answers freely and even went beyond what was asked. It was an unparalleled assertion of the royal prerogative. Richard had less success with the sheriffs and a deputation from London, who were pessimistic about the support they could provide in the event of a clash. The king was preparing for such an eventuality. In September he made de Vere justice of Chester.

Richard kept the judges' opinions secret, but by October the details had leaked out to his opponents. Those who believed themselves his targets struck first. At Waltham Cross in Hertfordshire, on 14 November, the Duke of Gloucester and the Earls of Arundel and Warwick formally laid charges against five key figures in Richard's entourage: Michael de la Pole, Robert de Vere, Robert Tresilian (the chief justice), Alexander Neville (the Archbishop of York) and Nicholas Brembre (a former mayor of London). The trio 'appealed' (prosecuted) the five, and hence became known as the Lords Appellant or simply the Appellants. At a council meeting at Westminster three days later, they confirmed their intentions to the king in person. Richard promised to hear the charges in the next parliament, scheduled for February 1388.

Acting on Richard's orders, de Vere hastily pulled together an army in Cheshire. Less courageously, de la Pole and Neville fled. On 12 December, at Huntingdon, the existing Appellants were joined by two others: the Earls of Derby (Henry of Bolingbroke, John of Gaunt's son) and Nottingham (Thomas Mowbray). Whereas the three seniors were motivated by a mixture of principle and personal grudges in varying degrees, the two juniors acted out of resentment at their exclusion from royal favour and a judgement about the likely winners of this clash. The Appellants split their army to encircle de Vere in Gloucestershire. The night of 19 December found de Vere at Chipping Campden and Gloucester nearby at Moreton-in-Marsh. Seeking an encounter with Gloucester's troops the following day, de Vere instead stumbled across Arundel's force at Burford and came off worse in a skirmish. At Radcot Bridge, over the Thames on the Berkshire-Oxfordshire border near Faringdon, de Vere found his way blocked by Derby and his men. The resulting battle was fought in thick fog and was a resounding victory for the Appellants. De Vere managed to escape, but most of his men were captured. The victorious Appellants entered Oxford and Richard retreated to the Tower of London. King and Appellants met in the Tower at the end of the month. Exactly what happened is debated, as there are conflicting accounts, one of which claims the Appellants deposed Richard for three days and only restored him when they were unable to agree whether Gloucester (his uncle) or Derby (his cousin) should reign in his stead. Much now depended on what happened in parliament.

The assembly which began at Westminster in February 1388 is known, aptly, by the name given it by a contemporary chronicler: the Merciless Parliament. In the writs, issued just before Radcot Bridge, Richard had tried to pack the Commons by including instructions to the sheriffs to return sympathetic MPs, but events rendered his effort futile. The court was ruthlessly purged and the favourites destroyed, the Appellants choosing new royal councillors. With three of the main targets in exile, there was little hope for the others. Brembre and Tresilian were both tried and executed early in the parliament. A further favourite, Simon Burley, was executed in May. Arrangements were made to sell the lands of the convicted to finance a renewal of the French war. When the parliamentary session ended in June, all attendees had to swear to uphold its decisions. The Appellants were determined to ensure that the Merciless Parliament was seen to be legitimate and to prevent its acts being easily undone. For Richard, it was an abject humiliation which he never forgot. His reconciliation with the Appellants was never more than a show; his true feelings were revealed in 1397. And as Edward II's delayed, ruthless vengeance led to his undoing, so Richard's brought about his own destruction.

In the summer of 1388, however, he had little choice but to acquiesce and bide his time. The main task which had brought the five Appellants together was complete and their unity began to crack rapidly thereafter. Their mediocre military record caused additional problems, with further setbacks in the French war. Although none of the Appellants were present in person, Scottish victory in the Battle of Otterburn on 5 August 1388 was a serious embarrassment. In parliament in the autumn, the Commons were unimpressed by a request for taxation to finance the naval war against the French, since they had been promised a break from such requests earlier in the year. Richard worked to separate the two junior, less committed Appellants, Nottingham and Derby, from the others. Largely keeping clear of politics, he avoided blame for the failures of 1388 and appeared to be reasonable and moderate.

At a council meeting at Westminster in May 1389, Richard declared himself of age to rule alone, replacing the councillors chosen by the Appellants with his own men. Thereafter, Richard seemed to have learned his lesson and took pains to bring harmony to his realm. For the next few years, the king carefully spread his patronage more widely, no longer relying on his narrow circle of favourites, most of whom were now in any case dead or in exile. He listened to advice and stopped reacting with anger whenever criticism was voiced. John of Gaunt returned from Spain in November, no longer a divisive figure but one who provided considerable support and stability for the king over the following years. Derby and Nottingham were back at court and the other Appellants kept any resentment to themselves. The years of strife seemed over.

Things were improving on the international front too. A truce was agreed with France, which further helped ease tensions. Richard was temperamentally disinclined towards the war, whose halting progress and enormous cost had entangled the English government ever more tightly as it dragged on. Peace was by no means universally popular and the parliament of 1394 opposed a proposed peace treaty. Nevertheless, after the death of Queen Anne in 1394, which left Richard devastated, the diplomacy of marriage helped matters. In May 1395, Charles VI of France offered his 6-year-old daughter Isabella as a bride. In March 1396, a thirty-year truce was agreed between England and France in Paris. After an extravagant meeting between the two kings at Ardres in northern France, at the end of October 1396, Isabella was handed over to Richard. They married in Calais on 4 November. Richard saw this as a diplomatic triumph. It certainly meant that he faced no further threats from France for the rest of his reign. The financial burden of war was dramatically reduced.

The first half of the 1390s was a much more tranquil period at home after the turbulence and recriminations of the later 1380s. Nevertheless, Richard sought to elevate the language and dignity of kingship, increasingly obsessed with his regality and a desire to show himself as set apart from his subjects by God. There is no clearer evidence of his desire to portray an image of powerful sovereignty than two works of art produced in the mid-1390s. One is the Wilton Diptych, an outstanding example of medieval Gothic art.[4] Here, the right-hand panel has a Virgin and Child surrounded by angels, one bearing the flag of St George aloft. The child leans forward to bless Richard II, who kneels in the left-hand panel, clad in crown and splendid robes. Behind him stand two Anglo-Saxon royal saints, Edmund the Martyr and Edward the Confessor, along with John the Baptist. The diptych speaks volumes about how Richard envisaged his role and the saints with whom he associated. In a different way, so does the enormous portrait of himself he had painted for Westminster Abbey, showing Richard crowned and enthroned, holding his orb and sceptre.

Richard was a devoted patron of Westminster Abbey. He had a particular devotion to Edward the Confessor, a royal saint associated with peace, whose shrine was housed there and lavished with offerings by the king. Richard completed the ambitious rebuilding works begun by Henry III but left unfinished on his death more than a century earlier. In 1395, a tomb was moved from the edge of Edward the Confessor's chapel in the abbey, to allow the construction of a suitable tomb with effigies in which Richard could later be laid to rest beside his beloved Anne. Interestingly, from at least 1385 Richard was also keen to promote the cult of his great-grandfather, pressing especially hard for Edward II's canonisation in the 1390s as he and his opponents drew very different lessons from that reign. After 1389, Richard became far more zealous about the enforcement of orthodoxy and combatting heresy, especially the increasingly popular teachings associated with John Wycliff. The piety and religious faith of Richard II were far more than the conventional type of most medieval kings. For Richard, piety and kingship were intertwined. The artistic depictions and his defence of orthodox faith show how Richard viewed kingship and testify to the nature of his court. Although this was a reign in which English literature flourished, Richard himself bore no direct responsibility, even if patronage did come from court circles. Royal tastes were focused elsewhere. The king spent large sums on clothing and jewellery. He was itinerant, often moving around the realm with his retinue, never a cheap activity for a king. Kingly splendour came at a cost and Richard's court absorbed considerable sums of money.

Raising taxation was tricky. The king worked hard on building bridges with the parliamentary Commons, partly to avoid being isolated again as he had been by the Appellants, but also because he needed their financial support. The traditional link between necessity and taxation, where a king was only expected to levy taxes to meet extraordinary expenditure such as that incurred during warfare, was gradually weakened in the 1390s. In 1397, Richard had the chancellor declare to parliament that granting taxes to allow the king to govern was part of their duty of obedience as subjects. Things were not always so smooth. In 1392, the mayor and aldermen of London refused the king a large loan. Richard responded by confiscating the city's liberties, which were only restored on payment of a fine, and the affair damaged his relationship with the Londoners.

After his return to England in 1389, John of Gaunt, Duke of Lancaster, was the most important, stable source of support Richard had. In choosing his close companions at court, Richard looked to men of existing noble blood, immune from the complaints levelled at de la Pole and de Vere for being raised above their station. Among his new circle of intimates, significant figures included Earls Edward of Rutland (heir of the dukedom of York) and John Holland of Huntingdon, Sir Thomas Percy (younger brother of the Earl of Northumberland) and Sir William Scrope (heir of the former Lord Chancellor). Others were also favoured as patronage was spread widely. Richard sought to build up an affinity, akin to that of the leading nobles in the localities. It was unusual for a king to develop a following of significant gentry in this way, but Richard was keen to avoid any repetition of his isolation in 1388. His followers had a special livery, the white hart emblem associated with the king and used as a badge to distinguish his retinue.

In 1394, Richard became the first king to visit Ireland since John in 1210. Plans had been mooted at various points since 1385, and in the mid-1390s a visit fitted into Richard's idea of a more prominent kingship across the British Isles. The English position in Ireland had been progressively deteriorating for eighty years. Effective peace on the French front meant a concentration of resources towards Ireland was no longer so risky. The announcement of the trip in June 1394 came just days after the death of Queen Anne; it is likely that the timing of the expedition was now a way for a distraught king to escape his grief. Leaving his uncle, the Duke of York, as keeper of the realm (Lancaster was in Aquitaine), Richard sailed from Milford Haven with a sizeable army on 1 October. Landing at Waterford, he went to Dublin, where he based himself until March 1395 with two trips to Drogheda. He managed to bring a significant number of Irish chieftains into the allegiance of the English crown before returning to Waterford. Setting sail at the start of May, after seven months in Ireland, he left to the Earl of March the difficult task of enforcing his settlement.

After this adventure, Richard spent much of the rest of 1395 in the Home Counties. Late in the year, the body of his old favourite Robert de Vere, who had died in Louvain in 1392, was brought back to England for reburial at Earls Colne in Essex. In a typically melodramatic gesture, Richard had the coffin opened so he could see his friend's remains and place gold rings on his fingers. 1396 saw the king on the road again, heading to the Midlands and Yorkshire before returning to the South-East and crossing over to France to meet Charles VI and marry Isabella. Superficially, as 1397 unfolded all still seemed calm. Yet things were about to change. One chronicler, writing in the next reign with the benefit of hindsight, records an abrupt shift:

> At the beginning of King Richard II's twenty-first year [June 1397], England seemed to be basking in peace and the future looked entirely favourable: the country had an impressive-looking king who had just married the daughter of the king of France and had thereby acquired not only great riches but a

truce to last for thirty years, and it had more, as well as more talented, lords than any other kingdom could boast. It was at this time, however, that through the rashness, cunning, and pride of the king, the entire kingdom was suddenly thrown into confusion.[5]

This chronicler, Thomas Walsingham, identified 1397 as the year Richard 'began to tyrannise and burden his people'. The context was the king's demand for forced loans, but it has been interpreted more broadly as a dramatic change in Richard's approach. The next two years would see Richard ascend to his zenith of power, only to plummet spectacularly to lose his throne and then his life.

Things were not as harmonious as Walsingham claimed in June 1397. The parliament of January–February 1397 had been tense and seen Richard lose his temper once more. The Commons and the Duke of Gloucester had not been amenable to sending a force against the Duke of Milan, something Richard wanted as part of his newfound friendship with King Charles of France. Worse, the Commons sent four articles to be considered by the king. He responded to two, ignored one, and went into a rage over the fourth. This objected to the excessive costs of the king's household and the number of resident bishops and ladies at court. Richard 'took great offence' and ordered the speaker of the Commons to find out who lay behind this demand.[6] The next day, the Commons handed over the name of Thomas Haxey and apologised in grovelling terms. The lords were induced to pass a law which was then applied retrospectively to Haxey to condemn him to death, although he was spared on the petition of the Archbishop of Canterbury and pardoned in May. The whole affair is slightly mysterious, not least because Haxey was not even a member of the Commons (he was in parliament as a proctor of the abbot of Selby, who sat as a lord spiritual), which has led to speculation about who was really behind the offending request.[7] Yet it shows that the harmonious front was cracking and criticism of the court emerging again.

On 10 July Richard dramatically ordered the arrest of Gloucester, Arundel and Warwick. All were taken by surprise. Quite why Richard chose this moment to act is hotly debated. One chronicle tells of Gloucester and Arundel plotting against the king, although this seems to have been a deliberate confusion on the part of the chronicler with the events of 1387, to explain otherwise inexplicable arrests. Despite the king's claim that they were being seized for new offences, there is little doubt his primary motive was revenge for 1388. In Gloucester's case, increasingly vocal opposition to

Richard's foreign policy was prompting the king's inner circle to incite action against the duke. The three once more had significant grievances and had been frozen out of the king's circle. Richard's strike was thus pre-emptive; a king who had already shown himself a master of the dramatic gesture now also revealed himself to be vindictive and dangerously unpredictable. At Nottingham in August, in an act of intentional irony, the three former Appellants were appealed for treason. Richard opted for another theatrical performance, having the trio tried in parliament. In a tidy reversal of fortune, the Revenge Parliament would undo the Merciless Parliament.

Richard left little to chance for the assembly which opened in Westminster on 17 September 1397. Unusually, lords were allowed to bring their retinues and Richard had several hundred Cheshire archers on hand to intimidate. There was a strong suspicion that Richard had rigged the membership of the Commons, given the change of personnel and outlook among MPs compared with the previous parliament in January, although the change is more likely explained by experienced former MPs having the wisdom to steer clear of a political crisis. With so many novices, the house would prove suitably compliant to Richard's wishes. The opening sermon, by the Bishop of Exeter, set the tone, with the theme 'there shall be one king over them all' (Ezekiel 37:22). The bishop announced a general pardon, excluding fifty unnamed individuals. Richard continually refused to identify them, leading over 500 concerned people to pay for individual pardons over the course of the following year. It was rule by fear.

Meanwhile, parliament revoked the pardons given to Gloucester, Arundel and Warwick in 1388 and impeached the Archbishop of Canterbury, Thomas Arundel. As Bishop of Ely, Arundel had accompanied Gloucester in 1386 to cajole Richard into returning to the Wonderful Parliament after he stormed off; now he was sentenced to forfeiture and exiled, replaced as archbishop by the king's treasurer, Roger Walden. The Earl of Arundel was beheaded. Warwick was sentenced to death, a sentence commuted to life exile on the Isle of Man after the earl burst into tears and begged for mercy. That left Gloucester. He had been sent to the custody of his former Appellant colleague, the Earl of Nottingham, in Calais, where Nottingham was now captain. An order was sent ordering Nottingham to produce Gloucester, but the response came back that the duke was already dead. Parliament condemned him regardless and a written confession was produced in justification. The circumstances of his death were highly suspicious. In Henry IV's first parliament, it was revealed that Gloucester had been murdered before parliament had begun, on Richard's orders. A ruthless king was taking no chances.

He went further, having statutes passed to ban the heirs of the condemned Appellants from sitting in parliament, requiring all future peers to swear to uphold the acts of this parliament before being granted their estates. On the final day, before an adjournment to Shrewsbury set for January 1398, Richard distributed new titles like confetti and created a headache for those trying to keep track of who was who in the reign. The Earl of Derby became Duke of Hereford and the Earl of Nottingham was raised to the dukedom of Norfolk. The Earls of Huntingdon, Kent and Rutland became respectively Dukes of Exeter, Surrey and Aumerle. Thomas Walsingham referred caustically to these new creations as the 'duketti'. There was also a new marquess and four new earls, along with a redistribution among all these men of the confiscated Appellant lands and titles. It was an unprecedented shower of titles and honours, a revolution in the peerage and local power structures. Obsessed with loyalty, the king also began inserting his own men into local offices, with a widespread replacement of sheriffs. Edward II had been accused of concentrating patronage far too narrowly and ignoring the need for support in the localities. Richard II intended to spread patronage liberally but ensure all its recipients were dependent on him, giving him power bases in the shires. He was determined to have unquestioning obedience. In spite of all this, by the time the Shrewsbury parliament met on 27 January 1398, discord was growing in court circles. Given the fate of their three former colleagues, Nottingham and Derby had cause to be ambivalent about Richard's revenge. On the first day of the assembly, the king forced through a statute repealing the acts of the Merciless Parliament of 1388. Further men were punished, a new definition of treason approved and a very generous tax granted, but the session lasted just four days. Richard was triumphant and unopposed, his revolution complete.

However, he was also paranoid. Richard's full concept of majesty had been unfolding for a decade, and now that it was at last revealed, so he felt in need of greater measures to defend it. The sheriffs' oaths became ever stricter professions of loyalty. Counties were compelled to submit themselves and their possessions to the king's pleasure, as well as promising to uphold the acts of the Revenge Parliament. The king had little time for council meetings or counsellors, relying increasingly on a core trio for advice and to enforce his will: John Bushy (speaker in the 1397–98 parliament), William Bagot and Henry Green. Richard did not care that resentment was growing, as evidenced by occasional unrest. This was a regime which delighted in ceremony with displays of sovereignty and subjection, and which tolerated no dissent. Here was Richard's idea of kingship, untrammelled sovereign rule to which all bowed down, with dissent silenced and his view supreme.

Nevertheless, Richard gave an impression of a man afraid. He took every opportunity to extract oaths and pledges of allegiance, travelling everywhere with his Cheshire archers. Increasingly, he drew nearly all his retainers from Lancashire and Cheshire, with Cheshire particularly favoured. The king had never forgotten the support of that county at Radcot Bridge and in 1397 he raised it to a principality. Cheshiremen received frequent favour and rewards; Cheshire has been termed the 'inner citadel' of Richard's kingdom. Richard spent a lot of his time in 1398 and 1399 in the western and northern Midlands, including repeated stays in places like Lichfield which had never previously been a major feature of royal itineraries. He felt much happier and safer in this part of his realm.

Yet he paid too little attention to rivalries within the nobility and it was a noble quarrel which began the chain of events which brought Richard down. The Dukes of Hereford and Norfolk (as Derby and Nottingham now were) fell out. According to Hereford's version, told to Richard in Staffordshire in January 1398 and the only side of the story we have, Norfolk had informed Hereford in December that the two of them were about to be 'undone' by the king. Norfolk also alleged a plot against the Duke of Lancaster and others from among the king's inner circle, as well as a plan to disinherit the duke's heirs. There was probably considerable truth behind these allegations. Once Norfolk discovered Hereford had betrayed his confidence, he panicked and laid an ill-considered trap to seize Lancaster as he made his way to parliament at Shrewsbury. Failure left Hereford free to present his story to parliament unchallenged.

Deprived of his offices of Earl Marshal and Admiral, Norfolk was brought before the king at Oswestry in late February. He denied Hereford's accusations, so both dukes were commanded to appear before a parliamentary committee. This met at Bristol in March and decided that, conclusive proof either way lacking, the law of chivalry would apply and the two would joust to resolve the matter. At Windsor in April, Hereford expanded his list of allegations to include financial misconduct and the murder of Gloucester. This was a mistake, for Richard had absolutely no interest in the investigation of that murder. Norfolk's demand for trial by battle was thus accepted and the event fixed for 16 September 1398 at Coventry. The stage was set, but like a consummate actor determined to be the star of the show, Richard changed the script. Victory for either Norfolk or Hereford would bring unwelcome consequences for the king. With the two protagonists mounted and about to charge, he dramatically halted proceedings and announced his verdict: Hereford was to be banished for ten years, Norfolk for life. Richard II was now master of his realm, his opponents vanquished and his sovereignty impregnable.

As in a Greek tragedy, this was hubris leading to nemesis. There was disquiet at Hereford's sentence, for he had been neither accused nor convicted of a crime. It cost Richard his most critical supporter, Hereford's father. For a decade, John of Gaunt had been the pillar of stability on which Richard's government depended. During the winter his health collapsed and he died on 3 February 1399. Reneging on a promise he had made after the aborted fight at Coventry, the king deprived Hereford, Gaunt's son and heir, of his inheritance as Duke of Lancaster and extended his banishment to a life sentence. Not only had Richard broken his word, he had attacked the accepted rules of inheritance and challenged the core interests of the nobility.

Fatally, Richard now left England. Accompanied by a sizeable retinue, including Hereford's eldest son (the future Henry V) as a hostage, he set sail from Milford Haven for a second visit to Ireland at the end of May, arriving in Waterford on 1 June. His last surviving uncle, the Duke of York, was left as keeper of the realm in England. Richard had written to the King of France at the start of May to inform him of his plans. Henry Bolingbroke (as Hereford is usually known in accounts of these events), in exile in Paris, immediately laid plans for an invasion, securing the backing of Charles VI's brother, the Duke of Orléans. How much of the plan Orléans knew is uncertain, but Henry was able to sail unimpeded from Boulogne to land at Ravenspur, on the Humber, at the end of June. Yorkshire was a good strategic landing place, despite the longer crossing from France, as there were several key duchy of Lancaster holdings in the area. Henry continued his voyage north to Bridlington, before making his way to Pickering, Knaresborough, and finally Pontefract around 14 July, his small force growing on the way. Ten days earlier, York had written to Richard relaying news of Henry's arrival. The messenger probably reached Dublin on the 10th, but problems rounding up ships meant another fortnight elapsed before the king landed at Milford Haven. At a meeting in Doncaster on the 16th Henry had won the crucial backing of the Percy family, the Earl of Northumberland and his son Henry ('Hotspur'). By the 20th, Henry was at Leicester pondering options, while York started moving towards Richard. Henry shadowed him and on 27 July the two men met where a previous king had been murdered in 1327: Berkeley.

York defected to Henry. Many of his troops had deserted, while it is worth remembering that he was Henry's uncle as well as Richard's. Together, Henry and York headed to Bristol, where the castle was immediately surrendered to them, and three hated royal councillors were promptly executed: the Earl of Wiltshire, John Bushy and Henry Green. Henry was now in control of a large portion of England, Richard's position fatally damaged before he could counterattack. Afraid of capture once he heard of York's capitulation, Richard chose to join with the Earl of Salisbury in North Wales. With a handful of trusted followers, who had as much to lose as the king, Richard slipped away from Carmarthen in the middle of the night. Discovering this the next morning, the steward of the household, the Earl of Worcester, broke his staff of office and permitted those left behind to depart. Richard made for Conwy. Henry headed for Chester, where the efforts of the Dukes of Exeter and Surrey on Richard's behalf to determine Henry's plans resulted in their arrest. Instead, Henry sent the Earl of Northumberland to Conwy.

Exactly what happened at Conwy is unclear. The official Lancastrian narrative has Richard agreeing to resign his crown in favour of Henry, while other more plausible sources suggest that at this stage Henry sought (and Richard conceded) rather less. Regardless, Richard realised the game was up. Northumberland sent news of Richard's surrender to Henry, and earl and king arrived in Flint on 15 August. The next day, Henry and Richard met at Flint Castle. Richard was taken to imprisonment at Chester the same day. On the 19th, Henry issued writs in Richard's name for a parliament to meet at Westminster on 30 September. On 20 August, the whole party began the journey to London. When they arrived on 1 September, Richard was sent to the Tower.

By 10 September, Henry's intention to claim the crown was in the open, but it had clearly been in his mind before then. It was a plan with significant obstacles, even if in 1399 the deposition of a reigning king was less radical because it had already happened before. The circumstances of 1399 created problems which had not existed in 1327. In removing Edward II, his deposers had an unchallenged replacement in the acknowledged heir, the king's eldest son. Richard II was childless, which created a much more complex situation. The senior male heir by primogeniture was not Henry (descended from Edward III's third son) but the 7-year-old Edmund, heir of the Earl of March (descended from the second son), although Edmund's descent through a female line complicated matters. Justification for removing Richard and giving Henry legitimate title was required. Practically, of course, Henry was laying claim to the crown by right of conquest, but to admit that openly would set far too dangerous a precedent. A solution was desperately needed as Richard was hardly going to surrender his throne willingly or easily. The need to validate replacing Richard with Henry preoccupied several Lancastrian chroniclers, the question of Henry's title to the throne likewise obsessing historians in the late nineteenth and early twentieth centuries.

Eventually the deposition of 1399 was, like that of 1327, a muddled compromise. The official Lancastrian version, the 'Record and Process', is a work of propaganda set down on the parliament roll to justify the usurpation. It has Henry going to Richard in the Tower on 29 September and the king cheerfully abdicating. Other sources suggest he gave in only under sustained pressure over two days. Officially, his reign was deemed to have ended on 29 September 1399. His abdication was read to parliament on the 30th. With more unease than the official record suggests, parliament accepted the deposition and agreed to Henry claiming the throne. The parliament summoned in Richard's name was dissolved and a new one called in Henry's. It met on 6 October and, after hearing a justification for what had happened from the restored Archbishop Arundel, was postponed for the coronation of King Henry IV on 13 October 1399.

As in 1327, a series of articles outlined why the king was unfit to rule. Whereas those directed at Edward II had hinted at too little attention to governance, those prepared for Richard II accused him of malevolent rule contrary to law and custom (although once more, the problematic word 'tyranny' was scrupulously avoided). There were certainly eerie similarities between the two depositions, kings brought down rapidly with almost no one willing to save them. Yet there were also key differences. Edward II knew how unpopular his regime was. Richard was sufficiently oblivious to wander off to Ireland with all his loyalists, strange for a man whose behaviour in other respects betrayed considerable fear. The deposition of Edward II led to widespread action, judicial and otherwise, against courtiers seen as responsible for the iniquities of the regime. This did not happen in 1399, even though people were given an opportunity to bring complaints to Henry IV's first parliament. Edward was seen as presiding over an unjust regime by giving free rein to avaricious favourites, whereas Richard was seen as an unjust king entirely to blame for the oppressions of his regime. Edward governed too little, Richard too much. The result was the same.

Apart from demoting some nobles to lesser titles, the new king opted for conciliation with Richard's closest followers. However, Henry IV was left with the problem of a 32-year-old deposed predecessor who might live for decades and become a focus for discontent. In late October, Richard was sent from the Tower to Gravesend, then Leeds Castle (Kent), and finally to Pontefract Castle. Henry presumably hoped Richard would fade quietly into oblivion in Yorkshire. This was wildly optimistic.

Henry had demoted the Dukes of Exeter and Surrey back to their original titles as Earls of Huntingdon and Kent, downgrading the Earl of Gloucester to Lord Despenser. In December 1399, these became the ringleaders with the Earl of Salisbury in a plot to free Richard. Henry found out. The rebels proclaimed Richard king as they headed along the Thames Valley, but found little support. Kent and Salisbury were lynched at Cirencester on 8 January 1400; Despenser was killed in Bristol on the 15th; and Huntingdon was captured and beheaded in Essex. There were further executions but no need for any additional action to quell the failed coup. The higher clergy who were implicated spent several months in prison. Although the king had won an easy victory with minimal effort, the shambolic rebellion secured Richard's fate. The new king was insecure while the old lived. Richard was discussed in council around 8 February, the implicit conclusion being that he had to die. No record of a direct order exists, but sometime in mid-February 1400 Richard was killed at Pontefract. As with Edward II, lack of detail and mysterious circumstances led to plentiful speculation about his death, but foul play (possibly starvation) was suspected and very probable. As in Edward's case, Richard's conveniently timed death from grief, as the Lancastrian sources would have it, stretched credulity.

The government, learning the lessons of 1327, had Richard's body prominently displayed on the journey south to prove that he was dead. This did not stop some believing he was still alive and the odd pretender claiming to be him, but he has never attracted the same number of bizarre survival myths as Edward II. Richard's funeral, attended by Henry IV, took place in St Paul's Cathedral on 6 March. He was taken to King's Langley for burial, in the Dominican Friary where Piers Gaveston had been laid to rest decades earlier. Richard's mortal remains spent little more than a decade at Langley. After Henry V succeeded his father in 1413, he had Richard exhumed and reburied in Westminster Abbey beside Queen Anne, as Richard had intended. Centuries of visitors left their mark: when the tomb was opened in 1871, Richard's lower jaw and a few other bones were gone, along with the majority of Anne's skeleton. The dean of Westminster had everything tidied up, while Queen Victoria suggested that the bronze cushions for the effigies (also purloined at some point) were replaced. It was a deference to majesty of which Richard would have approved. The last Plantagenet king was finally able to rest in peace.

Richard through the Centuries

The drama of Richard's reign left no shortage of commentators describing events and drawing morals from them.[8] Most chronicles are coloured by the deposition and take sides, mainly Henry IV's, hence the overall picture is negative, although Richard had sympathisers. Some of those who ended up hostile shifted position during the reign. Thomas Walsingham and John

Gower are the most obvious examples, relatively sympathetic portraits in the early years giving way to sharp, even vituperative condemnation after 1399. That said, Walsingham was never entirely uncritical of Richard even in his more sympathetic phase.

Walsingham was a monk of St Albans, a worthy successor to Matthew Paris in that abbey's tradition of historical writing.[9] Prolific, acute and acerbic, his line about Richard tyrannising his people is the single most influential comment any chronicler wrote about the reign. His post-1399 view of Richard is highly critical, as he became something of an apologist for the new Lancastrian regime. Two other anonymous authors provide a similar gloss on the end of the reign: the *Vita Ricardi Secundi*, written by a monk of Evesham Abbey in Worcestershire, and the *Continuatio Eulogii*, probably by a Franciscan friar in Canterbury. The author of the *Vita* saw Richard's death as justice (ignoring any hint of murder): 'since he had in the past so thoughtlessly condemned many people to die by the earthly sword, so it came about that in the end he himself died, childless and friendless, by the sword of hunger'. He went on to paint an unflattering portrait:

> King Richard was of average height, fair-haired, with a pale complexion and a rounded, feminine face which was sometimes flushed; he was abrupt and stammering in his speech, and, because he spurned the advice of his elders and betters and preferred to take counsel from the young, he was capricious in his behaviour. He was prodigious with gifts, extravagantly ostentatious in his dress and pastimes, and unlucky as well as faint-hearted in foreign warfare. Towards his servants he often displayed great anger; he was also puffed up with pride, consumed by avarice, and fond of burning the candle at both ends.[10]

This contains most of the main contemporary criticisms of Richard's character: effeminate, unsoldierly, extravagant, ill-counselled, greedy and mercurial. The intention was to damage Richard's reputation, so this cannot be taken at face value as a portrait of the king. We know, for example, that when his skeleton was measured in the nineteenth century it revealed him to have been around 6ft tall, definitely above average height for his time. The Lancastrian chroniclers were trying to fit Richard into the role of villain, downplaying his regal qualities.

The most avowedly Ricardian writers were French. Richard had brought peace with France, was married to the French king's daughter, and was well-disposed towards the Parisian court, which stood to lose by the change of regime. The most notable work in Richard's favour is the *Chronique de la Traison et Mort de Richart Deux Roy Dengleterre* (*Chronicle of the Treason and Death of Richard the Second King of England*). The author was a Frenchman who probably served in Queen Isabella's household in England. The positive portrayal of the king is often at the expense of believable fact. The *Traison and Mort* contains the story of the public protest by Thomas Merks, Bishop of Carlisle, which has him argue that 'my lord the duke [Henry] has more erred and offended against King Richard than has the king against him'. This was used to great effect by Shakespeare, but is historically very unlikely. Even less plausibly, the *Traison* has Richard hacked to death at Pontefract in a tale reminiscent of martyrdom. It is a very different approach to the English, Lancastrian chronicles, presenting a tragic hero much sinned against.[11]

There were dissident English voices, but these were mainly muted until 1413. Thereafter, with Henry V secure on the throne and having orchestrated Richard's reburial, the hostility began to diminish. Even Thomas Walsingham toned down his approach to Richard II. The picture became more nuanced as the fifteenth century advanced, with Richard's qualities acknowledged alongside his faults. When Edward IV seized the throne in 1461, the new Yorkist dynasty sought to denigrate Henry IV and highlight the illegitimacy of the Lancastrian usurpation of 1399.[12] In the official parliamentary justification of Edward IV's claim to the throne, it is stated uncompromisingly that Richard II was 'lawfully, rightfully and justly seised and possessed' of crown and kingdom before Henry's usurpation and the usurper's infliction of a 'most vile, heinous and lamentable death' upon his predecessor. The consequence was that the judgement 'of every Christian man sounds a loud lament in God's hearing in heaven and is not forgotten on earth, especially in this realm of England, which because of this has endured the burden of intolerable persecution, punishment and tribulation'.[13]

Thus did the new Yorkist regime introduce a theme which would be enormously influential in the Tudor interpretation of history and (via William Shakespeare and Walter Scott) into the twentieth century. This was the notion that the Wars of the Roses began with Richard II's deposition in 1399 and ended only with Henry VII's victory at Bosworth in 1485, making much of the fifteenth century a time of disorder and violence that concluded only with the stability provided by the Tudor dynasty. Historians have long since abandoned the idea that the fifteenth century was a time of near-permanent disorder, but the popular belief that the origins of the Wars of the Roses are found in Richard II's reign has proved harder to overcome. The Tudors used the Yorkist myth but changed the emphasis. Needing to undermine the Yorkist claim to the throne, Tudor apologists pushed the root cause back into Richard's 'tyranny', justifying the deposition of 1399. Richard II became a king whose misrule necessitated his removal, setting in motion decades of strife in England. This fitted into a broader picture in which Richard II and Richard III 'stood as the two poles of the Tudor historical sequence'. If the second Richard was not 'regarded as a monster' in the same way as the third, he was still a 'constructed type'. This construction was 'the stock image of the weak, overinfluenced minor, who failed on counsel, in religion, and in war, whose inability to rise above the deficiencies of his youth was the overriding reason for his downfall'.[14] The focus was on the final years of the reign and his perceived perpetual immaturity, an approach which was to have a lasting influence on his reputation.

During the early Reformation, Richard II became a Protestant role model, praised by William Tyndale and John Foxe. While never lauded to the same extent as King John, Richard was nevertheless reinvented as an Anglican hero. The villains of the reign were the (Catholic) bishops, who misled the king and connived in his removal. Henry IV oversaw much stronger action against religious dissent, including a statute of 1401 authorising the burning of heretics, which led Tudor Protestants to vilify him and praise his predecessor for not persecuting Wycliffites and other dissenters. The argument does not withstand scrutiny, for if Richard avoided executions, he still took increasingly more stringent steps in favour of orthodoxy. Nevertheless, that this most ostentatiously orthodox of kings could be appropriated to serve the cause of Protestant reformers is a reminder that the more negative portrait did not become absolutely dominant until later in the Tudor era.

Thereafter, it proved remarkably durable for centuries. Richard was dragged into significant political debates, aspects of his reign carefully deployed as precedent to serve a particular cause. The problem of an heirless sovereign with the attendant succession problems was especially topical in Elizabeth I's later years. The Virgin Queen herself famously declared an association with Richard II ('I am Richard II. Know ye not that?'). Richard's perceived tyranny was used by both sides in the Stuart era. Questions over his purported abuse of the royal prerogative also featured in heated Stuart debates over the role of parliament. Yet the same picture of the dangerous, immature king, a tyrant surrounded by foolish young advisors, was essentially repeated in histories of the seventeenth and eighteenth centuries. Some, like David Hume, were willing to be a little more tolerant of Richard's context, but the arguments were mitigation rather than defence.

Opinions about Richard began to diverge in the nineteenth century. Henry Hallam, comparing Richard II with James II, condemned Richard for his 'extreme pride and violence, with an inordinate partiality for the most worthless favourites'. The French historian Henry Wallon was much more sympathetic, partly because he gave priority to the French sources over the English ones.[15] Late Victorian constitutional historians steered between these extremes. William Stubbs, unsurprisingly, had a very clear understanding of why Richard was deposed: 'He had resolutely, and without subterfuge or palliation, challenged the constitution.' The cardinal sin, unforgivable in Stubbs' eyes and one which made Richard despotic, was meddling with parliament. Still, Stubbs was far more sympathetic towards Richard than towards Edward II, arguing that he fell 'not unpitied or undeserving of pity'. His reasoning quickly becomes apparent. 'The legislation again of Richard is marked by real policy and intelligible purpose: Edward II can scarcely be said to have legislated at all.' For Bishop Stubbs, too much government, even if exercised unwisely, was preferable to too little. However, he introduced a problematic strand to the debate in arguing that after his second marriage in 1396, Richard went mad: 'his mind, already unsettled, was losing its balance altogether'.[16] The king's mental stability has been a subject of discussion ever since.

As usual, Stubbs proved influential for those who followed. They too condemned Richard for 'autocracy' and 'despotism', but there is simultaneously a scarcely concealed admiration for his intellect and ability in building a powerful monarchy. For these writers, strong government was a good thing, so Richard had to be given credit for his attention to governance even if he overdid it somewhat. Typical here is T.F. Tout: 'it required both intelligence and character to pursue his purpose over many years, and Richard must not be denied the credit of his political acumen'. The main problem was that 'Richard's inability to live up to his ideals of autocracy is writ on the history of that short period'.[17] Tout then discusses Richard's misgovernment and failings, but Richard came to be treated far less negatively than Edward II because of the Victorian generation's belief that firm administration and structures were self-evidently positive. Such generosity was relative: Richard was still a tyrant or a despot, and a mentally unbalanced one at that.

One reason proposed for Richard's failure was his preference for the aesthetic over the military. Typical is A.R. Myers: 'He preferred beauty and refinement to war […] Richard found his tastes and qualities, from his patronage of art to his introduction and use of handkerchiefs, regarded as extravagant and effeminate.'[18] While Richard probably did invent the pocket handkerchief,[19] it seems a little unfair to use it as evidence of royal excess, but Myers is far from atypical. Bertie Wilkinson likewise argued that Richard failed because instead 'of the instincts of the warrior he possessed only the more exotic and less popular qualities of the aesthete, loving art, literature, and music, and the pleasures of the mind'.[20] As late as 1992, one historian could assert that Richard was 'one of England's less successful kings' because 'by inclination he was an artist rather than a warrior'.[21] Inevitably, a biography of Richard's militaristic father, the Black Prince, drew a comparison with another monarch accused of preferring 'un-kingly' pursuits:

> Edward II, who despite his bodily strength preferred menial occupations to knightly ones, and Richard II, with his highly developed aesthetic sense and love of refinement, whether in art or cookery, could not share their interests with their barons and courtiers; and on their barons their political power ultimately rested.[22]

In this approach, Richard was a failure because he did not meet warrior expectations of the king. What few seemed to wrestle with was the inherent contradiction of Richard being judged a failure for somehow succeeding to be too hard and too soft at the same time: tyrant, yet not aggressive enough.

Such tension is obvious in an opinionated biography by Anthony Steel (1941), for decades the standard life. At times, he introduces an anachronistic party political system into the fourteenth century. The chapter on 1389–97 is called 'The Policy of Appeasement'; while uncontroversial in the twenty-first century, the volume was published during the Second World War, only three years after Neville Chamberlain's concessions at Munich, which made it a rather loaded phrase. According to Steel, it was Richard's 'acute neurosis and suspicion' which 'dominated his last three years'. Psychoanalysis underpins Steel's entire assessment of Richard, which is generally hostile and judges him a schizophrenic: 'a schizoid mind of Richard's type suffers in times of mental stress from a feeling that the outer world has less and less reality […] By 1394 Anne was probably the only feature of the outside world which was altogether real to Richard.' V.H. Galbraith's 1942 review expressed doubts about Steel's psychologising, although indulged in its own by comparing Richard to 'the lonely boy at school, the non-cooperator, who hated rugger and cricket and refused to shout on the touchline'.[23] This says rather more about the public school outlook of Galbraith's generation than it does about a fourteenth-century king.

For a time, Steel's psychoanalytical approach was fashionable. Even Winston Churchill was uncharacteristically generous towards Richard II. After blaming childhood traumas and 'injuries and cruelties which he suffered at the hands of his uncle Gloucester and the high nobility', Churchill refers to Richard's posthumous popularity, a kindness in his verdict which he denied to Edward II:

> We have no right in this modern age to rob him of this shaft of sunlight which rests upon his harassed, hunted life. There is however no dispute that in his nature fantastic error and true instinct succeeded each other with baffling rapidity. He was capable of more than human cunning and patience, and also of foolishness which a simpleton would have shunned.[24]

A similar thesis, that Richard was a man damaged by his childhood who became a champion of the common interest against the nobility and elites, is likewise found in John Harvey's very sympathetic sketch. Harvey makes the bizarrely hyperbolic claim that 'the tragedy is not of Richard II only', but also of 'millions and millions of human beings, spread over 500 years of time and the whole surface of the globe'.[25] That Richard II's elevated notions of kingship could have saved the entire English-speaking world from centuries of aristocratic tyranny would most kindly be classified as extremely eccentric.

This approach led May McKisack to observe in 1959 that a 'cloud of romantic illusion has gathered round the name of Richard II'. McKisack firmly dispelled that cloud by outlining the illegalities and injustices of the king's last two years, arguing that 'Richard's supreme blunder in his final years was to cast the cloak of legality away and leave tyranny revealed in all its nakedness'. Comparing Richard with Edward II, she broke with established tradition in seeing Richard as the greater threat: 'the case for deposing him looked stronger than the case for deposing his great-grandfather', since 'Edward II had been a weakling and a fool; but Richard II had become dangerous, perhaps dangerously mad'. Her view allowed some mitigation, noting his more positive features as an 'exemplary husband, a loyal friend, a generous patron'. Finally, though, McKisack's verdict is stark and the exact opposite of Harvey's: 'His failure was a personal tragedy, but his success would have been the tragedy of a nation.' By now Richard's madness was deeply embedded in the historical tradition: 'If Richard was sane from 1397 onwards, it was the sanity of a man who pulls his own house about his ears.'[26]

McKisack's 'cloud of romantic illusion' reappeared around the next biography, Harold F. Hutchison's *The Hollow Crown* (1961). Hutchison's treatment of Richard is cloyingly romantic and at times lapses into gushing speculation verging on fiction. To argue that 'in a brutal age it was Richard's humanity which was outstanding' (the deaths of Arundel and Gloucester callously dismissed on the grounds that 'England was well rid of both') is a rather startling conclusion for a king who had his uncle murdered. Even for 1961, Hutchison's interpretation was old-fashioned and outdated, a strange picture of a humanitarian forced into misdeeds to respond to the nasty people all around him.[27]

Richard II, with John, is the only medieval king whose 'tyranny' was routinely cited by historians. That there was a strong accusation of tyranny from one of Richard's contemporaries helped make the slippery term acceptable. In 1968, Caroline Barron examined the accusations against Richard. Her conclusion was that one simple motivation underlay his approach: 'these are the acts of a man who was afraid; of a king, frightened into tyranny'. In response to hostility from his subjects, 'Richard tried, not to conciliate them, but to trample them underfoot, and, while he thus intimidated, milked and insulted his subjects and gave them increasing cause to hate and misunderstand him, he was vainly trying to hide from himself the fact that he was at their mercy.'[28]

The late 1960s and early 1970s saw considerable interest in Richard II. A 1971 volume of essays looked in detail at aspects of the reign which were often neglected.[29] A 1968 monograph by Richard H. Jones contends that Richard was brought down 'because he dedicated himself persistently to a programme of reform, the ultimate aim of which was to establish a régime of royal absolutism'. This was a king who in his final two years 'placed himself in a position of absolute authority' which generated fear in almost everyone.[30] The core problem was that Richard was constrained by the limits of his time and of medieval monarchy, which meant that absolutism was simply not possible as it would be in later centuries. The idea that Richard aimed at absolutism within the limits of the English monarchy, rather than at tyranny or despotism, was a break from the prevailing academic orthodoxy since Stubbs.

Gervase Mathew avoided the language of tyranny, although did assert that 'Richard's need for personal magnificence had probably always been combined with a ravaging extravagance'. He is clear, though, that Richard fell in 1399 because of his failure to command widespread support and his threat to the propertied classes: 'The safeguarding of inheritance and property-rights was an essential function of medieval kingship, so

Richard had alienated his natural supporters outside the court circle.'[31] Anthony Tuck drew a similar conclusion about the alienation of the lords: 'They thought that law should protect their lives and their property, and that Richard had overridden law and custom and was ruling by his will alone.' While less condemnatory than others, Tuck reasserts the language of tyranny for Richard's final years. Ultimately, it was mismanagement of the nobility and failure to recognise the need for cooperation which undid Richard, since the 'nobility could not make their will prevail for long if the king was determined not to cooperate, and in the end the only effective alternative was to remove the king'.[32] Likewise, in an examination of the Appellants, Anthony Goodman observed that the forfeiting and redistribution of noble lands and titles from 1397 'created a new group of the "disinherited", a source of embarrassment and danger'. The problem which faced the Appellants in 1386–88 and the disinherited in 1397–99 was that they 'were in a dilemma when the king behaved in a manner which they considered unjust and harmful to their interests'.[33]

There was no major shift in attitudes towards Richard in the later 1970s and 1980s, although Chris Given-Wilson did look in some detail at the question of Richard's creation of an affinity in the shires.[34] However, the 1990s was another golden age for Ricardian scholarship. In 1994, Given-Wilson produced a volume for the Manchester Medieval Sources Series which contained, in modern translation, a major selection of the principal sources for the years 1397–1400. Alison McHardy's companion volume was published in 2012 and covered the opening twenty years of the reign. Together with R.B. Dobson's collection for the Peasants' Revolt, this made available the main sources for the reign in a format which allows a lay reader to access the reign easily, a commendable luxury denied to students of most medieval kings.[35]

Published in 1997, Nigel Saul's *Richard II* immediately became the standard biography. He observed that 'Richard anticipated a number of the initiatives that were later to serve the Yorkists and early Tudors well', the problem being that the circumstances of the late fourteenth century were not conducive to their immediate success. However, 'Richard's political legacy could thus hardly be considered sterile'. Yet as with Edward II, Richard failed in 'the essence of successful kingship', that is 'the delicate task of managing the nobility and harnessing their power and influence to the crown'. He brought about his own downfall: 'It was Richard himself who had raised the crown to such dizzy heights of power and fame; and it was Richard himself who created the conditions in which [...] he was brought down.' In a detailed, careful study, though, Saul does succumb to the temptation, on a couple of extended occasions, to psychoanalyse Richard, which is a problematic approach at a distance of six centuries with no reliable clinical data. He sees Richard's behaviour as explicable psychologically as 'situation dependent'. This became pronounced in later years especially: 'as he became more powerful in the 1390s, so he became more aloof, and possibly also more arrogant'. Ultimately, Saul deems Richard to have had an 'essentially narcissistic' personality, which explains the aggression and anger with which he responded to criticism and his burning desire for revenge. By the end of the reign, this meant that 'his grasp on reality was becoming weaker'. That, ultimately, informs Saul's final verdict on Richard II: 'in the theatre of medieval monarchy there was no keener actor than Richard. His tragedy was that he mistook the illusion of the stage for the reality of the world around him.'[36]

For Alison McHardy, the psychological verdicts of both Steel and Saul were 'too extreme and melodramatic'. She preferred to suggest that Richard's behaviour was 'the result of a serious lack of self-confidence'. McHardy argued that Richard 'was not mad, nor was he even neurotic'. Further, his 'personality was not especially complex, nor were his characteristics unique, or even unusual'. The core problem was that Richard had 'the classic symptoms of an inferiority complex', which was a real problem for a king, as he was unable to 'cope with criticism, by responding calmly, and even learning from it'. In other words, Richard lacked the necessary attributes for successful kingship.[37]

McHardy's piece was in one of three volumes of essays about Richard II's reign which appeared in the period 1997–2000. Although most of these essays focused on specialised aspects of the reign, there were also some revisionist thoughts about Richard himself. James L. Gillespie, noting that the general historical consensus meant 'a reflection upon the military aspects of Richard II's reign would be rather like a study of Margaret Thatcher's Marxist ideals', nevertheless reassessed Richard as a military leader. While Richard never campaigned in France (part of the reason for his negative military reputation when set against Edward III and Henry V), Gillespie examined his military record in Scotland and Ireland. He observed that 'military imagery' was 'an essential feature of Ricardian kingship' and that while no one 'can claim Richard II was a great warrior', he did 'demonstrate strategic sense on both Scotland and Ireland which historians have been slow to credit'.[38] Chris Given-Wilson re-examined Richard's relationship with the higher nobility, observing that while the king failed to 'contain conflict' and that this was 'undeniably to some extent his own fault', that 'historians have been led to argue that it was almost entirely his fault is a measure of the success of his opponents' propaganda'.[39] Yet the rehabilitation was partial. Studying how Richard transformed parliament from 'an instrument of opposition to a tool of royal power', Gwilym Dodd concluded that the king's 'success in bringing parliament under his control' was nevertheless doomed as it 'relied on fear and compulsion' and 'derived from political insecurity and weakness'.[40] To say that Richard was a better warrior than conventionally believed and was not solely responsible for noble conflict was not to exonerate him from the charges of failure to work constructively with the political community as expected of a medieval king.

Richard's character continued to fascinate. Caroline Barron, author of the 1968 article about Richard's tyranny, appeared to repent of the term, now arguing that Richard was no worse than other medieval kings and questioning the justice of his deposition.[41] Gerald Harriss, identifying the king's 'deep-personal insecurity', unusually avoided undue speculation on the causes to deal with its manifestation in a fierce defence of the royal status.[42] Other twenty-first century historians were less reticent to analyse him against new theoretical frameworks. Christopher Fletcher's monograph took as its starting point the argument that 'interpretations of the reign of Richard II have for centuries been more or less consciously influenced by this king's unmanly reputation', as his 'unmanly character has provided the cement with which historians have filled the gaps in their interpretations'. Setting the reign in a detailed discussion of masculinity theory and concepts of manhood, Fletcher draws the conclusion that Richard aspired to conventional manly ideals. Since 'a young man of noble status proved his manhood by responding to the challenges of his enemies, averting the threat of shame', Richard's 'attitude to chivalry and warfare was entirely in accordance with this approach to manhood'. His opponents resorted to a 'rhetoric of youth' in order to challenge his authority, the ambitions of his uncles in the 1380s preventing the king undertaking 'manly' pursuits. Ultimately, in 'his final tyranny', the king ended up 'creating the conditions of his deposition by his pursuit of manly vengeance'.[43] The crises of the reign, and Richard's ultimate failure, thus stemmed from his desire to prove himself a man.

Fletcher's book was a reminder that by the twenty-first century the ground had shifted. For younger generations in particular, older models of masculinity and the idea of 'effeminacy' as somehow inappropriate for a man were increasingly toxic. Much more relaxed about the fluidity of gender roles and unwilling to accept the need to conform to gender stereotypes, for them a focus on Richard's 'unmanliness' made little sense. In scholarly literature, there were signs of a greater focus on Richard's performance and failings as king than on psychological assessments and dissections of character. Emphasis was placed on the consequences of Richard's concentration on a small circle of friends and the resulting alienation of the wider nobility. As Jonathan Sumption observed, if Richard was 'intent on a major redistribution in favour of the Crown and a new nobility which shared his own exalted idea', then he had cause to succumb to the increasing paranoia which marked his actions from 1397; after all, 'no English king had succeeded in ruling for very long without the support of the higher nobility'.[44]

In his biography of Richard's supplanter, Chris Given-Wilson concluded that 'Henry's kingship was qualitatively different from Richard II's'. The comparison was favourable to Henry, whose 'most significant achievement was the restoration of the consensual style of politics practised by Edward III' and who 'acknowledged the limitations of royal power'.[45] As it became accepted that 'strong' kings worked with their nobility and parliaments in pursuit of a common purpose, so Richard's overbearing, interventionist style in his two final parliaments came to look more like a failure of kingship, demonstrating a 'fundamental loss of control on the part of the king' who was no longer able to 'work with the community to ensure the compromise between his demands and those of his subjects'.[46] Some believed this had always been Richard's true nature. In a study of the Earl of Warwick in the context of his West Midlands heartland, A.K. Gundy challenged the idea that Richard learnt from the experience of the 1380s. For her, the early 1390s was not the period of tranquillity others have suggested: 'far from ruling in a harmonious or successful manner, Richard changed only his tactics, not his attitudes.'[47] This book revived the idea of Richard ruling tyrannically, arguing that a royal affinity was necessarily a sign of bad kingship and tyranny, since the king was effectively buying support. As Gwilym Dodd observed in critiquing the approach, this is too simplistic, extrapolating too much from a local case study, ignoring the culture of loyalty and service which underpinned late medieval politics.[48] Yet the tyranny debate continues precisely because it is such an ill-defined term which means different things to different people, muddying rather than clearing the waters.

The reign continues to be the focus of intensive research, as shown by the 2022 volume of essays to honour Nigel Saul.[49] Although there have been changes in emphasis, Saul's essential portrait of Richard (psychological diagnosis aside) has not been seriously challenged in any of the popular biographies published since 1997. Laura Ashe's short volume is a study of the culture and literature of the reign rather than a biography, from which

Richard is often frustratingly absent. It is strongest in discussing Richard's ideas of majesty and the artistic results of these, but Ashe's Richard becomes little more than a literary character – 'the idea of him may be the only real object of study there is' – which is problematic.[50] Kathryn Warner's biography has a much clearer narrative focus. As in her biography of Edward II, the idea that Richard 'was born to be king of England and did not choose the position' is anachronistically modern; at the very heart of Richard's understanding of kingship was precisely the fact that he was born into a sacred office. Likewise, the idea that 'Henry IV was, in many ways, no great improvement on Richard' rather ignores recent work on Henry which suggests that his different, consensual style was indeed different and more successful than has traditionally been allowed. However, Warner's overall picture is sympathetic without whitewashing Richard, accepting that 'in the last years of his life he ruled tyrannically and greedily and made himself grossly unpopular'.[51] She also mercifully avoids trying to psychoanalyse the king, settling for recounting his tantrums and actions without feeling the need to theorise about them.

Despite being one of the most intensively-studied late medieval kings, the historical Richard II remains elusive, a contradictory figure who always seems just beyond the historian's grasp. That this is the case is due, in large part, to the fact that his fictional alter-ego is one of the most influential characters ever to strut upon the English stage and has long overshadowed the real man upon whom he is based.

Richard in Popular Culture

It is impossible to escape the problematic legacy of Shakespeare when considering how Richard II has been (and still is) viewed in the popular imagination. Although the sequence was not written in chronological order, *Richard II* is the first of eight plays treating the crisis of monarchy in the years 1399–1485. It presents the Tudor thesis in dramatic form, with 1399 ushering in a period of instability and violence which is ended only by Henry Tudor's triumph at Bosworth in the final play, *Richard III*. Shakespeare thus does not deal with Richard simply as an interesting character in his own right, but as the figure whose actions and resulting downfall initiated a cycle of warfare and misery in England. The play deals only with the very end of a twenty-two-year reign. Yet for all Shakespeare altered, distorted and even invented history, it is nevertheless an acutely insightful play in which the playwright's 'characterization of the king and his understanding of what mattered to him probably bring us closer to the historical figure than many a work of history'.[52]

What Shakespeare instinctively understood was the vital part majesty and the royal dignity had in Richard's view of kingship. For all the moments of doubt and agony, Richard's core tragedy is that in his mind his person and his office are one, which means that he can accept no dissent or criticism that he does not see as a challenge to his crown. In one of the most moving scenes, Richard 'unkings' himself.

> I give this heavy weight from off my head
> And this unwieldy sceptre from my hand,
> The pride of kingly sway from out my heart.
> With mine own tears I wash away my balm,
> With mine own hands I give away my crown,
> With mine own tongue deny my sacred state,
> With mine own breath release all duteous oaths.

Even in surrender, Richard is controlling the action. His kingship can only be undone by his will, for he is the king; yet, as he claims elsewhere,

> Not all the water in the rough rude sea
> Can wash the balm from an anointed king.

Shakespeare's success was to capture this key element of Richard, the king who believed that kingship was something sacred, irrevocable and which set him apart. One particular soliloquy, a sombre musing on kingship, has proved especially influential.

> Within the hollow crown
> That rounds the mortal temples of a king
> Keeps Death his court

'The Hollow Crown' has frequently been used as a title in works about this period. In modern times, *Richard II* has been a popular Shakespeare play to perform, with the RSC putting on more than thirty productions since 1870. Jeremy Irons (1986), Alex Jennings (1990), Sam West (2000) and David Tennant (2013) have all trodden the boards in the title role at Stratford-upon-Avon. Screen versions of Richard have overwhelmingly been in film or television adaptions of the play, with Ian McKellen, Derek Jacobi, Fiona Shaw and Mark Rylance all taking the lead role. The BBC has done more than half a dozen adaptions, the most recent with Ben Wishaw as Richard in *The Hollow Crown* (2012). There have been versions elsewhere in the English-speaking world, principally in Australia and the USA, as well as more unlikely adaptions for German, Russian and even Hungarian audiences.

So dominant is Shakespeare's play as a fictional interpretation of the reign that few authors have trespassed into this territory. Compared to the other kings in this volume, there is a notable dearth of fiction which has much of a role for Richard II. There are no significant appearances for him on the silver screen outside of performances of Shakespeare. There is a 1932 play, *Richard of Bordeaux*, by 'Gordon Daviot' (a pen name of Elizabeth MacKintosh, better known by her alternative pseudonym Josephine Tey). It covers a broader spectrum of the reign, from 1385 onwards, with the love between Richard and Anne at its centre. The other main theme, easier to draw out over this longer timeframe, is Richard's desire for peace with France, setting him at odds with his more pugnacious uncles and nobles. While perfectly defensible as historical interpretation, beneath this approach lies the strongly pacifist sentiment of a society still deeply scarred by the First World War. There is a sharp contrast between this sensitive, gentle, pacifist Richard and Shakespeare's regal narcissist. It was well received when first performed and made a star of leading actor John Gielgud. Yet although it crossed the Atlantic from the West End to Broadway, and was later adapted for both TV and radio, *Richard of Bordeaux* has proved far less enduring than Shakespeare's version. A 1985 play by Anthony Minghella, *Two Planks and a Passion*, fictionalised a 1392 royal visit to York for the city's passion plays but has had limited impact.

Richard himself has not inspired many novelists. *Within the Hollow Crown* (1941) by Margaret Campbell Barnes fictionalises the reign but is very much of its time. Hilda Lewis' work for young adults, *The Gentle Falcon* (1952) tells the story of the closing years of the reign through the eyes of an English servant of Richard's second wife, Isabella. The portrait of the king is in tune with academic thinking of the time. He is a king on the brink of madness, who has never overcome the loss of his first queen, Anne. Extravagant, interested in the arts and uninterested in war, this Richard is a capricious, brooding figure who cannot trust others, yet is capable of flashes of generosity and kindness even as he essentially neglects Isabella. An unusual perspective is found in *A Bloody Field by Shrewsbury* (1972) by Edith Pargeter (better known by the pen name under which she wrote the Cadfael series, Ellis Peters). This deals with the opening of Henry IV's reign up to the 1403 Battle of Shrewsbury, but the start covers Richard's deposition and death through the eyes of Henry of Monmouth, Henry IV's eldest son and the future Henry V. As his father seizes the throne, the young Henry looks fondly back on the deposed king and recalls his kind treatment of him. It is worth recalling that once he became king, Henry V had Richard reburied in Westminster Abbey; this interpretation is thus an intriguing reminder that not all Lancastrians were necessarily hostile to the memory of Richard II.

From the twenty-first century, Paul Doherty's Brother Athelstan series is set in the early years of Richard's reign. However, as the king was still a boy at this point, greater emphasis is placed on John of Gaunt in the stories. The most extensive modern treatment in fiction comes in three books by the American novelist Mercedes Rochelle. *A King under Siege* (2018) covers the Peasants' Revolt and the Appellant crisis, while *The King's Retribution* (2020) and *The Usurper King* (2021) treat Richard's revenge and fall and the start of Henry IV's reign. The odd anachronism and historical slip aside, they are well-written and well-paced to capture the excitement and drama. They also include events which are not typically treated in fiction (such as the Carmelite friar accusing John of Gaunt at Salisbury in 1384, Richard's desire to canonise Edward II and Haxey's petition in 1397). Considerable research lies behind the novels, which reflect the spirit of the surviving sources and employ plausible scenarios to fill in the gaps. The Richard who emerges from these pages, although fictional, is a recognisable version of the historical figure: loving husband, loyal friend, prone to bouts of temper, vengeful and acutely aware of his majesty. The one flight of fancy is the use of a legend about Richard escaping to survival in Scotland, but it is pardonable in this fictional setting where it works well as part of the plot. Despite the paucity of novels about him, Richard has here found an author who does him justice.

Intriguingly, even if he has failed to excite novelists, Richard II (or at least his Shakespearean incarnation) is still considered familiar enough to feature in comparisons in national newspapers. In December 2021, when British prime minister Boris Johnson was coming under sustained pressure over allegations of corruption and illegal parties in Downing Street, he held a press conference with England's chief medical officer. In an opinion piece for *The Guardian*, the columnist Marina Hyde scathingly summarised the event:

At a Downing Street briefing this week, the chief medical officer explained: 'What we've got is two epidemics on top of each other.' Yeah, and two press conferences on top of each other.

One is being held by Chris Whitty; the other is being gibbered through by a knock-off Richard II, surrounded by useless cronies and unsuccessfully begging parliament for money.[53]

Quite what Richard, so obsessed with regality and appearance, would have made of comparison with the notoriously scruffy Johnson can only be imagined. Yet it reveals much about the residual modern view of Richard as the Shakespearean anti-hero oblivious to reality, listening only to his clueless inner circle, ignoring the realm collapsing around him.

Verdict

Like Edward II, it is hard to argue that Richard II was anything other than a failure given his reign ended in deposition. In some respects, the events of 1399 were far more radical than those of 1327, for they required the political community to acquiesce in the replacement of the king by someone other than his son and heir. That Henry IV was able to achieve this, albeit not entirely smoothly, demonstrates the extent of Richard's failure. Yet Richard's fate is more puzzling than that of his great-grandfather. Edward II's reign was one long succession of crises, the outright hostilities interspersed with periods of cold war. Richard II's reign was not. Yes, there were crises, but there were also long periods of peace. Edward II's throne looked under threat most of the time, but no one could have predicted in 1395 that Richard's was at risk.

Indeed, there were successes in Richard's reign. He can hardly be held accountable for the Peasants' Revolt, in which seething problems from his grandfather's reign came to a head, but he acted with courage and showed a degree of initiative sorely lacking in most of his adult advisors. After 1389, he seemed to have learned the lessons of the Appellant crisis and England mainly enjoyed a stretch of domestic harmony. The pursuit of peace with France was a logical policy with a successful outcome, although it is true that it was not popular with those, including the king's uncles, who longed for the glory days of Crécy and Poitiers. Richard was certainly not averse to military campaigns, as he demonstrated in Scotland and Ireland, although his military wisdom is questionable, not least when he left the south of England wide open to potential French attack in 1385. Yet the war with France had dragged on for decades, most of the tangible gains had been lost, and it was an immense drain on finances. The logic of Richard's peace policy can be defended without recourse to attacking his lack of courage or military interest. It achieved the desired result and freed Richard to concentrate on domestic matters.

Unfortunately, Richard thus freed destroyed himself. Whether calling what happened in 1397–99 'tyranny' is helpful is in the eye of the beholder, but the forced loans, the blank charters, the reliance on a Cheshire militia and the endless demand for oaths and sureties suggested to his subjects a king who was out of control, which meant few had any interest in saving his crown when the crisis came. His treatment of the Appellants and their heirs, and above all the perceived injustice towards Henry Bolingbroke, alarmed a landed society who were deeply concerned that the king was undermining the established basis of landholding and inheritance. In this regard, Richard's failure was very similar to his great-grandfather's, in that he failed to grasp the need to work with his nobility towards a common end. After a rocky period in the 1330s, culminating in a crisis in 1341, this was something Edward III had learned and it made the middle of his reign a conspicuous success, his nobility focused together on the French war. Richard had no such unifying focus to bring his lords together and he seemed unable or unwilling to stop the strife among them at the most critical moments. He gave too many of them a vested interest in his removal, not least the man who took his crown.

It is pointless to do what so many have attempted and psychoanalyse Richard in order to explain what went wrong. Six hundred and more years later, with no clinical evidence, such attempts will always be speculative and tell us more about the purposes of the historian than about Richard. We can only draw on the evidence of what happened. On the one hand, it is clear that Richard was immensely loyal to his friends (even when it was politically foolish) and that he was a loyal, loving husband who was distraught by Anne's early death. On the other hand, he had a liking for theatrical performances, he was prone to bouts of temper, and he was capable of coldly calculated acts of ruthless vengeance. His petulance in the 1380s and his use of fear in the late 1390s both demonstrate that he had no understanding of the need to work with parliament and the political community rather than try to dominate or rule in spite of them. If he cast his net far wider than Edward II, who tended to fixate on a single individual or family, Richard II nevertheless invested too much in a group of favourites. In both 1388 and 1399, those excluded from his inner circle turned on the king. The attempt to use the judiciary to undo his enemies in 1387, as well as the cruel revenge exacted against Arundel, Warwick and Gloucester in 1397, made the king appear dangerous and unpredictable. Far from upholding justice and the rule of law, he was attempting to reinterpret the law to assert his own sovereign power.

That is the essence of his failure. 250 years after Richard was stripped of his throne, another king would declare, in the process of losing both his throne and his head, that 'a subject and a sovereign are clean different things'. Recognising the very different contexts of 1399 and 1649, we should be cautious of drawing too many parallels between Richard II and Charles I, but both ultimately had a concept of kingship which was incompatible with that of their subjects. Richard would not have disagreed with Charles' words. He attempted to introduce an augmented kingship, where parliament did his will, the nobility was purged and recreated to be a group loyal to him, and where his authority was sovereign, free from dissent or challenge. This was at odds with the understanding of the English political community, where kingship was something more contractual, requiring the king to accept counsel from his 'natural' advisors (the higher nobility) as well as his chosen ones, upholding justice and respecting the law, not least the law of inheritance. Richard's idea of a king was not shared by many of his subjects, especially the powerful ones, and he paid the price. Henry IV's very different style was a conscious reaction against Richard's approach, and Henry died peacefully in his bed, his throne safely passed to his son.

Richard II was thus the architect of his own failure. He was a man who in the 1390s had shown himself capable of wise, courageous policies and ruling competently, even if his concept of majesty caused some concern. For whatever reason, his sudden avenging of ten-year-old humiliations in 1397 led him to establish a style of rule which was superficially dominant but fundamentally flawed. He challenged the basic understanding of English kingship and alienated or worried too many people in the process. One unsuitable king had already been deposed in the fourteenth century, so it required no great leap of imagination to do it again. Richard's tragedy was that he could have taken another path and when everything collapsed around him, he had no one to blame but himself.

Chapter 5

Richard III: A Villainous King?

Even by the standards of a country which has turned archaicised ceremonial into an art, the events of Thursday 26 March 2015 were bizarre. As a slightly bemused international media observed, only the English could manage something akin to a ceremonial funeral, complete with four preceding days of obsequies, for a king who had lain dead more than five centuries. On Sunday 22nd, with somewhat questionable taste, Richard III's hearse had conveyed him to Leicester Cathedral via Bosworth battlefield, scene of the defeat which had cost him his throne and his life in 1485. For three days he lay in repose, visited by thousands, before the archbishops of Canterbury and Westminster presided over a nationally-televised reburial in a specially-constructed tomb inside the cathedral. Retrieved from under a car park in 2013, the bones of the last Plantagenet king were finally laid to rest in a royal tomb.

It did wonders for Leicester's tourist industry, but it was an extraordinary sequence of events. Richard had been dead more than half a millennium. That the rediscovery and eventual reinterment of his mortal remains aroused such excitement, interest and disputes demonstrated the hold he continued to have on popular imagination even after the passage of so many years. No other monarch comes close. It is impossible to imagine that, were the bones of Henry I miraculously relocated at Reading, many people would care, let alone that there would be anything remotely approaching the same level of ceremony accompanying their reburial. Indeed, it is hard to envisage anyone initiating the search. Richard III reigned for less time than any post-Conquest monarch except Edward V and Edward VIII, his reign the shortest of any sovereign who made it as far as a coronation. Yet there are almost as many books about him as most other kings combined. An entire historical society is devoted to defending his reputation, while numerous volumes have been devoted to attacking it. At the heart of it all is not Richard's performance during his brief time as king, but rather the question of how he assumed the crown and above all whether or not he murdered his nephews. Richard III is inseparable from the Princes in the Tower, and the raging debates over his guilt or innocence make him a polarising king like no other.

Reviled as the most evil king ever to sit upon the throne and lauded as a persecuted great ruler slandered by the Tudors, Richard has divided opinion for centuries.

Richard's Life and Reign

Richard was born on 2 October 1452 at Fotheringhay in Northamptonshire. He was the eleventh of Duke Richard of York and Cecily Neville's twelve children and their eighth son, although four of his older brothers had died in infancy. When he was born, there was considerable congestion on the road between Richard and the throne, and no one would have predicted he would one day be king. As the fourth surviving son of a duke, even a duke of the blood royal, he was not of great interest to chroniclers and his childhood is poorly recorded. It is likely that he resided with his mother's household, mainly at Fotheringhay, and had the conventional noble upbringing of a younger son.

His father was one of the leading figures in a realm descending into crisis. In the summer of 1453, the Hundred Years' War effectively ended in French victory. Final defeat added to an already febrile atmosphere in England, where York was at odds with Henry VI's inner circle, including Queen Margaret and Edmund Beaufort, Duke of Somerset. The king himself was a feeble character who reigned but did not rule, and in August 1453 his mental health collapsed. York, the realm's premier duke, became protector during the king's incapacity, but when Henry recovered, outright hostilities commenced. The first Battle of St Albans (22 May 1455) marked the effective start of the Wars of the Roses, with York victorious and Somerset killed. York was briefly protector again, but the queen was determined to thwart him. Four years of tension followed St Albans until open conflict resumed.

At Ludlow on 12 October 1459, the royal army confronted troops led by York, his two eldest sons, and the Earls of Salisbury and Warwick. These troops refused to fight against the king in person, forcing York and the others to flee into exile, leaving their supporters to be condemned and forfeit their lands. In October 1460, York returned to claim the throne in parliament. A compromise was worked out whereby Henry VI would remain king for life and then be succeeded by York. As this involved disinheriting her son Edward, it was anathema to Queen Margaret. Armies were raised again and at the Battle of Wakefield (30 December 1460), York and his second son Edmund were killed. Margaret won a follow-up victory in the second Battle of St Albans (17 February 1461).

147

The 8-year-old Richard was swiftly sent overseas, into the care of the Duke of Burgundy, along with his 11-year-old brother George. Their exile was brief. The eldest brother, Edward, Earl of March, was 18 and took up York's claim to the throne. A fortnight before the queen's victory at St Albans, Edward's troops had defeated a Lancastrian army at the Battle of Mortimer's Cross (2 February 1461). Marching to London, Edward was proclaimed king on 4 March. On Palm Sunday, 29 March, Edward achieved a decisive victory over the Lancastrians in a snowstorm at the Battle of Towton, the bloodiest pitched battle ever fought on British soil. The queen and her son fled abroad, while Henry VI was not captured until 1465, but the Yorkist cause was triumphant. George and Richard were back in England in time for their brother's coronation as King Edward IV on 28 June. Before that ceremony, the two were knighted and George, now heir to the throne, was created Duke of Clarence.

Richard, second in line, was created Duke of Gloucester in November 1461. As the king was only 19, it could reasonably be expected that he would have a son who would succeed as an adult, thus displacing Richard in the succession. In any case, Richard was still only a child, so did not have much of a role in the early years of his brother's reign, beyond being created Admiral of England in October 1462. His known movements are sketchy, although by 1465 he was placed in the household of the greatest lord in England. Richard Neville, Earl of Warwick, is popularly known as Warwick the Kingmaker for his crucial role in the period 1455–71, and at this point had been a mainstay of the Yorkist cause for a decade. However, the king's foolishness was to change that, with momentous consequences for all three brothers.

Edward IV was a womaniser with a later reputation for enjoying sensual pleasures. Yet when he married, he did so impetuously and secretly. In the mid-1460s, Warwick was negotiating Edward's marriage with the French. Then, in the autumn of 1465, it emerged that the king had already married in May 1464. His bride was Elizabeth Woodville, widow of the Lancastrian John Grey, Lord Ferrers. Whatever the lustful monarch's motivations, it was a baffling move which caused no end of problems. It embarrassed Warwick, but it also alarmed him and many others in the aristocracy. In addition to two sons from her first marriage, Elizabeth also had twelve siblings. Providing for the queen's large family would absorb most of the available royal patronage. Warwick, who had two daughters, was not impressed, especially when Edward refused to allow his brother Clarence to marry the elder daughter, Isabel.

In late 1468, when he turned 16, Richard left Warwick's household. In October of that year, he was granted forfeited lands in Somerset and Wiltshire, while in May 1469 he was given the duchy of Lancaster estates of Clitheroe and Halton. The king needed to provide for his youngest brother and perhaps secure his loyalty, given that the other brother was causing trouble. Warwick and Clarence had united against the king. In July 1469, Clarence married Warwick's daughter Isabel in Calais. Earl and duke issued a manifesto against Edward and invaded. A royal army was defeated at the Battle of Edgecote (24 July). Alongside several others, the queen's father and one of her brothers were executed without trial. Although not at the battle, the king was captured at Olney in Buckinghamshire and imprisoned in Warwick's castles at Warwick and then Middleham (Yorkshire). However, Warwick, Clarence and the Archbishop of York (George Neville, Warwick's brother) proved unequal to the task of governance or halting a breakdown in public order, so by October Edward was back in control in London.

Richard benefited from all this. He became Constable of England and Warden of the West March on the Scottish border. Moreover, he was set to work restoring order, emerging as a key figure in his brother's regime, although his effectiveness in the critical year of 1470 was blunted when he became distracted by inheritance disputes in the North. Nevertheless, Edward was short of commanders. Warwick and Clarence had defected to the Lancastrians and fled to France. Supporting Henry VI's restoration, Warwick had his younger daughter Anne married to Henry's son Edward. In the autumn of 1470 Warwick and Clarence invaded England, forcing Edward and Richard to flee to the Low Countries. Henry VI was restored to begin a brief second reign ('the Readeption'), which was an abject failure given that he was basically a puppet of others and was in no state to rule, mentally or physically.

Aided by the Burgundians, Edward invaded to reclaim his throne. Clarence changed sides again to rejoin his brothers. At the Battle of Barnet (14 April 1471), Edward and Richard were victorious. Warwick was killed. Final victory came with the Battle of Tewkesbury (4 May), at which an army led by Queen Margaret was crushed and her son Edward slain. Leading figures captured during the battle or removed from sanctuary in Tewkesbury Abbey were tried by Richard (as Constable) and the Duke of Norfolk (as Earl Marshal), then executed. The Yorkists were taking no chances and Richard showed no compunction about ruthless action against those who had acted against his brother. Soon afterwards, Henry VI died in the Tower of London, almost certainly murdered on Edward's orders. Restored, Edward IV could begin his second reign in the knowledge that all viable threats to the throne had been extinguished.

As the accusations have been so important in shaping Richard's reputation, it is necessary to dwell briefly on the allegations that he was responsible for the deaths of both Henry VI and his son, Prince Edward. These stories grew in the telling in Tudor times, to the extent that some versions have Richard killing Henry with his own hands. It is part of a narrative which seeks to show how Richard ruthlessly cleared his way to the throne, the murderer of 1483 prefigured in the murderer of 1471. It does not withstand scrutiny. The queue between Richard and the throne was growing ever longer, Edward IV having had children, so by 1471 he can have had little realistic hope of succeeding. Contemporary evidence suggests that Prince Edward was killed on the battlefield at Tewkesbury; even if it was after the fighting, he was in arms against the Yorkists and cannot have expected mercy in defeat. Henry VI was almost certainly murdered, but it was the king who gave that order (explicitly or otherwise), and it is very unlikely that a royal duke carried it out. Richard was not squeamish and supported his brother's judgements, but it is ridiculous to attribute every murder or shady death between 1471 and 1485 to him. 1471 was not, as the most hostile commentators seem to believe, a warm-up act for 1483. Ultimate responsibility in 1471 lay with Edward IV.

Richard, the loyal brother, was duly rewarded for his support. His loyalty had been as much necessity as choice, his fortunes inextricably tied to Edward's, but it still contrasted with Clarence's betrayal and opportunistic side-switching. Richard received a large swathe of Warwick's former lands in the North and northern Midlands. Clarence opposed Richard's marriage to Anne, Warwick's daughter and widow of Henry VI's son, but the king forced him to yield and the marriage took place in 1472. Next Clarence had to be compelled to share the Warwick inheritance with his younger brother, Edward forcing his acquiescence. With some exceptions, Richard acquired the northern part of the inheritance and Clarence the southern. Technically, both the king's brothers benefited from Warwick's fall and the defeat of the Lancastrian cause. In practice, Clarence was tainted by his past disloyalty and it was Richard who was more favoured. True, Edward had a habit of capriciously revoking royal grants and reassigning them, which when it affected him must have caused Richard as much resentment as it did Clarence. Richard, however, was much more adept at hiding any disappointment and complying with the king's wishes. He himself could be ruthless in securing his rights at the expense of others.

Now an adult, Richard was at something of a physical disadvantage compared with his oldest brother. Edward IV was tall, handsome and charming, although somewhat corpulent in later years as his indulgent lifestyle took its toll. Richard was of only average height and slender build. If the bones discovered at Leicester are his, he had a curvature of the spine which would have affected his appearance. It is far from the stooping hunchback of Shakespearean legend, but would have been noticeable. We can readily dismiss some of the more ludicrous slurs of Tudor times, which include an impossible two-year pregnancy for Duchess Cecily and Richard being born with a mouthful of teeth. Nevertheless, in appearance he differed considerably from his commanding, majestic brother.

Throughout his brother's second reign, Richard was Admiral and Constable of England, both significant offices with considerable powers. He was also Warden of the West March, although during the 1470s not an entirely helpful one; his more bellicose attitude towards Scotland contrasted with the king's desire for peace on this front to allow him to concentrate on a French war. While Richard's estates were not exclusively northern, the majority were and it was in the North that Richard became especially dominant, a power base where he built up a loyal following as he expanded his lands and influence through careful deals. By the end of the reign, he was easily the leading noble in northern England. This pre-eminence brought the potential for conflict with the Stanley family in Lancashire and the Percy family in Northumberland, which required the king to broker agreements recognising his brother's primacy while ensuring he respected the sensitivities of these key nobles. Nevertheless, Edward recognised the value of Richard's role in the North. It brought peace and stability in a turbulent region, without the king needing to expend much personal effort on the area. In return, Edward had to accept that Richard was an ambitious nobleman who sometimes exceeded or reinterpreted his brief.

As Richard, Duke of Gloucester, rose ever higher during the 1470s, so George, Duke of Clarence, fell ever lower. Both brothers had been displaced in the succession by the birth of two sons to Edward IV: Edward, Prince of Wales, in 1470 and Richard, Duke of York, in 1473 (a third son, George, Duke of Bedford, was born in 1477 but lived only two years). The stain of disloyalty never left Clarence and by the start of 1478, he found himself facing trial in parliament for treason. Even if Clarence had behaved foolishly and impetuously, few contemporaries seemed to think the charges justified and there was widespread criticism of what became a show trial. Found guilty, Clarence was executed in the Tower of London on 20 February; whether this was by drowning in a barrel of malmsey wine, as the famous story has it, is not provable one way or the other. Whatever Shakespeare later claimed, Clarence's downfall was not part of some evil plan on Richard's part and the blame lies squarely with the king. The queen's family had been the main targets of Clarence (and Warwick), and it seems much more plausible that their machinations lay behind the duke's demise. Of course, Richard supported Edward in his destruction of Clarence and exacted a price for doing so, benefiting considerably from his brother's downfall. However, that does not mean that it was part of some Machiavellian plot to get the throne: the king was only thirty-five and had two sons, so removing Clarence would hardly have helped Richard in a quest to be king. His incentive was the increased lands, offices and status which would naturally come his way and augment his position as the leading nobleman in the realm. Ultimate culpability for Clarence's demise lay with Edward, not Richard, who merely supported the king in a calculated move to improve his own position, and as a careful modern study has made clear, it 'deserves to remain a blot on Edward's reputation'.[1]

After Clarence fell, Richard's position was an impressive one. From the mid-1470s, he based himself primarily in the North. The Yorkshire castle of Middleham is especially associated with him, but during the 1470s he acquired a succession of other lordships and castles in that county, among them Richmond, Scarborough, Sheriff Hutton and Skipton-in-Craven. He also held Barnard Castle in County Durham and Penrith in Cumberland, developed a close relationship with the major city in the North, York, and became sheriff of Cumberland for life. In addition to building a landed base, Richard devoted considerable effort and resources to creating an affinity, investing in a large circle of northern retainers. The white boar badge was his symbol, marking out his followers, and this retinue was to be important during his time as king.

From 1480, Richard's position in the North and his military reputation were significantly enhanced when he was appointed the king's lieutenant in the North, responsible for putting into action Edward's move from peace to a bellicose policy towards Scotland. Now at peace with the French, Edward IV instead picked a quarrel with James III of Scotland (1460–88). The nominal point of contention was James' failure to hand over his son, the future James IV, to marry Edward's daughter Cecily. The English king had already paid the dowry, but as Prince James only turned 7 in March 1480, demanding the marriage take place then was somewhat premature and something of a smokescreen. Richard was the obvious person to place in charge. In 1480 only border skirmishing took place, as in both 1481 and 1482 the intention was that the king would lead the campaign in person. Although preparations were made on that basis, on neither occasion did Edward deign to appear, leaving everything in the hands of his younger brother, supported by the Earl of Northumberland. The 1481 effort was fairly inconsequential, that of 1482 more significant.

At Fotheringhay in June 1482, Edward and Richard reached an agreement with Alexander, Duke of Albany and estranged brother of James III. The intention was to install Albany as an English puppet on the Scottish throne. Edward used this agreement as an excuse to once more avoid going north in person, leaving Richard and Albany to head to York and then launch the campaign in July. The town of Berwick-upon-Tweed (which had been handed to Scotland in 1461 by Henry VI's queen, Margaret of Anjou, in return for Scottish support) surrendered at once to avoid being sacked, but the castle held out in Scottish hands. Richard's and Northumberland's armies won various engagements, but were unable to tempt a Scottish force into any engagement. At the end of the month, Richard found himself in Edinburgh, occupying the town, but he had no one with whom to negotiate. The Scottish nobility had staged a coup days earlier and imprisoned their king in Edinburgh's impregnable castle. Richard was forced to have his demands announced publicly to a ghost town before retreating to Berwick. Over the coming months, terms were agreed with the Scots, which included the surrender of Berwick Castle. After centuries of switching between Scottish and English crowns, this 1482 transfer of the border town into England was to prove permanent.

Otherwise, the 1482 campaign was expensive and achieved little. The king, however, chose to portray it as a huge success. Richard was feted for his achievements, and in the parliament of January–February 1483 received unprecedented grants in Cumberland and the disputed border territories, hailed as a military hero and rewarded accordingly. With his position and reputation riding high, he had the potential to become a very powerful figure in northern England, a region in which his brother showed little personal interest. Fate, however, was to turn the duke's attention away from the North and set him on another path.

Edward IV died unexpectedly on 9 April 1483, just short of his 41st birthday. His oldest son, now Edward V, was only 12, which raised the tricky question of a minority government or regency. There was no established precedent for this, with the previous occasions on which a child became king (1216, 1377 and 1422) all handled differently. The new king had grown up among his maternal family, but the Woodvilles were not popular and there were fears in some quarters about the influence they might exercise over Edward V. The various factions of the nobility had been united by their loyalty to Edward IV, but with him dead and a child on the throne, the minority promised to be a challenging period. At Westminster, as Edward IV was sent off to be buried at Windsor, the widowed queen and her faction took control and opted for a hasty coronation. With the date set for 4 May, nothing else was agreed as the realm's major figures headed towards London. Anthony, Earl Rivers (Queen Elizabeth's brother) was accompanying Edward V from Ludlow, where the Prince of Wales' household was based. Gloucester was on his way from Yorkshire. In London, meanwhile, William, Lord Hastings, Edward IV's household chamberlain, had earlier clashed with the Woodvilles and thus opposed them having a lead role in any minority. He was apparently pressing for a regency under Gloucester. The rest of the council, under the queen mother's influence, preferred rule by a council without a designated regent.

Events were about to spiral out of the council's control. On 29 April, Gloucester arrived at Northampton to meet Henry Stafford, Duke of Buckingham. The king was some fifteen miles to the south in Stony Stratford. The size of his entourage had already been considerably reduced following a successful intervention in council by Hastings. Rivers and some of his companions rode to dine with Gloucester and Buckingham that evening. Relations between Gloucester and the dowager queen's family appear to have been amicable up to this point. Yet the following day would see Gloucester strike against the Woodvilles, the beginning of the dramatic few months on which his entire reputation hinges.

Early on the morning of 30 April, Rivers and the others staying with Gloucester and Buckingham at Northampton were woken and arrested. The two dukes headed for Stony Stratford, where they arrested more of Edward's companions and took the king into their protection. Letters were sent ordering the postponement of the coronation. The prisoners were dispatched to safe confinement in the North. On the scheduled coronation date, 4 May, Gloucester and Buckingham entered London with the king, Gloucester presenting himself very visibly as Edward's defender. Four days later, he formally assumed the office of Lord Protector.

What caused Gloucester to act in this way? His own position, for public consumption at least, was that he had responded to a Woodville conspiracy aimed against himself, the king and the kingdom. When he entered London, he displayed four carts full of weapons claimed to have been seized from those involved in this conspiracy. He also sought the execution of Rivers and others for treason, based on their role in this alleged conspiracy, although the council demurred. In Gloucester's official line, this was a pre-emptive strike. Others saw an ambitious man staging a coup and taking advantage of the circumstances. At issue is whether there was genuinely a conspiracy, or if not whether Gloucester sincerely believed there was. Was Gloucester then a saviour of the realm or a calculating cynic enacting a ruthless scheme to seize power? It can be argued in numerous ways, typically dependent more upon the arguer's general attitude to Richard of Gloucester than the evidence. When Richard settled on the crown is hotly contested. More than five centuries and endless repeats of this debate later, there is no way to determine the answer with any certainty with the evidence we have. For all his protestations of loyalty to Edward V, the way events unfolded naturally arouse suspicion that Richard was acting his part superbly to win the crown.

At the time, some (like Buckingham and Hastings) were very favourable to Richard becoming Protector, a large majority were probably cautiously ambiguous, and some (including, obviously, the Woodvilles) were adamantly opposed. While the king was sent to take up residence in the Tower, ostensibly for his safety, Queen Elizabeth claimed sanctuary in Westminster Abbey with her daughters and her younger son, Duke Richard of York. Throughout May and early June, Gloucester remained publicly loyal to the king and officially acted in his name. His use of propaganda was especially skilful and would later be honed even further, Richard being 'the first English king to use character assassination as a deliberate instrument of policy'.[2] He would make particular use of charges of sexual immorality and debauchery against his brother and others. Richard was on shaky ground; as the father of two acknowledged bastards, he was hardly a monk.

The Protector took steps to destroy the Woodvilles, seeking to round up those still at large. None of the family had been tried, never mind convicted, but their lands and offices were treated as though they were already condemned. Buckingham benefited greatly from the subsequent redistribution of patronage. Naturally enough, the Woodvilles, especially those still at liberty, were almost certainly seeking to destroy Gloucester. Whether any threat they posed was credible is another question. We can only speculate as to whether Gloucester actually believed that it was, but on 10 June, he wrote to York, England's second city and a reliable stronghold for him in his northern heartland, to request their aid against the queen mother's family, claiming they were plotting to murder him and Buckingham. The following day, letters were sent to the Earl of Northumberland and the heir of the Earl of Westmorland, requesting troops urgently. Whatever his motivations and ultimate intentions, Gloucester was now preparing for a showdown with the Woodvilles. Again, we cannot know for certain whether he had by now decided to make a bid for the throne as part of destroying the family, or whether the throne had even been his aim all along. All that is definite is that on 13 June, the situation escalated dramatically.

On that Friday, at Gloucester's instigation, a small subgroup of the royal council met at the Tower of London. We know only three things for certain, which are agreed by the conflicting accounts which survive.

Gloucester declared that there was a conspiracy against him; at least three councillors – Thomas Rotherham (the Archbishop of York and Edward IV's final chancellor), John Morton (the Bishop of Ely) and Oliver King (Edward IV's secretary) – were arrested; and the meeting ended with the death of Lord Hastings, subjected to immediate execution without trial. Gloucester's mistrust of the arrested trio is explicable, if not necessarily justifiable. Yet the instantaneous demise of Hastings, one of Gloucester's most vocal advocates a mere six weeks earlier, is mystifying. Ever since, the Protector's motives have been hotly debated, although there are only two really plausible scenarios. One is that Hastings knew or believed that Gloucester's sights were now set on the throne and bluntly told him that he would not acquiesce in usurpation. The other is that Gloucester was aware that Hastings would oppose his bid for the crown and struck pre-emptively. In either case, this was extrajudicial murder and caused outrage and consternation. The coordinated attack on potential opponents at this meeting strongly suggests that by now at the very latest, Gloucester was planning to become king.

This is obvious with hindsight, but Edward V's coronation was still planned for 22 June, just nine days away. Over the weekend, Richard persuaded the rest of the council, presumably shaken by events at the Tower, that this ceremony would require the presence of the Duke of York. On Monday, the 16th, Thomas Bourchier (the Archbishop of Canterbury) led a delegation to the queen mother in Westminster Abbey. He persuaded her (aided by troops stationed round the building and the House of York's reputation for not respecting sanctuary) to hand over young Richard, who was sent to join his brother in the Tower. The coronation was now postponed until 9 November, while a parliament summoned for 25 June was also cancelled. Most ominously, the traditional dating of letters using the king's regnal year was replaced by the calendar year (1483 instead of 1 Edward V). There was considerable anxiety in London, which would have been heightened had there been knowledge of what was happening in the North. In response to Gloucester's letters, troops were being raised in Yorkshire. Before this army headed south, steps were taken to neutralise whatever threat the captive Woodvilles and their allies might pose. Rivers and others were executed without trial on 25 June at Pontefract Castle. The assembled force headed to join Gloucester, although by the time they set out he had a new title.

Back in London, government had stopped, with letters no longer being issued under the great seal. Buckingham became the principal beneficiary from Hastings' fall. In return, he was allied even more closely to Gloucester, who now took to riding regally through the streets. Finally, on Sunday, 22 June (the intended date of the now postponed coronation), Gloucester declared his hand. A large audience was gathered at St Paul's Cross to hear the preacher proclaim Gloucester's title to the throne, but the approach was misjudged. Sources suggest that on this, the first occasion the duke openly claimed the crown, it was declared that Edward IV was illegitimate and that his children were thus debarred from the succession. This went down badly and Gloucester had to move quickly to shift his ground and limit the damage.

Buckingham began canvassing support for Gloucester's claim and on 26 June, the intrigue ended as the duke was formally petitioned to take the throne. The composition of the group who did the petitioning is not clear, although it is highly likely that it was stage managed from behind the scenes rather than being spontaneous. The basis for Gloucester's title was officially set down for the record in the parliament of January 1484. Abandoning the allegation of Edward IV's illegitimacy, which had proved an unpopular approach and could hardly have pleased Gloucester's mother (who would outlive all her sons), Edward's own conduct became the basis for removing Edward V. In essence, the story was that before his clandestine marriage to Elizabeth Woodville (itself questionable because of its secret nature), Edward IV had been pre-contracted to another widow, Eleanor Butler. This made his marriage to Elizabeth bigamous, hence their children were illegitimate and could not inherit the throne. Richard of Gloucester was thus his brother's legal heir. The evidence suggests that this version was not widely believed, but however reluctantly, people acquiesced in the ending of Edward V's short reign. Receiving the petition in London, Gloucester was taken to Westminster Hall for a ceremony which inaugurated his reign as King Richard III. Again, it is a matter of debate and speculation whether this had been Richard's plan ever since Stony Stratford, or whether he had decided to displace his nephew more recently. It was a dubious claim to the throne at best and he must have known that the road ahead would not be straightforward.

The coronation took place ten days later, on 6 July, attended by a majority of the nobility. After the interlude of Edward V, Richard III's initial household and administration showed considerable continuity from Edward IV's. Richard began a royal progress through his realm, heading west as far as Gloucester and Worcester before swinging north towards York. Yet although he had left London behind, he could not so easily escape the thorny problem of his nephews who remained there. Edward and Richard were still living (or, more accurately, imprisoned) in the Tower of London and were a serious threat to King Richard. Many, perhaps most, saw Edward V as the rightful king and Richard III as a usurper. The boys were always going to be a focus for opposition to Richard. Risings and efforts to free them while the king was on his tour of the realm convinced him that he could never be secure while they had this potential to be a rallying point for his enemies.

What happened to the two Princes is one of the most contentious questions in English history; practically any sentence written about this matter will attract someone's ire. Over the years, Richard has been roundly condemned as their murderer by his opponents while all manner of ingenious (if mostly implausible) alternative culprits have been put forward by his apologists. We have one basic fact: the boys were never seen again after the autumn of 1483. Theories about what happened to them and who was responsible could fill an entire library. Yet quite simply, by far the most likely scenario is that they were killed on Richard's orders. While in a court of law the verdict might be the Scottish one of 'not proven', the balance of probabilities in the court of history tells strongly against Richard. The princes were too great a threat to Richard to be allowed to live. That they disappeared strongly suggests that they were no longer alive, as there was little benefit to Richard in keeping them alive but hidden; the pretenders who emerged in Henry VII's reign can easily be dismissed as imposters. No one would have presumed to kill them without Richard's knowledge, nor indeed without his orders, be they implicit or explicit. It was Richard who was threatened by their continued existence, who benefited by their removal, and who was in a position to order their murders. There was, it is true, no formal announcement of death or display of the bodies, but as one historian has put it, 'the funeral of two children would have been, in modern terms, a public relations disaster'.[3] If murdering a deposed king was no novelty, the killing of two innocent children was of a very different order to killing compromised adults like Edward II and Richard II. The moral outrage it would have generated necessitated it being done in secret and the bodies disposed of covertly. In the end, of course, the murders removed the immediate threat but created a different one. A king with a dubious claim to the throne who had had his nephews killed was going to have problems with enemies who could rally support on moral grounds.

From 29 August until 20 September, Richard was in York. It was an expensive visit full of lavish ceremony, the king in the supportive capital of the North. During the stay, Richard's young son Edward was invested as Prince of Wales in York Minster. However, the enjoyment of the stay quickly vanished as Richard headed south again. He knew the South was restless and for more than a fortnight he stayed at Pontefract, within reach of his loyal northern retainers should matters turn ugly further south. Eventually, he continued his journey to Gainsborough and then Lincoln. It was at Lincoln on 10 October that king ordered action against the serious revolt he was now facing, summoning his forces to meet at Leicester.

Buckingham's Rebellion, as it has come to be known, is a confusing and sometimes murky affair.[4] It was not one coherent rising spearheaded by the Duke of Buckingham, rather a series of interlocking local disturbances in which he was later identified as the leading rebel, even though it was underway before he defected. Focusing on Wales and the South-West, he had nothing to do with the rebellions in the South and South-East and struggled to raise troops. Why Buckingham turned against Richard has long baffled commentators. Since they had joined forces at the end of April, the duke had been Richard's most important and steadfast ally. As reward, he had received lands and offices in considerable quantity, allowing him to develop a particularly impressive base in Wales and the West Country. For him to defect made little sense, for there is no chance he would have done as well for himself under any other regime, let alone any better. The argument that he was overcome by remorse, at either his own or Richard's actions, lacks conviction. More believable, if still doubtful, is that he wanted the crown himself; descended from Edward III through the female line, he may have seen Richard's troubles as his opportunity. As ever in this reign, we are left trying to discern motives from hearsay and rumour, but there is no doubt that his moving into armed opposition was a serious blow to Richard.

The rebellion had the potential to be extremely serious, even fatal, for Richard. A large number of Edward IV's household and loyalists in the South had not reconciled themselves to the usurpation. A major cause of the rebellion was rumours about the fate of the Princes. Most of southern England rebelled, although the range of motivations, a lack of coordination and simple bad luck (Buckingham was in part undone by the flooding of the River Severn trapping him) led to ultimate failure. Buckingham was captured and executed at Salisbury on 2 November. Henry Tudor, up to this point a relatively obscure, marginal figure, was given support by Brittany to launch an invasion, but his landing at Plymouth in early November came too late, after defeat was assured. Richard had survived, but the extent of opposition to his kingship had been laid bare.

There were executions, but Richard avoided a bloodbath. Some who submitted were pardoned, albeit not without cost, while others were deprived of estates and titles. When parliament met in January 1484, unreconciled rebels, many of whom had fled abroad, were subjected to acts of attainder (whereby they were judged guilty and their lands confiscated). Richard's title to the throne was set down for the official record. He began to work on consolidating his position and by March, he had reached an agreement with the Dowager Queen Elizabeth which saw her and her daughters emerge from sanctuary. At this point, he appeared to have achieved a degree of security, yet less than eighteen months later he would lose everything at Bosworth.

In hindsight, it can be very easy to let this dominate our entire view of the reign, but defeat at Bosworth was not inevitable and Richard was an active king who took his responsibilities seriously. Some modern advocates have taken this too far and present him as a great reformer and governor; the reality is that his reign was too brief to achieve much. That said, he came to the throne with a far greater level of experience than anyone since Henry IV, who, like Richard, had spent years as a major lord before seizing the crown. Richard was also far more familiar with his realm, especially the North, than any other fifteenth-century king. Henry VI and Edward IV had spent most of their time in London and the Thames Valley, whereas Richard was much more itinerant, making particular use of the centrally-located castles at Nottingham and Pontefract and travelling widely. He was understandably reluctant to allow anyone to replace him as the greatest noble in the North. Prince Edward was nominally given the lead northern role, then after his death there was a blurred mix of responsibilities between the Earls of Lincoln and Northumberland, the genesis of the council of the North which developed more fully under the Tudors. Yet Richard still intended to take the lead role himself, drawing on his extensive military experience. His hostility to Scotland led to a renewal of the Auld Alliance between Scotland and France. An unsatisfactory and fragile truce was agreed between Richard and James III in the autumn of 1484, only after Richard had decided against another full-scale military campaign.

Throughout 1483 and 1484, the windfall from confiscations combined with the income from his own landed interests gave Richard some financial security. From the start, he proclaimed he would not seek to burden his subjects; he politely refused gifts on his post-coronation tour and declined to seek a tax from parliament (which it would almost certainly have granted) in 1484. Later in the reign, finances became much tighter and he had to resort to forced loans. Throughout, Richard dispensed patronage liberally, too liberally in the eyes of some later chroniclers. As was expected of a medieval king, a substantial amount of this patronage went to the Church and religious foundations. Notably, he founded a chantry at York Minster to be staffed by a college of a hundred priests, part of the special favour he showed towards York's recently completed cathedral. (This has led to speculation that, with Westminster Abbey and St George's Chapel in Windsor both short of space, Richard intended York Minster to be his mausoleum.) Yet he patronised and founded colleges and religious livings across the country, on a particularly large scale even for a late medieval king, and had Henry VI's remains moved from Chertsey to Windsor. There is plentiful evidence that Richard was conventionally pious, attentive to his devotions and obligations, as shown both by his patronage and by his surviving religious books.

For all the competent exercise of his kingship, Richard's fundamental weakness was dynastic. His young son Edward died in April 1484, with Queen Anne following him to the grave in March 1485. The question of Richard's heir became urgent, but it was an immensely problematic question for the king. The young Earl of Warwick, another Edward, Clarence's son, was the obvious candidate. Unfortunately, removing the legal machinations which had stripped him of his inheritance gave the boy a better claim to the throne than Richard, since Warwick was the son of the king's older brother and thus higher in the line of succession. So while hoping to father another son, the king's preference probably fell for now on his nephew John, Earl of Lincoln, adult son of Richard's older sister Elizabeth, Duchess of Suffolk. Yet the future of the Yorkist dynasty hung by a very slender thread, largely because Richard had removed almost all the viable contenders for the throne in securing his own crown.

In the absence of anyone else, a previously marginal figure suddenly became a realistic contender. Henry Tudor, who styled himself Earl of Richmond, had the flimsiest of claims to the throne which requires especially close reading of the bewilderingly complex royal family tree. Nevertheless, he had backing from Brittany and France, who had their own reasons to want to destabilise England. As his aborted invasion had shown in November 1483, he was becoming a figurehead for Richard's opponents. The king could not rest secure with Tudor across the Channel, accompanied by many fellow exiled rebels. Richard's northern retinue became more important than ever. Historians have perhaps been too quick to accept the anti-northern prejudices of southern chronicles, but the rebellion in the South had been so widespread that Richard had no choice but to bring northerners in to fill many of the vacated offices there. He could not trust his brother's Yorkist following, which left him little room to manoeuvre. For the rest of his short reign, he always had to act under the shadow of the threat from over the Channel, knowing his domestic support was far from reliable. Northerners were looked on with great suspicion in the South, which made Richard's reliance on his retinue problematic.

Henry had designs on marrying Elizabeth of York, Edward IV's daughter. This would neatly unite the claims of Lancaster and York, posing a considerable threat to Richard while boosting Henry's legitimacy. The old Yorkists in exile with him would be able to overlook the extreme weakness of his claim by descent, if he was thus tied to Edward IV's family. For that reason, Richard (in desperate need of children) seems to have given serious consideration to the controversial idea of marrying Elizabeth himself after Anne's death. Rumours that he had poisoned Anne circulated and had to be denied; they were baseless, but their existence suggests Richard was in trouble.

Richard had spent most of his reign at risk, but the danger was now becoming more acute. The man who had used propaganda so well in his bid for the throne was now losing the propaganda war with Henry Tudor. Richard's enemies made particular capital out of the demise of his nephews. If Henry did not inspire a popular uprising to join him when he did finally invade, his support coming from exiled rebels with foreign backing, his propaganda did probably prevent many turning out to support Richard: absenteeism would prove fatal for the king. That he could not be sure of his subjects led him to place considerable effort into preventing or repelling any invasion by Henry and his supporters, but it was expensive and impractical for the king to keep his forces together for long periods.

Henry finally landed at Milford Haven on 7 August 1485 and made his way across Wales to Shrewsbury. He picked up some additional supporters, although there was no sudden rush of popular support flocking to his cause. Richard's army mustered at Leicester. Battle was joined near Market Bosworth in Leicestershire on 22 August. So famous is this battle, so steeped in legend, that it is disconcerting to realise that it is among the worst-recorded in English history, with no contemporary eyewitness accounts. For many centuries, even the location was incorrectly identified. What is clear is that Richard gambled everything and fought bravely, but his tactics seem to have been flawed. The defection of Lord Stanley to Henry proved decisive. Richard was killed, Henry Tudor taking his crown as King Henry VII. It was not quite the end, for the new king would face challenges and pretenders in the years ahead, but for all practical purposes the Wars of the Roses were over.

Richard's naked body was slung across a horse and taken to Leicester. There, it was put on public display to prove that he was dead. Afterwards, without ceremony or even a coffin, it was interred in the Franciscan Church (Greyfriars). A few years later, Henry felt secure enough to have a memorial erected in the Church, but in 1538, at the dissolution of the monasteries,

Leicester Greyfriars was demolished. While one local legend held that Richard III had been dug up and thrown into the River Soar, most believed his body continued to lie in his forgotten grave. By the twenty-first century, this place lay beneath the urban sprawl of modern Leicester. Philippa Langley, chair of the Scottish branch of the Richard III Society, conceived the idea of searching for the king's remains. In 2011, she persuaded Leicester City Council and the University of Leicester to back the project, and with the funding shortfall made up by eager society members, an archaeological dig began in a car park in August 2012. It seemed a hopelessly quixotic venture. Yet less than a fortnight into the dig, a male skeleton with curvature of the spine and battle wounds was excavated. The University of Leicester soon went public and announced that they had possibly found Richard III. After months of scientific tests and DNA comparisons with modern descendants, it was finally declared on 4 February 2013 that 'beyond reasonable doubt, the individual exhumed at the Greyfriars in September 2012 is indeed Richard III, the last Plantagenet king of England'.[5] While acceptance of the identification was not universal, dissenters were in a small minority.[6] The story was considered so compelling that in 2022 it was even made into a controversial film, *The Lost King*.

An unseemly squabble erupted over where his body would be laid to rest. While several places attracted support in online petitions, the tussle quickly became one between supporters of Leicester Cathedral and York Minster. In the end, a judicial review launched by distant relatives of Richard III was dismissed by the judge and his remains went to Leicester. More arguments then erupted over the form Richard's tomb was to take before he became the only medieval king to have his burial screened live on national television. Tens of thousands turned up to Leicester for a week of ceremonies which cost some £3 million, a testimony to the extraordinary interest Richard III continued to generate more than 500 years after his death.

Richard through the Centuries

The literature on Richard III is so vast that an effort to read it all would probably lead to madness. Such is the division he causes that almost every word in the records has been picked over countless times, interpreted and reinterpreted to make every possible nuance serve as justification for a particular view of the king. Part of the problem is that writers on both sides of the debate are prone to using the sources partially, defending the passages which suit their purpose and dismissing problematic sections as propaganda.

Since the moment he usurped the throne in 1483, there has been no shortage of people wanting to express their opinion about Richard III.[7]

The only major source from before Bosworth is an account written by the Italian Dominic Mancini at the end of 1483.[8] Mancini had been in London during the events from Edward IV's death to Richard III's coronation and wrote up his version when he returned to the Continent. Although he is frustratingly vague when it comes to dates and wrong when he does use them (he misdates Edward IV's death), and was probably hampered by his lack of English, Mancini's account is valuable because he was on the scene and had no vested interest in English politics. He preserves the dramatic nature of that summer and records the rumours and opinions which reached him. The other main contemporary source is the 'second continuation' of the Crowland Chronicle. The textual history is complicated, but the account was written or completed in 1486 and ended up in the chronicles of Crowland Abbey in Lincolnshire. Whoever the author was, he had a distinct southern bias, as evidenced in his comments about Richard's granting of confiscated lands after Buckingham's rebellion, where he notes that the king redistributed these 'among his northerners whom he had planted in every part of his dominions, to the shame of the southern people who murmured ceaselessly and longed more each day for the return of their old lords in place of the tyranny of the present ones'. (This points to a wider problem with our sources, which are all southern.) Nevertheless, the continuator could be fair to Richard, as when he noted that the king 'never acted sleepily but incisively and with the utmost vigilance'.[9] If Richard is treated less kindly than Edward IV, this account is sober, well-informed and generally avoids explicit commentary on Richard's character. Even so, it is hard to find much sympathy for his actions during the usurpation. As the only contemporary narrative source for the whole reign, this chronicle is of considerable importance. Taken together, Mancini and Crowland provide 'strong *contemporary* evidence that Richard was disliked and mistrusted in his own time'.[10]

This is especially significant when we come to the question of later sources. Whatever Richard's advocates might wish, we cannot reject the early Tudor accounts in their entirety. They must be used with extreme caution, but they are not complete fabrications, even if the main sources did largely demonise Richard in order to emphasise Henry VII's qualities and the moral validity of his claim to the throne. In the earliest years, this was not official propaganda, but a desire to court favour on the part of individual writers. The classic example is John Rous, a Warwickshire antiquary who, during Richard's reign, wrote of the king as a 'mighty prince' and 'good lord' whose just rule earned 'the great thanks and love of all his subjects great and poor'.[11] After Bosworth, demonstrating extensive moral flexibility, Rous wrote a damning account, in which 'King Richard, who was excessively cruel in his days, reigned for three years [*sic*] and a little more, in the way that Antichrist is to reign.'[12] Here are all the most scurrilous parts of the myth later deployed to full effect: the unnatural birth with hair and teeth, the murder of Henry VI, the poisoning of Queen Anne. That Rous could write such diametrically opposed accounts within a few years of each other, to appeal to the king of the day, says all that is necessary about his reliability.

Much more devastating for Richard's reputation were the major works of the sixteenth century. It is almost obligatory to talk of 'Tudor bias', but it is worth reiterating that this was not an official, state-sponsored version of history. It is instructive to compare the way in which Richard's parliament of 1484 and Henry's first parliament in 1485 justified the titles of men who had come to the throne by dubious means and with dubious claims. Richard's version spins a sordid tale of illegitimacy, adultery, false marriages and even witchcraft to decry Edward IV and refute the right of his sons to reign. Henry is much more restrained, settling for references to 'Richard III, late in deed and not by right king of England' without much in the way of character assassination.[13] Henry VII himself expended little energy on demonising his vanquished predecessor, partly because there was little need. Those who wrote critical accounts of Richard were not his official spokesmen. That is not to say it would have been possible, never mind a good idea, for a Tudor writer to pen positive things about Richard III. Yet Henry VII was not standing over these authors like some inflexible teacher, dictating to them or demanding they say certain things in order to pass their exam, which is the impression sometimes given in discussions of 'Tudor bias'.

The two most influential Tudor authors in retrospect were an Italian, Polydore Vergil, and the future Lord Chancellor, Thomas More. Vergil was an internationally renowned humanist whose history of England was finished in 1513 but not published until 1534. His account of Richard's reign is the longest and fullest we have. There is plenty of embellishment and even outright invention, but he draws upon genuine research (Vergil seems to have had access to the Crowland Chronicle as well as London material) and is far from a hatchet job. Much more problematic is Thomas More's work, which comes in several versions and only extends to the autumn of 1483. It is unfortunate, as one modern commentator has observed, that this 'least authentic of the early accounts of Richard' has had 'the greatest influence on subsequent opinion, whether positive on the orthodox, or negatively on those who require dogma to disbelieve'.[14] More's Richard is a monster, a malevolent hunchback constantly plotting. Alone of these early sources, More has a lengthy, graphic account of the demise of the Princes in the Tower, which is almost certainly fiction but has had undue influence in subsequent centuries. Precisely because he was a gifted writer, able to use subtlety and innuendo as well as blunt attack, More's work has been catastrophic for Richard's reputation. Whether intended as history, or whether this most playful of writers was writing literature or satire, is much debated. Its impact on its subject's image can hardly be overstated.

Vergil and More were both deployed (or plagiarised) by Edward Hall, whose 1548 *Union of the Two Illustre* [Illustrious] *Families of Lancaster and York* was an unashamed apologia for the Tudor monarchy. Embellishing his sources, with more sensationalist and florid prose, Hall's derivative work was the main source used by Shakespeare, so was arguably the most destructive piece of them all. The Richard who emerged from the Tudor period had a terrible reputation, but it is worth observing that he had hardly entered it with a good one. If the attempts to turn him into a monster and rewrite the 1470s can be safely dismissed, when it comes to his reign we need to recall that these post-Bosworth works did not invent a wicked Richard III from nothing, but rather 'were building upon a foundation of antagonism to Richard III which ante-dated his death'.[15]

As the Tudor dynasty became extinct with the death of Elizabeth I, so the first doubts about the traditional picture were tentatively voiced. The Scottish Stuarts who now assumed the throne had no vested interest in the reputation of an English king who had died more than a century ago. It was hardly to be expected that the hostile view would change overnight, especially as opinions were heavily influenced by Shakespeare, who was still alive. Yet before his death in 1622, Sir George Buck penned a robust defence of Richard III which cleared him of the main charges, based on original sources. It was published in a badly-edited abridgement by his nephew in 1646, with a proper edition not produced until 1979.[16] Although a tedious read, given the author's habit of meandering off the point on lengthy tangents, it is noteworthy as the first serious attempt to defend Richard. Such efforts remained very much in the minority during the seventeenth century. Indeed, Oliver Cromwell was cast as a new Richard III by opponents who believed he was scheming to take the crown. Cromwell's 'tyranny' was compared by royalists to that of a Richard who is every bit the Shakespearean villain. The title of one tract published in 1649 gives a sense of Richard's image at the time: *Plantagenets Tragicall Story: or, the Death of King Edward the*

Fourth: with the unnaturall voyage of Richard the Third, through the Red Sea of his Nephews' innocent bloud, to his usurped Crowne. In Restoration drama, Richard continued to be portrayed as a tyrant and compared to the now hated Cromwell.

Richard's reputation suffered a major blow in 1674, when workmen demolishing a staircase at the White Tower in the Tower of London uncovered the skeletons of two children, buried 10 ft (3 metres) deep. Immediately, these were identified as the remains of Edward V and his brother and buried in Westminster Abbey as such in 1678. This hasty identification was immensely problematic. In part, the conclusion was reached because the bones were found in a place which seemed to match the description in More's fanciful account of their demise, conveniently overlooking More's statement that they were later moved. For a hurried, secret burial, 10 ft is incredibly deep. Scientific tests in 1933 were flawed because they presupposed the bones to be those of the princes, so important questions (such as the sex) were not investigated. Many modern historians are cautious, if not sceptical, about accepting these results, and without further examination the charges are at best not proven. In the seventeenth century, however, it strengthened the case against Richard III.

Yet the doubts started to grow stronger in the eighteenth century. Aside from the cantankerous David Hume, who upheld the traditional picture because he preferred to rely on the likes of More rather than research the medieval period himself, there was a sympathetic shift towards Richard. A history of York published in 1736 used previously overlooked local records, which caused the author, Francis Drake, to see a very different, northern, view of the king from the traditional, southern picture. The most famous revisionist work of this period was Horace Walpole's *Historic Doubts on the Life and Reign of Richard the Third* (1768), which caused such interest that the entire original print run sold out on the first day. It also aroused considerable controversy, the unpleasant nature of which caused Walpole's resignation from the Society of Antiquaries. Yet it was an important volume regardless, for it outlined a case which was to have considerable influence for more than a century. Walpole's method was to examine ten murders attributed to Richard. Observing the tendency of historians to lazily repeat assumptions passed on through the generations (which did not go down well with historians), Walpole examined these cases and, as the title suggests, cast doubts on Richard's guilt. It was a landmark work in the study of Richard III, although rather less attention has been given to the fact that in the aftermath of the French Revolution, Walpole recanted his views about Richard's innocence in 1793.

Five years earlier, William Hutton had approached Richard fairly even-handedly. He did see Richard as the evil genius behind Clarence's downfall and argues that Richard's designs on the crown began in 1477. When it comes to the usurpation, Hutton is almost admiring as he claims that there is no other instance of 'a prince forming a design upon the crown, laying so able, and deep a scheme, in which were so many obstacles; surmounting them all, and gaining the beloved option in eight weeks!' Examining Richard's character as king, he sees that 'in many instances, it appeared in an amiable light', although after listing Richard's virtues he balances them with the main charges for the prosecution: the murders of Clarence, Hastings, Rivers and the princes.[17] The attempt at balance is testament to a desire to move away from the tradition of an irredeemable monster to a more nuanced portrait.

Such an approach was developed in Sharon Turner's multi-volume history of England at the start of the nineteenth century, a work based in detailed research and a willingness to recognise the different customs and outlooks of past ages. Turner clears Richard of responsibility for the death of Henry VI and Clarence, stating bluntly that 'most of the actions of Richard III have been mis-stated, and his motives blackened'. The account of the events leading to Richard's seizure of the throne is sympathetic without being a whitewash, with Turner viewing it a 'treasonable and immoral action', but adding the mitigation that Richard was no worse than others. He was simply 'the most fearless, determined and unshrinking'.[18] A thorough discussion of the fate of the Princes in the Tower holds Richard culpable, although there is a surprising lack of condemnation as Turner seeks to understand the king's position. Richard is admired for his qualities and presented as a product of his age.

After Turner, the general approach of the nineteenth century was a more sympathetic view of Richard III, the odd defender of the traditional view notwithstanding. The villain who had hacked his way to the throne in Shakespeare and his sources was no longer credible in many eyes, even if the charges against him concerning his nephews were still widely believed. Among the notable work of these years was a two-volume biography by, appropriately enough, the wife of the vicar of Middleham. Caroline Halsted was certainly thorough, with more than eighty appendices across the two volumes containing supporting documents and sources. Ultimately, her 800 and more pages of discussion led her to express the hope that 'further discoveries, by throwing yet more light upon the dark and difficult times in which Richard III flourished, will add to the proofs which already exist of his innocence as regards the great catalogue of crimes so long and so unjustly laid to his charge'.[19] The Richard of the nineteenth century was fast becoming a slandered innocent.

This more indulgent view of Richard suffered a massive blow in 1878. In his intensive work on the early Tudor records, James Gairdner came to the conclusion that the traditional view of Richard was correct on the grounds that discarding tradition was 'like trying to learn an unknown language without a teacher'. Such an elevated view of tradition is more typically the preserve of theologians than medieval historians, but Gairdner argued forcefully that the picture of More and Shakespeare was reliable despite all the doubts raised over the previous decades by others. Richard is throughout an embodiment of evil and malice. However, Gairdner does not follow More and Shakespeare slavishly. He dismisses, for example, the idea that Richard plotted Clarence's downfall, laying the blame squarely with Edward IV and seeing the worst charge against Richard as being that he 'did not demonstrate' afterwards. 'That he was regarded as a tyrant by his subjects seems […] indisputable', but 'he was not destitute of better qualities'.[20] The concessions are grudging and conditional, but they are there. Gairdner goes a long way to restoring the Shakespearean villain as a historical character, but his work is not entirely without nuance and it is not quite the work of demonisation some have tried to make it.

Sir Clements Markham would have disagreed. His robust defence of Richard in 1891 led to a spat with Gairdner in the pages of the *English Historical Review* and was the basis of his 1906 book.[21] If Gairdner tended towards demonology, Markham steered dangerously close to hagiography; as A.R. Myers observed, 'it is as impossible to believe in his crowned angel as it is in Shakespeare's crowned fiend'.[22] The received image of Richard was one great Tudor plot, at the centre of which was the arch-villain Cardinal John Morton, Henry VII's Archbishop of Canterbury. As far as Markham was concerned, Morton was the true author of Thomas More's history, and it was he who rewrote history to demonise Richard. Dismissing this work, Markham naturally clears Richard of all charges concerning murders and plots in the 1470s in slightly injured tones. His reference to the 'so-called usurpation' makes his thoughts on the matter abundantly clear. Accepting the pre-contract story, he has Richard dutifully claiming his just inheritance from the illegitimate young Edward V. Through wishful thinking, he denies Hastings was summarily executed, instead defying all evidence to have him arrested on Friday 13 June and executed after (an entirely unrecorded) due process on Friday 20th. In this alternate reality, the princes survived into the reign of Henry VII, who was the true culprit behind their murder. Markham's Richard III is akin to a Disney hero, boldly saving the day and then tragically smeared by his tyrannical successor. Unfortunately, despite being passionately argued and its enormous popularity thereafter, the historical credibility of his work is not much greater than that of a Disney film.

In the short term, Gairdner prevailed in the academic world. Charles Oman, Chichele Professor of Modern History at Oxford, bluntly asserted that Edward IV had Henry VI 'the saintly and feeble prince murdered, by the hands of his young brother Richard, Duke of Gloucester'. Gairdner had only hinted at that murder. When it came to the Princes in the Tower, Richard apparently 'sent back a secret mandate to London, authorising the murder of his little nephews', who 'were smothered at dead of night in their prison in the Tower', apparently 'between the 7th and the 14th of August, 1483'. The existence of such a mandate is pure conjecture (it would have made centuries of debate redundant), as is the manner of death and the date, which has never been even vaguely known; this is as fanciful as Markham. Oddly, Oman immediately contradicts himself when he ends by saying that the crime's 'manner and details were never certainly known'. His summary talks of 'the prince who had wrought so much evil, and won his way to power by such unscrupulous cunning and cruelty'. 'There have been worse kings in history', Oman opines, without naming any, but 'the consequences of his first fatal crime drove him deeper and deeper into wickedness, and he left a worse name behind him than any of his predecessors.'[23] Interestingly, William Stubbs, not a man to hold back his moral criticism, was much more ambiguous in his acceptance of Gairdner. Noting that there can 'be little doubt of his great ability' and that 'he was not without the gifts which gained for Edward IV the lifelong support of the nation', Stubbs observed that 'Richard III yet owes the general condemnation, with which his life and reign have been visited, to the fact that he left none behind him whose duty it was to attempt his vindication'.[24]

If Gairdner won short-term academic opinion, though, it was Markham who won the popular mind of the twentieth century. Book after book was published trying to redeem Richard's reputation and claim he is much misunderstood. After a century of such an approach, the idea that he is still maligned is wearing rather thin, but the volumes of defence continue to appear, essentially rehearsing the same arguments over and over. At the more extreme end of the spectrum, Richard becomes almost the greatest man ever to rule England, a paragon of virtue whose brilliance is only unrecognised because of malicious Tudor propaganda. Of course, there are also those, albeit far rarer, who react against this and consciously try to present a mirror image of Richard the devil incarnate. With echoes of Gairdner versus Markham, two volumes were published on the 500th anniversary of Richard's accession in 1983 which it is hard to believe were about the same man. Jeremy Potter's *Good King Richard?* and Desmond Seward's *Richard III: England's Black Legend* reveal their approaches in their titles. There is something about Richard which causes writers to abandon any sense of balance or proportion. He even managed to be voted into eighty-second place on the 2002 BBC poll of *100 Greatest Britons*, between Geoffrey Chaucer and J.K. Rowling.

The main aim of most of Richard's fan club has been to prove that he was not responsible for the murder of the Princes in the Tower. Over the years, arguments ranging from the ingenious to the curious to the bizarre to the downright deranged have been put forward in his defence. Every potential inconsistency is exploited, every source micro-analysed, often with little understanding of the fifteenth-century context and a good deal of speculation to fill in gaps. The main purpose is to find an alternative candidate for the crime, which normally ends up with two main suspects: the Duke of Buckingham and Henry VII. Neither case withstands critical scrutiny. It is inconceivable that a subject, no matter how mighty, would have disposed of the king's nephews without the king's knowledge and consent, which rules out Buckingham. (There is often a strange double standard here, with those arguing a deposed king, Henry VI, could only have been killed on the orders of the new king, Edward IV, failing to apply the same logic to the princes.) The idea that the princes somehow survived until after Bosworth is untenable. Given the public relations disaster caused by the belief that he had killed them, Richard could simply have produced the boys alive to discredit these allegations. That he did not, and that no one ever saw them after autumn of 1483, makes it virtually impossible that they were still alive for Henry VII to kill in 1485. Henry may have been ruthless, cruel and one of the most unlikeable men ever to wear the English crown, but there is simply no evidence that he was implicated in the death of the princes. Only wishful thinking and special pleading can overlook the most obvious and plausible scenario.

The efforts to exonerate Richard have also been based upon arguments about his character. His loyalty and his virtues are praised, his detractors condemned as unfair character assassins, typically overlooking that Richard was a formidable character assassin himself. Particular attention is given to Richard's purported administrative abilities and genius as a king, which often ignores the realities of the fifteenth century, the extent to which he built on the work of his predecessors, and the limited amount possible in such a short reign. His single parliament has been portrayed as some great reforming assembly. Even in respectable academic journals, one could read the historically unsustainable view that Richard was a 'singularly thoughtful and enlightened legislator, who brought to his task a profound knowledge of the nature of contemporary problems, and an enthusiastic determination to solve them in the best possible way, in the interests of every class of his subjects'.[25]

In 1924, the Liverpool surgeon Saxon Baxter founded The Fellowship of the White Boar, a small group of amateur enthusiasts convinced that history had treated Richard III unfairly. This remained an exclusive group until rebranded as The Richard III Society in 1959. There is also an affiliated branch in the United States. Officially, the society challenges the 'traditional' narrative and promotes further research into Richard and his times, although some amateur Ricardians undoubtedly hold an entirely uncritical view of the king which refuses to hear anything bad against him, evidence notwithstanding. Over the years, however, the society has furthered its official aim by funding and producing important editions of sources for the reign, and eminent scholars as well as amateurs write articles for its journal, *The Ricardian*.

One of the most influential Ricardian scholars of the twentieth century was Paul Murray Kendall, a professor of English at Ohio University. His *Richard the Third* (1955) is the most robust defence of the king among biographies which can claim to be the product of serious research. It is beautifully written, at times reading like a novel, which is problematic because on occasion it becomes one. His vivid description of the Battle of Barnet caused one commentator to remark sardonically that the 'incautious reader might be forgiven for thinking that the author himself was present at the battle'.[26] This is the general problem with the book, that it often straddles the boundary between history and historical fiction with effortless ease. It was an important work and still has value, but like so much written about Richard, must be used with caution.

Academic historians were rather more critical, but in mid-century most were relatively sympathetic and willing to accept that 'there was a sound constructive side to Richard III' and that he 'was very far from being the distorted villain of tradition'.[27] Not all mid-century academics inclined this way, with J.R. Lander making Gairdner look restrained when he claimed Richard became 'in the highest degree schizophrenic, a criminal self-righteously invoking the protection of the Almighty'.[28] Later twentieth century academic work is often labelled 'traditionalist', although that is a slippery term. It is true that nearly all academic historians believe that Richard usurped the throne with a baseless justification. Likewise, there is near unanimity that the princes most probably died on Richard's orders.

However, the idea that Richard was preternaturally wicked is generally dismissed. There is a much greater focus on understanding Richard in his context, recognising his abilities and the constraints he faced without absolving him of culpability for his actions. Such an approach is 'traditionalist' only for those who want Richard to be a saint, cleared of everything.

The basic starting point is the work of Charles Ross, who placed Richard III in a broader Yorkist context. Turning Richard III into an evil monster in Tudor times required Edward IV's reign to be a golden age, in which Edward was almost saintlike compared to his scheming, demonic brother. Ross, however, wrote biographies of both Edward and Richard, which allowed him to present the continuities between the reigns. His final verdict on Edward is scathing. 'He remains the only king in English history since 1066 in active possession of the throne who failed to secure the safe succession of his son. His lack of political foresight is largely to blame for the unhappy aftermath of his early death.'[29] Of course, Ross holds Richard accountable for his own errors, given his 'usurpation had been, and was nakedly seen to be an unashamed bid for personal power'. Richard was also responsible for the murder of his nephews, although Ross observes that what was more important than what may or may not have happened was 'the consequences of what many of his subjects believed to have been a peculiarly atrocious crime, even by the rather tarnished standards of the fifteenth century'. Equally, however, 'there is no good reason to doubt that Richard was a genuinely pious and religious man' who 'proved himself an energetic and efficient king'. If Ross is negative overall, he is insistent that the context is crucial in judging Richard, who 'must be seen in the context of his own age and, more particularly, of the record of his own family'. Both his father and brother were respectively an aspirational and an actual usurper who had no issue with using violence, including fratricide in Edward IV's case. 'No one familiar with the careers of King Louis XI of France […] or Henry VIII of England would wish to cast any special slur on Richard, still less to select him as the exemplar of a tyrant', hence to 'put Richard thus into the context of his own violent age is not to make him morally a better man, but at least it makes him more understandable'.[30]

Placing Richard in this context is what the main academic writers on the reign have tried to do subsequently, shifting the focus away from the circular debate about his motivations and character to analyse him as a fifteenth-century nobleman and king. Rosemary Horrox looked in considerable detail at Richard's affinity and use of patronage, both before and during the reign, casting particular light on the problems he had with loyalty after

1483 which alienated him from many Yorkists and compelled him to rely on his loyal northern followers. Her final verdict is harsh, as she noted that of all medieval depositions, 'it was the one which, with whatever justification, could most easily be seen as an act of naked self-aggrandisement', 'the first pre-emptive deposition in English history' justified not by the fact 'that Edward V had failed, but the likelihood that he might fail'. Ultimately, 'Richard III was the only failed usurper of the Middle Ages'. Writing a short biography three decades later, Horrox returned to that theme of failure, a view embodied in the very title (*Richard III: A Failed King?*). Horrox sees Richard as a failure because 'a young man with no claim to the throne' was able 'to amass enough support to overthrow the reigning king'. This was not 'a reactivation of the Wars of the Roses', but 'a violent splintering of the House of York' in which 'the former servants of Edward IV rejected his brother's seizure of power'. Ultimately, Richard 'can with justice be seen as a *failed* king, who in the end destroyed whatever it was that he has sought to rescue and preserve, losing his crown, and his life, in the process'.[31]

A.J. Pollard produced important work on Richard's northern affinity and connections. In an early article, 'The Tyranny of Richard III', he examined how Richard might have been understood as tyrannous by contemporaries and Tudor writers. He later acknowledged the title was intentionally provocative, for he was not arguing that Richard was a tyrant, but that fifteenth- and sixteenth-century writers in the South had grounds to portray him as such on their own terms. The interplay between North and South, as well as Richard's northern retinue and sphere of influence, was extensively studied by Pollard in several works. As he accepted, however unpopular Richard's introduction of northerners into the southern shires was, he had very little choice after Buckingham's Rebellion, given the lack of reliable locals to employ; this was 'tyranny' by force of circumstances rather than by design or inclination. Pollard also wrote a lavishly illustrated volume on *Richard III and the Princes in the Tower* (1991), one of the most sensible contributions to the popular debate.[32] However, such immersion in the world of bitter argument over Richard III can be exhausting. With a volume of his collected essays in 2001, Pollard consciously chose to stop writing directly about Richard: 'It would be accurate to say that I have arrived at the position where sceptically I distrust both traditions about Richard III and have retreated to cynical agnosticism.'[33]

The most prolific academic writer on Richard, who has shown no signs of such despondency, has been Michael Hicks. Starting with the published version of his doctoral thesis, a biography of Clarence (1980), he has written articles or books on most of the main figures of the period. Following Ross in stressing the importance of contextualising Richard, Hicks has paid particular attention to Richard's time and behaviour as Duke of Gloucester. While he dismissed the ducal saint of the more ardent Ricardians, Hicks acknowledges Richard the duke as 'a remarkably successful and far from conventional member of the late medieval nobility'.[34] Given his conspicuous loyalty to Edward IV, in 1483 the Woodvilles were 'unaware how formidable he was, how vigorous, intense, egotistical, ambitious, aggressive, ruthless, and uncompromising he had always been away from court'. In the weeks before seizing the crown, Richard was skilful enough to do 'nothing irrevocable and might indeed have withdrawn from the brink until the last days of Edward V's reign'. Contextualising Richard, Hicks finds Richard a successful fifteenth-century noble, 'a remarkable man who made more of himself by sheer determination and assertion than his physical limitations should have permitted', although of course, 'he was not perfect; nobody ever is'. Yet what 'changed a successful (but historically obscure) career into a notorious reign was the supreme gamble of his usurpation'. 'Kingship was the pinnacle of his career and also his ruin.'[35]

This is nothing more than a flavour of the main works, for a full analysis would require a multi-volume study in itself. Even within the academic world, there remains considerable division. It can be found in the different opinions presented even in the same 1993 volume of essays.[36] The sources are all there for those who want to try their hand at interpreting the king, including some excellent collections of key excerpts. Many have, and as one author has observed, 'there will always be a market for partisan work on Richard III', with the result that what 'needs to be rescued is not Richard's reputation, but the validity of historical interpretation'.[37] Therein is the core problem with any attempt to reach a balanced historical verdict on Richard III, for he left the realm of history long ago to become the lead character in the morality plays of his interpreters. Whether he is a saint, a devil or something in between is determined more by the moral of the tale than by the reality of King Richard III.

Richard in Popular Culture

The battle over Richard III's image has involved the interpretation of portraits as much as texts. All the known ones were painted after Richard's death, but the main controversy has come to focus on the most famous, which survives in several copies. This is Richard, dressed in black against a red background, fiddling with a ring on his finger. The most familiar is in the National Portrait Gallery in London, but this is a late sixteenth-century copy. There is an earlier version (pre-1520) in the Royal Collection, possibly based on an image from Richard's lifetime. The right shoulder has clearly been overpainted to make it higher than the left to create the 'hunchback' of popular Tudor legend. Richard's defenders have used this obvious alteration as evidence that the Tudors consciously distorted reality to create their monster. (Ironically, when the Leicester skeleton was found to have scoliosis, a curvature of the spine, many of those who so objected to the 'hunchback' portrayal saw this as proof that it was Richard.) This portrait has had a major impact on perceptions of Richard III. It is probably one of the most instantly recognisable images of an English monarch, alongside Holbein's portrait of Henry VIII.

It was this Richard that Shakespeare placed upon the stage. Richard III is one of the greatest Shakespearean villains, encompassing all the worst elements of the Tudor version of his story. Yet while creating an evil, scheming genius, the Bard avoided an overly simplistic character. Shakespeare's Richard carries the audience with him in asides and soliloquies, inviting the viewer into his dastardly plans. Cunning and bitterness mingle in Richard, who is the Tudor monster perfected, wading through blood to seize the crown. The play does not stand alone, being the last in the series of eight which begins with *Richard II*. The future Richard III first makes his appearance in *Henry VI: Part 2*, demonstrating considerable swordsmanship during the first Battle of St Albans, an impressive feat for someone who would have been 2 at the time. He has a much greater role in *Henry VI: Part 3*, not least as Henry VI's killer. Although the sequence was not written in order, in dramatic terms *Richard III* is the culmination of Richard's bloody path to the throne which takes him across the pages of three plays.

Despite being one of Shakespeare's longest works, second only to *Hamlet*, *Richard III* has proved enduringly popular with performers. In modern times, it has been staged frequently by the RSC at Stratford-upon-Avon. Christopher Plummer (1961), Ian Holm (1963), Ian Richardson (1975), Anthony Sher (1984), David Troughton (1995) and Robert Lindsey (1998) have been among those who have taken the lead role in performances. Elsewhere, Richard has been played by the likes of Ian McKellen (National Theatre, 1990), Kenneth Branagh (Sheffield Crucible, 2002) and Kevin Spacey (Old Vic, London, 2011). Notwithstanding the multiple settings, all have given interpretations of Richard which conform to the received tradition of the malevolent hunchback. Few, however, can rival the most familiar film version, directed by Laurence Olivier (1955). Taking the title role himself, Olivier gave a memorably hammed-up performance which left a lasting impression. The part of Edward IV was taken by Cedric Hardwicke, who was then 62 (more than quarter of a century older than Edward would actually have been during Clarence's downfall in 1477–78); there has been a tendency to opt for a wise, gentle older man to play Edward in order to highlight the difference with Richard, blatantly ignoring history. (That said, most actors playing Richard have also been older; Richard died at 32, but Olivier was 47 in 1955.) Shakespeare's Richard has continued to make occasional appearances on television, including the 2016 BBC version of *The Hollow Crown*, where he was played by Benedict Cumberbatch.

In the twenty-first century, however, the character of Richard became problematic with its mocking portrayal of disability. Elizabethans associated physical disability with moral deformity, an attitude abhorrent to us today but one which creates serious questions when analysing and interpreting the play. Much of the dialogue relies upon Richard seeking revenge for his physical deformity, the kind of hyperbolic portrayal by Olivier intended to emphasise the evil nature of the character. Modern interpretations must be sensitive to this problem and recognise a very different understanding of disability. In 2022, the RSC cast a disabled actor in the lead role for the first time, Arthur Hughes having radial dysplasia and identifying as 'limb different'.

Richard III has also lent itself to cinematic reinterpretations which underline the theme of tyranny. In 1995, Ian McKellen starred opposite Annette Bening (as Elizabeth Woodville) in a version which transplanted the play into 1930s Europe, against the growing menace of fascism. While not a version of the play, the BBC series *House of Cards* (1990) brings the theme of a devious plotter into the arena of modern politics at the end of the Thatcher era. Based on a 1989 novel by Michael Dobbs, it sees government chief whip Francis Urquhart (Ian Richardson) ruthlessly scheme his way into 10 Downing Street, quoting *Richard III* along the way, although his wife Elizabeth (Diane Fletcher) has more in common with Lady Macbeth than Anne Neville. While this was fiction, there have indeed been times in recent British politics when *Richard III* has appeared more like a political manual for leadership hopefuls than a play.

More light-heartedly, *Richard III* is well enough known to be satirised. In *The Eyre Affair*, the first novel in Jasper Fforde's *Thursday Next* series, it is performed at the Ritz Theatre in Swindon every Friday night, as it has been for fifteen years: 'Richard III was one of those plays that could repeal the law of diminishing returns; it could be enjoyed over and over again.' 'All the actors were pulled from an audience who had been to the play so many times they knew it back to front', an audience which joins in, heckles and hams it up with those on stage.[38] There is, as in all satire, a reflection of reality here, for Richard is one of Shakespeare's most familiar characters and perhaps only *Macbeth* has as recognisable an opening line. On a deeper level, Fforde's portrayal reflects how, thanks to Shakespeare, Richard has often become a caricature, a consummate stage villain rather than a real person.

If Shakespeare's is by far the most renowned dramatisation for the prosecution, the most acclaimed for the defence is Josephine Tey's novel *The Daughter of Time* (1951). Tey was a pseudonym of Elizabeth MacKintosh and this was easily her most successful work, appealing as it does to all diehard Ricardians. Bored while laid up in hospital, a Scotland Yard detective, Alan Grant, sets to work on the 'case' of the Princes in the Tower, aided by a friend. As is explicitly acknowledged towards the end, this is a fictionalised form of Clements Markham's case from half a century earlier. Grant is prompted into his investigation by looking at Richard's portrait, which he thinks reveals Richard to have been kind and gentle rather than a cruel murderer. It is hardly a scholarly approach, although arguments outside the fictional world have been constructed on similarly preposterous foundations.

In general, the large number of novels which feature Richard III have followed popular history in being sympathetic to the king. From Margaret Bowen's *Dickon* (1929) onwards, authors have typically highlighted Richard's traumatic upbringing and play down or even totally ignore the question of the princes; there are simply too many to mention and few stand out. Some have made him part of a wider panorama, such as Sharon Penman in *The Sunne in Splendour* (1982). Philippa Gregory's twin books, *The White Queen* (2009) and *The White Princess* (2013) posits an alternative scenario in which young Richard of York survived, while also portraying a Princess Elizabeth who loved Richard III and resented having to marry Henry VII; the novels were later adapted as mini-series for television. Perhaps most interestingly, Kate Sedley set her Roger the Chapman series against the 1470s and 1480s, making Richard a significant background character. The series shows an appreciation of some of the core tensions of Richard's career, as one example shows:

> 'But you hate the north,' I protested, 'and I understand that His Grace rarely comes south since Clarence's execution. They say his hatred of the Queen's family is as strong as ever.'
> 'True,' Timothy admitted. 'But I love that man and I miss him. I'm even willing to live among barbarians in order

to serve him. So...' He spread his hands and gave me a sheepish grin.

I knew what he meant. Richard of Gloucester had always exerted the same fascination over me.[39]

The tension between horror of northerners and the affection Richard could inspire is weaved through this.

Some have tried to resolve the greatest controversy of Richard's life by staging courtroom proceedings. In 1984, Channel 4 screened *The Trial of King Richard III*, a mock trial at the Old Bailey in which Richard was tried (*in absentia*) for murdering his nephews and acquitted by a jury. In 2018, Lady Justice Hallett presided over another trial of the king at the Novello Theatre in London, to raise money for the Shakespeare Schools Foundation. Comedian Hugh Dennis acted as foreman of a jury formed of the audience, which was asked to vote on a verdict. Of course, almost all the evidence about the case would be inadmissible in a modern court of law, being largely opinion, hearsay and balance of probabilities, but the format highlights the fascination this aspect of Richard's life still retains for many people.

A consequence of this is the popularity of alternative reality versions of the story, both humorous and more serious. In the first episode of the BBC comedy *Blackadder* (1983), Richard III (played by Peter Cook) is a kindly, loving uncle who is mistakenly slain by the incompetent Edmund Blackadder (Rowan Atkinson) at Bosworth. He is then succeeded by his nephew as Richard IV (Brian Blessed), and only after his demise years later does Henry Tudor rewrite history. Of course, the premise is flawed, for Richard would not have been king had his nephew lived and been eligible for the throne, but it gently satirises a deeper popular desire for the reality to be a Tudor myth. Four years later, the *Jonny Quest* comic used a similar storyline in Winters of Discontent, in which the protagonists accidentally go back in time to find the princes alive, well and adored by their uncle who is likewise loved by his subjects. John M. Ford's novel *The Dragon's Waiting* (1983) set a recognisable sketch of Richard's ascent to power in a world where magic exists and the Duke of Milan is a vampire. Richard then wins Bosworth and continues as king. Blood-drinking undead rulers aside, it is interesting that this novel has a European dimension which rarely features in either history or fiction. More time travel is involved in Margaret Peterson Haddix's novel for young adults, *Sent* (2009), part of a series in which children are kidnapped by twenty-first-century time travellers; in this case, the two children turn out to be the Princes in the Tower.

Perhaps the strangest place Richard has found his way into popular culture is in a country he never knew existed, Japan. In 2001, the video game company Konami released *Yu-Gi-Oh! The Duelists of Roses* for PlayStation 2. Part of a series based on a manga about trading card gaming, this particular game (as the English version of the title suggests) took the Wars of the Roses for its plot, albeit very loosely interpreted. Meanwhile, between 2013 and 2022, a manga series by Ana Kayyo called *Requiem of the Rose King* was published in a Japanese magazine and then as individual volumes (subsequently translated and issued in English). This also inspired an anime version which began to air on Japanese television in 2022. Roughly based on Shakespeare, the central character is an intersex Richard III who fights against his demons on the way to the throne. That Richard's story has even become a part of Japanese manga and anime says much about its enduring popularity. His reputation has spread across the globe, where he is both hero and villain, fictional character as much as historical king.

Verdict

As the last English king to die in battle, a battle fought against his own subjects, Richard III was evidently a failure. Yet the result of the Battle of Bosworth was far from a foregone conclusion and had Richard won, it is unlikely he would appear in this volume. Had Henry Tudor died on that August day in 1485, it is hard to see who was left to lead the opposition to Richard. Perhaps Richard would have been able to recover his authority. Counterfactual musings are of limited use, of course, but in Richard's case it is worth remembering just how much hinged on a single battle, for he was a capable man with the potential to be a capable king.

The monster found in sixteenth-century accounts and perfected by Shakespeare has long ceased to be credible. Placing Richard in his fifteenth-century context reveals a man who for the most part was no worse (or better) than his noble contemporaries. He was indeed ambitious, violent and unscrupulous, but he hardly stands out for that in the age of Richard of York, Edward IV, Warwick the Kingmaker, Clarence, Buckingham, the Woodvilles and Henry VII. They were no cast of angels. We cannot seriously entertain Richard's guilt regarding any of the crimes and murders prior to 1483. He proved effective in the North, was conspicuously loyal to his brother, and adeptly built himself into a powerful regional lord. He constructed a northern affinity who were loyal to him and he could inspire considerable devotion. Even as king, given the constraints within which he worked, he generally conformed to most of the expectations of the role and proved an able ruler.

Yet for all the special pleading of his champions, he was no saint. He was a leading nobleman during the Wars of the Roses and behaved accordingly. To accept that he was ruthless and brutal in an age when other lords were ruthless and brutal too is not a moral exoneration. That Edward IV was also prone to dispensing with due process cannot be used to excuse Richard III from the judicial murders of Rivers and Hastings. The murder of his nephews was an act which surpassed even the violent standards of that age, and by far the most likely scenario is that the Princes in the Tower met their end on Richard's orders. This crime is the one which really set him apart, even if it is hard to see how he could have let them live and had any hope of resting secure on his throne. Beyond that, however, there have certainly been far worse men to wear the crown of England. Fearful southerners and Tudor propagandists may have made him a tyrant, but tyranny is a slippery, subjective term and not one any sober historian can apply to Richard.

There is little doubt that in the right circumstances, Richard III could have been a competent king. The problem was that the circumstances in which he came to the throne, with a questionable title aggravated by the murder of his nephews, turned many Yorkists against him and meant he was never able to establish his authority fully. While he may genuinely have feared for his position under a Woodville-dominated Edward V, it is hard to see that his actions in June 1483 were motivated by anything other than ambition. It was a coup for which the justifications were feeble and unbelievable. Whatever his potential competence as king, he could never overcome the manner in which he assumed the title. If enough of the nobility were prepared to be complicit in the destruction of the adult Woodvilles, or at least not openly object, the subsequent killing of two boys was entirely different. However insecure Richard's position would have been had the boys lived, the slaying of innocent children was as morally reprehensible in the fifteenth century as it is today. That someone with the most tenuous claim imaginable to the throne was able to galvanise enough support to defeat him at Bosworth is evidence of Richard's failure to heal the deep wounds caused by his usurpation. He was no inhuman monster, but for all his previous good service and for all his abilities, Richard III let ambition get the better of him and took the throne illegitimately. He failed because he could never overcome that illegitimate beginning.

Conclusion

The Worst Monarchs?

Stephen, John, Edward II, Richard II and Richard III. All were failures as kings. Only two managed to pass the thrones on to their sons, although in tumultuous circumstances which left children as monarch. Three lost their crowns and another would probably have done so had he not died. The five failed for different reasons and in different ways, but all fell short of contemporary expectations of kingship. An inability to preserve peace was the most obvious sign of their failure. All five faced civil war, and in every case these were civil wars provoked by their own actions (although we might question whether the alternatives to Stephen and Richard III would also have caused civil war). Contemporaries liked kings who waged successful wars against France or Scotland, not ones who fought their own subjects. The causes were many and deep-rooted, but it is in this domestic discord that the failure of the kingship of these five is laid bare.

If they were undisputed failures, does this make them the worst kings of the Middle Ages? This is a difficult question. In some cases, fortune plays a significant role. Other kings performed badly or made major mistakes on occasion, yet survived. Henry III had a turbulent reign and provoked considerable opposition, especially in the 1250s and 1260s, but he survived to pass on his throne peacefully. Had Richard III won Bosworth, maybe he would be viewed very differently. Henry VI, who was a disastrous king, would certainly be included had he ever really been more than a crowned puppet. The civil war resulting from his reign was a far bloodier affair than that of Stephen's time, but Henry escapes censure because it is hard to hold him personally responsible. To judge who were the worst of England's eighteen medieval kings is thus not easy, a judgement call rather than an exact science.

That caveat notwithstanding, the list of worst medieval monarchs will always justifiably include John, Edward II and Richard II. All three had the ability to be competent kings, but they proved totally unable to rule well or in accordance with contemporary expectations. Where kingship called for the exercise of justice and mercy, these three were often arbitrary and vindictive. Where a king was meant to take counsel and spread patronage widely, John trusted no one and gave nothing, Edward fixated on individuals and gave them everything, and Richard surrounded himself with friends who would not challenge him. Where a king was meant to be an inspiring warrior, John lost most of his continental inheritance, Edward was an abject failure against the Scots, and the most that can be said for Richard is that he didn't lose any battles (an easy feat when he didn't fight any). All three reigns ended in disaster, the harsh judgement of posterity on each being fair. There is little point dwelling on whether or not they were tyrants, for the concept of tyranny is too problematic and in the eye of the beholder. What is beyond doubt is that the three ruled badly, failed to respect the rules of English kingship, and brought about their own demise.

Stephen and Richard III are trickier. Stephen's reign was overwhelmed by civil war, a bewildering sequence of sieges and shifting allegiances. Yet compared to the civil wars of the other reigns considered here, this was a remarkably 'gentlemanly' conflict: there were none of the executions, judicial murders and acts of brutality which would disfigure later centuries. If the other four are condemned for lack of mercy and for cruelty, Stephen is often criticised for being too merciful and not ruthless enough. Although it did not help him as king, he seems to have been one of the more likeable men to wear the English crown, and contemporaries recognised his kingly qualities. His tragedy was that Henry I left the succession unsettled and that civil war was almost inevitable as a result; had he come to the throne in different circumstances, Stephen could have been a good king. The same is true of Richard III. He had been a notably successful lieutenant for his brother in the North and clearly had the ability to be king. Unfortunately, he stole a crown that wasn't his, tried to cover up that fact through slander and insinuation, then committed the unpardonable act of having his nephews murdered. Like Stephen, ambition proved his undoing. Unlike Stephen, the brutal way in which that ambition was realised meant he lost the hearts of many of his subjects and could not retain his crown. Both were competent men capable of ruling well. If Stephen and Richard III were failures, they do not number among the worst monarchs.

The ambiguity about Stephen is reflected in his position (or lack thereof) in popular memory. He is the one of these five kings most people will know nothing about, because he does not fit the part of the villain. The others are much more familiar among the 'bad kings' of popular imagination. All are perhaps better known through their fictional alter-egos than as historical figures: it is the John of Walter Scott and Robin Hood, the Edward II of Marlowe, and the Richard II and Richard III of Shakespeare who have become most familiar. Yet if they distort the historical reality, they are not complete fabrications. These characters are grounded in a recognisable reality and the generally hostile views of their contemporaries, which is why they have endured. It is Richard III who has become most problematic, for it seems he must always be either saint or demon, adored or despised. It is slightly baffling that a king who had one of the shortest reigns in English history has become such a massively polarising figure, but it just shows that the development of historical reputations can be an unpredictable, strange process.

Historians will continue to ask new questions and revise past opinions, as they ask different questions which make sense in their own time. Novelists and screenwriters will continue to look for new angles and ways of challenging traditional narratives. The fortunes and reputations of these five kings will continue to ebb and flow. Yet they will do so only so far. It is unfair to number Stephen and Richard III among the worst of kings, although they were not ultimately successful and they can be redeemed only to a certain point. There can be no such redemption for John, Edward II and Richard II, whose self-inflicted catastrophes mean they are justifiably remembered as some of the worst monarchs to rule England.

Notes

Full publication details are contained in the bibliography.

Introduction

1. Jean Dunababin, 'Government', in *The Cambridge History of Medieval Political Thought, c. 350–c. 1450*, ed. J.H. Burns (1989), pp. 477-519.
2. John of Salisbury, *Policraticus*, ed. Cary J. Nederman (1990).
3. William of Pagula, 'The Mirror of King Edward III', trans. Cary J. Nederman, in *Medieval Political Theory: A Reader*, ed. Kate Langdon Forhan and Cary J. Nederman (2006), pp. 200-206; Thomas Hoccleve, *The Regiment of Princes*, ed. Charles R. Blyth (1999).
4. Roy Strong, *Coronation* (2005); H.G. Richardson, 'The Coronation in Medieval England: The Origin of the Office and the Oath', *Traditio* 16 (1960), 111-202.
5. For example, the anointings of Saul and David in 1 Samuel 10:1 and 16:13, and 2 Samuel 2:4.
6. An introduction to some of the complexities is R.R. Davies, *The First English Empire: Power and Identities in the British Isles, 1093–1343* (2000).
7. J.R. Maddicott, *The Origins of the English Parliament, 924–1327* (2010).
8. Gwilym Dodd, *Justice and Grace: Private Petitioning and the English Parliament in the Late Middle Ages* (2007); *Early Common Petitions in the English Parliament, c. 1290–c. 1420*, ed. W. Mark Ormrod, Helen Killick and Phil Bradford (2017).
9. Clare Valente, *The Theory and Practice of Revolt in Medieval England* (2003).
10. For an excellent study of medieval chronicles, see Chris Given-Wilson, *Chronicles: The Writing of History in Medieval England* (2004). See also Antonia Gransden, *Historical Writing in England*, 2 vols. (1974–82).
11. Anthony Seldon, *Blair* (2nd edition: 2005), p. 703.

Chapter 1: Stephen

1. *The Anglo-Saxon Chronicles*, ed. and trans. Michael Swanton (1996), p. 265.
2. *The Chronicle of John of Worcester Volume III*, ed. and trans. P. McGurk (1998), p. 216.
3. *Chronicle of John of Worcester III*, p. 272.
4. Henry of Huntingdon, *The History of the English People 1000–1154*, ed. and trans. Diana Greenway (1996), pp. 74-75.
5. This story is told in Richard Oram, *David I: The King who Made Scotland* (2004), pp. 167-89.
6. *Anglo-Saxon Chronicles*, pp. 263-64.
7. Henry of Huntingdon, *History*, pp. 66, 87.
8. William of Malmesbury, *Historia Novella: The Contemporary History*, ed. Edmund King and trans. K.R. Potter (1998), pp. 29, 45, 71.
9. *Gesta Stephani*, ed. and trans. K.R. Potter and R.H.C. Davis (1976), pp. 68-69.
10. Björn Weiler, 'Kingship, Usurpation and Propaganda in Twelfth-Century Europe: The Case of Stephen', *Anglo-Norman Studies* 23 (2001), pp. 301, 308.
11. Marjorie Chibnall, *The Empress Matilda: Queen Consort, Queen Mother and Lady of the English* (1991), p. 198.
12. *Polychronicon Ranulphi Higden Monachi Cestrensis*, 9 vols. (1879), vol. 8, p. 478.
13. Ralph Holinshed, *Chronicles of England, Scotland and Ireland* (2nd edition: 1587), online at The Holinshed Project (http://www.cems.ox.ac.uk/holinshed/).
14. Samuel Daniel, *The Collection of the History of England* (5th edition: 1685), p.79.
15. David Hume, *The History of England from Julius Caesar to the Revolution in 1688*, 6 vols. (1879 edition), vol. 1, p. 345.
16. Paul de Rapin, *History of England*, trans. Nicholas Tindal, 13 vols. (1727), vol. 2, p. 220.
17. William Stubbs, *The Constitutional History of England in its Origin and Development*, 3 vols. (1874-78), vol. 3, pp. 348, 353.
18. J.H. Round, *Geoffrey de Mandeville: A Study of the Anarchy* (1892), pp. 24, 35, 36.
19. H.W.C. Davis, 'The Anarchy of Stephen's Reign', *English Historical Review* 18 (1903), 630-41. The opposing arguments about the 'waste'

question are summed up in Emilie Amt, *The Accession of Henry II in England: Royal Government Restored 1149–1159* (1993) and Graeme J. White, *Restoration and Reform 1153-1165: Recovery from Civil War in England* (2000).

20. Walter Carruthers Sellars and Robert Julian Yeatman, *1066 and All That* (1930), pp. 20-21.
21. For example, A.L. Poole, *Domesday Book to Magna Carta 1087–1216* (2nd edition: 1954), p. 132.
22. R.H.C. Davis, *King Stephen* (3rd edition: 1990), pp. 29, 79, 92, 93, 124.
23. H.A Cronne, *The Reign of Stephen: Anarchy in England 1135–54* (1970), pp. 3, 67, 71, 83, 110.
24. John T. Appleby, *The Troubled Reign of King Stephen* (1969), pp. 68, 146, 156, 191, 203, 204, 207.
25. C. Warren Hollister, 'Stephen's Anarchy', *Albion* 6 (1974), 233-39; *The Anarchy of King Stephen's Reign*, ed. Edmund King (1994).
26. W.L. Warren, *Henry II* (Yale edition: 2000), p. 20.
27. Marjorie Chibnall, *The Empress Matilda: Queen Consort, Queen Mother and Lady of the English* (1991).
28. Keith J. Stringer, *The Reign of Stephen: Kingship, Warfare and Government in Twelfth-Century England* (1993), pp. 13, 27, 88.
29. Jim Bradbury, *Stephen and Matilda: The Civil War of 1139–53* (1996), pp. 27, 216, 218.
30. Weiler, 'Kingship, Usurpation and Propaganda'.
31. David Crouch, *The Reign of King Stephen, 1135–1154* (2000), pp. 319, 342.
32. Donald Matthew, *King Stephen* (2002), p. 195.
33. Edmund King, *King Stephen* (2010), p. 339.
34. David Carpenter, *The Struggle for Mastery: The Penguin History of Britain 1066–1284* (2003), p. 164.
35. Simon Schama, *A History of Britain, 3000 bc – ad 1603* (2000), p. 120.
36. Oram, *David I*, pp. 132, 138.
37. Marjorie Chibnall, 'Introduction' in *King Stephen's Reign (1135–1154)*, ed. Paul Dalton and Graeme J. White (2008), p. 8.
38. Catherine Hanley, *Matilda: Empress. Queen. Warrior* (2019); *Henry of Blois: New Interpretations*, ed. William Kynan-Wilson and John Munns (2021); Judith A. Green, 'The Charters of Geoffrey de Mandeville', in *Rulership and Rebellion in the Anglo-Norman World, c.1066–c.1216*, ed. Paul Dalton and David Luscombe (2015), pp. 91-110.
39. Carl Watkins, *Stephen: The Reign of Anarchy* (2015), pp. 85-86.

40. Matthew Lewis, *Stephen and Matilda: Cousins of Anarchy* (2019), pp. ix-x, 55, 59, 82, 233.

41. The quotes in the following paragraphs are from Ellis Peters, *One Corpse Too Many* (1979), pp. 82, 168, 254, 259; *The Fourth Cadfael Omnibus* (1993), pp. 24, 245; *The Fifth Cadfael Omnibus* (1994), pp. 180, 288, 278, 356, 360; and *The Seventh Cadfael Omnibus* (1997), p. 372.

42. Sharon Penman, *When Christ and His Saints Slept* (1994), pp. 314, 414, 491, 487-88.

Chapter 2: John

1. Eleanor and Herbert Farjeon, *Kings and Queens* (1932).

2. 'The Phony King of England' is a song by Johnny Mercer in the Disney Film *Robin Hood* (1973), sung by Phil Harris as Little John.

3. Nicholas Vincent, 'Isabella of Angoulême: John's Jezebel', in *King John: New Interpretations*, ed. S.D. Church (1999), pp. 174-75.

4. J.C. Holt, *The Northerners: A Study in the Reign of King John* (1961), p. 34.

5. Nick Barratt, 'The Revenue of King John', *English Historical Review* 111 (1996), 835-55.

6. *Memoriale Fratris Walteri de Coventria*, ed. William Stubbs, 2 vols. (1872-73), vol. 2, p. 203.

7. Holt, *Northerners*, p. 100.

8. *Matthaei Parisiensis, Monachi Sancti Albani, Chronica Majora*, ed. Henry Richards Luard, 7 vols. (1872-83), vol. 2, p. 669.

9. W.L. Warren, *King John* (Yale edition:1997), p. 13.

10. Gransden, *Historical Writing I*, p. 321.

11. For summaries of the chronicles for John's reign, see Gransden, *Historical Writing I*, pp. 318-355; Holt, *King John*, pp. 16-23; and David Carpenter, *Magna Carta* (2015), pp. 70-97.

12. Carole Levin, 'King John and Early Tudor Propaganda', *The Sixteenth Century Journal* 11 (1980), 23-32.

13. John Speed, *Historie of Great Britaine* (3rd edition: 1632), p. 572.

14. Daniel, *Collection*, pp. 128, 144.

15. James Tyrrell, *The General History of England*, 5 vols. (1700–4), vol. 2, pp. 805-6.

16. Hume, *History of England*, vol. 1, p. 520.

17. William Stubbs, *Historical Introduction to the Rolls Series* (1902), pp. 239, 442, 487.

18. John Richard Green, *A Short History of the English People* (1882), pp. 122-23, 229-30.
19. Kate Norgate, *John Lackland* (1902), pp. 58, 181, 286.
20. James Henry Ramsay, *The Angevin Empire* (1903), p. 502.
21. Edmund B. D'Auvergne, *John, King of England* (1934), p. 8.
22. V.H. Galbraith, 'Good Kings and Bad Kings in English History', *History* 30 (1945), 128-29.
23. Maurice Ashley, *The Life and Times of King John* (1972); Alan Lloyd, *King John* (1973); John T. Appleby, *John, King of England* (1959); J.A.P. Jones, *King John and Magna Carta* (1971).
24. Doris Mary Stenton, *English Society in the Early Middle Ages (1066–1307)* (2nd edition: 1959), p. 46.
25. J.C. Holt, *King John* (1963), pp. 6 (for chickens quote), 7.
26. Graham E. Seel, *King John: An Underrated King* (2012), 58, 181, 286.
27. Winston S. Churchill, *History of the English-Speaking Peoples*, 4 vols. (1956–58), vol. 1, pp. 177-86.
28. Poole, *Domesday Book to Magna Carta*, p. 425.
29. C. Warren Hollister, 'King John and the Historians', *Journal of British Studies* 1 (1961), pp. 7, 16.
30. Holt, *King John*, pp. 16, 27; Holt, *Northerners*, pp. 174, 255; J.C. Holt, *Magna Carta* (3rd edition: 2015).
31. Sidney Painter, *The Reign of King John* (1949), pp. 19, 94, 226, 227.
32. Warren, *King John*, pp. 71, 259.
33. Ralph V. Turner, *King John* (1994), pp. 19, 94, 226, 227.
34. Jim Bradbury, 'Philip Augustus and King John: Personality and History', in *King John: New Interpretations*, ed. Church, pp. 347, 361.
35. Charles Petit-Dutaillis, *The Feudal Monarchy in France and England* (1936), p. 215.
36. Sellar and Yeatman, *1066 and All That*, p. 24.
37. John Gillingham, *Richard the Lionheart* (1978), p. 278; John Gillingham, *The Angevin Empire* (2nd edition: 2001), pp. 85, 125.
38. Frank McLynn, *Lionheart and Lackland: King Richard, King John and the Wars of Conquest* (2006).
39. Simon Sebag Montefiore, *Monsters: History's Most Evil Men and Women* (2008), pp. 80-81.
40. Barratt, 'Revenue of King John', 855.
41. Essays by J.L. Bolton, Paul Latimer, Nick Barratt and V.D. Moss in *King John: New Interpretations*, ed. Church; S.D. Church, *The Household Knights of King John* (1999); Paul Webster, *King John and Religion* (2015).

42. Stephen Church, *King John: England, Magna Carta and the Making of a Tyrant* (2015), pp. xx, xxi, 248.
43. Nicholas Vincent, *John: An Evil King?* (2020), pp. xvi, 101, 102.
44. Marc Morris, *King John: Treachery, Tyranny and the Road to Magna Carta* (2015).
45. Frédérique Lachaud, *Jean sans Terre* (Paris, 2018), p. 353.
46. Pictures of a selection of this memorabilia are found in the British Library book accompanying the octocentenary exhibition: *Magna Carta: Law, Liberty, Legacy*, ed. Claire Breay and Julian Harrison (2015).
47. Carpenter, *Magna Carta*, p. 72.
48. Studies of the Robin Hood legend include J.C. Holt, *Robin Hood* (1989); A.J. Pollard, *Imagining Robin Hood* (2004); and David Crook, *Robin Hood: Legend and Reality* (2020).

Chapter 3: Edward II

1. Carpenter, *Struggle for Mastery*, p. 525.
2. Michael Prestwich, *The Three Edwards: War and State in England, 1272-1377* (2nd edition: 2003), p. 71.
3. Christine Carpenter, *The Wars of the Roses: Politics and the Constitution in England, c.1437–1509* (1997), p. 40.
4. Christopher Given-Wilson, *Edward II: The Terrors of Kingship* (2016), p. 66.
5. *The Register of Thomas de Cobham, Bishop of Worcester 1317–27*, ed. Ernest Harold Pearce (1930), p. 97.
6. Claire Valente, 'The Deposition and Abdication of Edward II', *English Historical Review* 113 (1998), 852-81.
7. W. Mark Ormrod, *Edward III* (2011), p. 53.
8. The extent of Edward's hostility is questioned in Samuel Lane, 'The Deposition of Edward II: The Kenilworth Embassies', in *Fourteenth Century England XII*, ed. James Bothwell and J.S. Hamilton (2022), pp. 65-77.
9. Jill Barlow, Richard Bryant, Carolyn Heighway, Chris Jeens and David Smith, *Edward II: His Last Months and Monument* (2015).
10. For an analysis of the debate over the death (or survival) of Edward II, see the thorough and judicious discussion in Seymour Phillips, *Edward II* (2010), pp. 520-606, with which I am in agreement.
11. For more detailed analysis of Edward in the chronicles, see Phillips, *Edward II*, pp. 9-15 and Gransden, *Historical Writing in England II*, pp. 1-57. See also *The Reign of Edward II, 1307-27*, ed. and trans.

Wendy R. Childs and Phillipp R. Schofield (Manchester University Press, Manchester, 2022).

12. *Vita Edwardi Secundi*, ed. and trans. Wendy R. Childs (2005), pp. 69, 153, 232; Chris Given-Wilson, '*Vita Edwardi Secundi*: Memoir or Journal?' in *Thirteenth Century England VI*, ed. Michael Prestwich, R.H. Britnell and Robin Frame (1997), pp. 165-76.

13. *The Chronicle of Geoffrey le Baker*, trans. David Preest (2012).

14. This is the translation of Phillips, *Edward II*, p. 10.

15. Ian Mortimer, 'Sermons of Sodomy: A Reconsideration of Edward II's Sodomitical Reputation', in *The Reign of Edward II: New Perspectives*, ed. Gwilym Dodd and Anthony Musson (2006), pp. 48-60. This is challenged in Kit Heyam, *The Reputation of Edward II, 1305-1697: A Literary Transformation of History* (2020), pp. 42-43.

16. *Chronica Monasterii de Melsa*, ed. Edward A. Bond, 3 vols. (1866–68), vol. 2, p. 355. The usual translation is 'the vice of sodomy', but for problems with this see Heyam, *Reputation of Edward II*, p. 43.

17. Paul E.J. Hammer, '"Absolute and Sovereign Mistress of her Grace?" Queen Elizabeth I and her Favourites, 1581–1592', in *The World of the Favourite*, ed. J.H. Elliott and L.W.B. Brockliss (1999), pp. 38-53.

18. Roger Lockyer, *Buckingham: The Life and Political Career of George Villiers, First Duke of Buckingham, 1592-1628* (1981), pp. 101-102.

19. Elizabeth Cary, *The History of the Life, Reign, and Death of Edward II* (1680).

20. Stubbs, *Constitutional History*, vol. 2, pp. 327-29.

21. T.F. Tout, *The Place of the Reign of Edward II in English History* (1914), pp. 9, 11, 12.

22. James Conway Davies, *The Baronial Opposition to Edward II: Its Character and Policy* (1918), pp. 76, 80.

23. *Thomas Frederick Tout (1855–1929): Refashioning History for the Twentieth Century*, ed. Caroline M. Barron and Joel T. Rosenthal (2019).

24. Hilda Johnstone, *Edward of Carnarvon 1284–1307* (1946); *Letters of Edward Prince of Wales 1304–1305*, ed. Hilda Johnstone (1931).

25. John Harvey, *The Plantagenets* (1948), p. 132.

26. Churchill, *History of the English-Speaking Peoples*, vol. 1, p. 228.

27. May McKisack, *The Fourteenth Century, 1307–1399* (1959), pp. 95-96.

28. *Vita Edwardi Secundi*, ed. N. Denholm-Young (1957), p. ix.

29. J.R. Maddicott, *Thomas of Lancaster, 1307–1322: A Study in the Reign of Edward II* (1970); J.R.S. Phillips, *Aymer de Valence, Earl of Pembroke, 1307–1324: Baronial Politics in the Reign of Edward II* (1972).

30. Harold F. Hutchison, *Edward II: The Pliant King* (1971), pp. 12, 151.
31. Chalfant Robinson, 'Was King Edward the Second a Degenerate?', *American Journal of Insanity* 66 (1910), 445-64.
32. Maddicott, *Thomas of Lancaster*, p. 83.
33. Hutchison, *Edward II*, p. 147.
34. Caroline Bingham, *The Life and Times of Edward II* (1973).
35. Prestwich, *Three Edwards*, p. 72.
36. Natalie Fryde, *The Tyranny and Fall of Edward II, 1321–1326* (1979).
37. Phillips, *Edward II*, p. 531.
38. Nigel Saul, 'The Despensers and the Downfall of Edward II', *English Historical Review* 94 (1984), p. 32.
39. Mary Saaler, *Edward II, 1307–1327* (1997), pp. 146, 147.
40. John Boswell, *Christianity, Social Tolerance, and Homosexuality* (1980), pp. 298-300.
41. Schama, *History of Britain*, p. 213.
42. Michael Prestwich, *Plantagenet England, 1225–1360* (2005), pp. 178, 180.
43. Roy Martin Haines, *The Church and Politics in Fourteenth-Century England: The Career of Adam Orleton, c.1275–1345* (1978); Mark Buck, *Politics, Finance and the Church in the Reign of Edward II: Walter Stapeldon, Treasurer of England* (1983); Roy Martin Haines, *Archbishop John Stratford: Political Revolutionary and Champion of the Liberties of the English Church, ca.1275/80–1348* (1986).
44. J.S. Hamilton, *Piers Gaveston, Earl of Cornwall, 1307–1312: Politics and Patronage in the Reign of Edward II* (Detroit, 1988), p. 109; Pierre Chaplais, *Piers Gaveston: Edward II's Adopted Brother* (1994).
45. Roy Martin Haines, *King Edward II: His Life, His Reign, and Its Aftermath, 1284–1330* (2003), pp. 332, 337.
46. Paul Doherty, *Isabella and the Strange Death of Edward II* (2003); Ian Mortimer, *The Greatest Traitor: The Life of Sir Roger Mortimer, Ruler of England 1327–1330* (2003).
47. G.P. Cuttino and Thomas W. Lyman, 'Where is Edward II?', *Speculum* 53 (1978), 522-43, is an intriguing study in which the title question is left unanswered.
48. Andy King, 'The Death of Edward II Revisited', in *Fourteenth Century England IX*, ed. James Bothwell and Gwilym Dodd (2016), pp. 1-21; J.S. Hamilton, 'The Uncertain Death of Edward II?', *History Compass* 6/5 (2008), 1264–78; Phillips, *Edward II*, pp. 539-99.
49. W.M. Ormrod, 'The Sexualities of Edward II', in *Reign of Edward II*, ed. Dodd and Musson, pp. 22, 46.

50. Phillips, *Edward II*, pp. 4, 124, 308, 394, 448, 452, 607, 612.
51. Given-Wilson, *Edward II*, pp. xi, 104, 105, 109.
52. Kathryn Warner, *Edward II: The Unconventional King* (2014), pp. 261-62; Stephen Spinks, *Edward II: The Man. A Doomed Inheritance* (2017).
53. Heyam, *Reputation of Edward II*, p. 278.
54. Michael G. Cornelius, *Edward II and a Literature of Same-Sex Love: The Gay King in Fiction, 1590–1640* (2016), pp. 261, 262, 263, 268.
55. Cornelius, *Edward II*, p. 106.
56. Cornelius, *Edward II*, p. 29.
57. Michael Jecks, *No Law in the Land* (2009), p. 35; Michael Jecks, *Prophecy of Death* (2008), pp. 225, 227.
58. The quotes which follow are from *The Peacock's Cry* (2016 e-book); *Dark Serpent* (2016), p. 23; *The Poison Maiden* (2007), p. 118; and *Devil's Wolf* (2017), pp. 17, 91-92.

Chapter 4: Richard II

1. Gwilym Dodd, 'Richard II and the Fiction of Majority Rule', in *The Royal Minorities of Medieval and Early Modern* England, ed. Charles Beem (2008), pp. 103-59.
2. Miri Rubin, *The Hollow Crown: A History of the Britain in the Late Middle Ages* (2005), p. 121.
3. *Knighton's Chronicle, 1337–1396,* ed. and trans. G.H. Martin (1995), p. 355.
4. *The Wilton Diptych*, ed. Dillian Gordon (2015).
5. *Chronicles of the Revolution, 1397–1400*, ed. and trans. Chris Given-Wilson (1993), p. 71.
6. *The Parliament Rolls of Medieval England*, 16 vols. (2005), VII, p. 314.
7. A.K. McHardy, 'Haxey's Case, 1397: The Petition and Its Presenter Reconsidered', in *The Age of Richard II*, ed. James L. Gillespie (1997), pp. 93-114.
8. On the sources for Richard's reign: *Chronicles of the Revolution*, pp. 3-12; Gransden, *Historical Writing II*, pp. 118-93; John Taylor, 'Richard II in the Chronicles', in *Richard II: The Art of Kingship*, ed. Anthony Goodman and James L. Gillespie (1999), pp. 15-35.
9. *The Chronica Maiora of Thomas Walsingham (1376–1422)*, trans. David Preest (2005); James G. Clark, *A Monastic Renaissance at St Albans: Thomas Walsingham and his Circle, c.1350–1440* (2004).

10. *Chronicles of the Revolution*, p. 241.
11. *Chronicles of the Revolution*, pp. 191, 234.
12. Simon Walker, 'Richard II's Reputation', in *The Reign of Richard II*, ed. Gwilym Dodd (2000), pp. 119-28.
13. *Parliament Rolls of Medieval England*, XIII, p. 14.
14. Margaret Aston, 'Richard II and the Wars of the Roses', in *The Reign of Richard II: Essays in Honour of May McKisack*, ed. F.R.H. du Boulay and Caroline Barron (1971), pp. 289, 316.
15. Henry Hallam, *View of the State of Europe during the Middle Ages* (1871), p. 384; Henri Wallon, *Richard II*, 2 vols. (1864).
16. Stubbs, *Constitutional History*, vol. 2, pp. 514, 533-35.
17. Tout, *Chapters*, IV, pp. 31-32.
18. A.R. Myers, *England in the Late Middle Ages* (1952), p. 35.
19. George B. Stow, 'Richard II and the Invention of the Pocket Handkerchief', *Albion* 27 (1995), 221-35.
20. B. Wilkinson, *The Later Middle Ages in England, 1216–1485* (1965), p. 157.
21. C. Warren Hollister, *The Making of England, 55 BC-1399* (6th edition: 1992), p. 227.
22. Richard Barber, *The Black Prince* (1978), p. 238.
23. Anthony Steel, *Richard II* (1941), pp. 174-75, 216; V.H. Galbraith, 'A New Life of Richard II', *History* 26 (1942), p. 226.
24. Churchill, *History of the English-Speaking Peoples*, vol. 1, p. 285.
25. Harvey, *Plantagenets*, p. 161.
26. McKisack, *Fourteenth Century*, pp. 496-98.
27. Harold F. Hutchison, *The Hollow Crown: A Life of Richard II* (1961), p. 239.
28. Caroline M. Barron, 'The Tyranny of Richard II', *Bulletin of the Institute of Historical Research* 61 (1968), p. 18.
29. *Reign of Richard II*, ed. du Boulay and Barron.
30. Richard H. Jones, *The Royal Policy of Richard II: Absolutism in the Later Middle Ages* (1968), pp. 6, 88.
31. Gervase Mathew, *The Court of Richard II* (1968), pp. 151, 164.
32. Anthony Tuck, *Richard II and the English Nobility* (1973), p. 225.
33. Anthony Goodman, *The Loyal Conspiracy: The Lords Appellant under Richard II* (1971), pp. 71, 176.
34. Chris Given-Wilson, *The Royal Household and the King's Affinity: Service, Politics and Finance in England, 1360–1413* (1986).
35. *Chronicles of the Revolution*; *The Reign of Richard II*, ed. and trans. A.K. McHardy (2012); *The Peasants' Revolt of 1381*, ed. R.B. Dobson (2nd edition: 1983).

36. Nigel Saul, *Richard II* (New Haven, CT, 1997), pp. 202, 391, 434, 440, 441, 442, 459, 460, 467.

37. A.K. McHardy, 'Richard II: A Personal Portrait', in *Reign of Richard II*, ed. Dodd, pp. 16, 24, 30, 31.

38. James L. Gillespie, 'Richard II: King of Battles?', in *Age of Richard II*, ed. Gillespie, pp. 139, 160.

39. Chris Given-Wilson, 'Richard II and the Higher Nobility', in *Richard II*, ed. Goodman and Gillespie, p. 128.

40. Gwilym Dodd, 'Richard II and the Transformation of Parliament', in *Reign of Richard II*, ed. Dodd, p. 84.

41. Caroline M. Barron, 'The Deposition of Richard II', in *Politics and Crisis in Fourteenth-Century England*, ed. John Taylor and Wendy Childs (1990), pp. 132-49.

42. Gerald L. Harriss, *Shaping the Nation: England 1360–1461* (2005), p. 489.

43. Christopher Fletcher, *Richard II: Manhood, Youth, and Politics, 1377–99* (2008), pp. 7, 12, 277-78, 280.

44. Jonathan Sumption, *Divided Houses: The Hundred Years War III* (2009), p. 848.

45. Chris Given-Wilson, *Henry IV* (2016), pp. 532-33, 540.

46. Phil Bradford, 'A Silent Presence: The English King in Parliament in the Fourteenth Century', *Historical Research* 84 (2011), p. 210.

47. A.K. Gundy, *Richard II and the Rebel Earl* (2013), p. 240.

48. Gwilym Dodd, 'Tyranny and Affinity: The Public and Private Authority of Richard II and Richard III', in *The Fifteenth Century XVIII: Rulers, Regions and Retinues – Essays Presented to A.J. Pollard*, ed. Linda Clark and Peter W. Fleming (2020), pp. 1-16.

49. *Creativity, Contradictions and Commemoration in the Reign of Richard II: Essays in Honour of Nigel Saul*, ed. Jessica A. Lutkin and J.S. Hamilton (2022).

50. Laura Ashe, *Richard II: A Brittle Glory* (2016), p. 103.

51. Kathryn Warner, *Richard II: A True King's Fall* (2017), pp. 308, 309.

52. Saul, *Richard II*, p. 467.

53. *The Guardian*, 17 December 2021.

Chapter 5: Richard III

1. Michael Hicks, *Edward IV* (2004), p. 200.

2. Charles Ross, *Richard III* (1980), p. 183.

3. Rosemary Horrox, *Richard III: A Failed King?* (2020), p. 48.

4. Louise Gill, *Richard III and Buckingham's Rebellion* (1999).

5. Matthew Morris and Richard Buckley, *Richard III: The King under the Car Park* (2013), p. 7. See also Philippa Langley and Michael Jones, *The King's Grave: The Search for Richard III* (2013); *Finding Richard III: The Official Account*, ed. A.J. Carson (2014); and Michael Pitts, *Digging for Richard III: How Archaeology found the King* (revised edition: 2015).

6. For a dissenting view, see Michael Hicks, *The Family of Richard III* (2015), pp. 180-97.

7. On the sources and historiography: A.R. Myers, 'Richard III and Historical Tradition', *History* 53 (1968), 181-202; Alison Hanham, *Richard III and His Early Historians, 1483–1535* (1975); Ross, *Richard III*, pp. xxxiii-lxvii; Michael Hicks, *Richard III: The Self-Made King* (2019), pp.3-24. For extracts from the sources, a good start is the three volumes by Keith Dockray: *Henry VI, Margaret of Anjou and the Wars of the Roses: A Source Book* (2000); *Edward IV: A Source Book* (1999); and *Richard III: A Source Book* ().

8. Domenico Mancini, *De Occupatione Regni Anglie*, trans. Annette Carson (2021).

9. *The Crowland Chronicle Continuations: 1459–1486*, ed. Nicholas Pronay and John Cox (1986), pp. 163, 171.

10. Ross, *Richard III*, p. lxi.

11. Cited in Ross, *Richard III*, p. xxxvi.

12. Cited in Hanham, *Richard III*, p. 123.

13. *Parliament Rolls of Medieval England*, XV, pp. 13-18, 97–102.

14. Hanham, *Richard III*, p. 189.

15. Ross, *Richard III*, p. lxii.

16. *The History of King Richard III by Sir George Buck, Master of the Revels*, ed. Arthur Noel Kincaid (1979).

17. William Hutton, *The Battle of Bosworth Field* (1788), pp. lxiv-lxv, lxxxiii-lxxxiv.

18. Sharon Turner, *The History of England during the Middle Ages* (2nd edition: 1825), vol. 3, pp. 371, 455.

19. Caroline Halsted, *Richard III as Duke of Gloucester and King of England*, 2 vols, (1844), vol. 2, p. 506.

20. James Gairdner, *History of the Life and Reign of Richard the Third* (2nd edition: 1898), pp. xi, 36, 246.

21. Clements R. Markham, 'Richard III: A Doubtful Verdict Reviewed', *English Historical Review* 6 (1891), 250-83; Clements R. Markham, *Richard III: His Life and Character* (1906).

22. Myers, 'Richard III', p. 200.
23. Charles Oman, *A History of England* (1895), pp. 259, 268, 271.
24. Stubbs, *Constitutional History*, vol. 3, pp. 231-32.
25. H.G. Hanbury, 'The Legislation of Richard III', *American Journal of Legal History* 6 (1962), p. 113.
26. Ross, *Richard III*, p. 21.
27. E.F. Jacob, *The Fifteenth Century, 1399–1485* (1961), p. 645.
28. J.R. Lander, *Government and Community: England 1450–1509* (1980), p. 330.
29. Charles Ross, *Edward IV* (1974), p. 426.
30. Ross, *Richard III*, pp. 79-80, 104, 128, 147, 175, 228, 229.
31. Rosemary Horrox, *Richard III: A Study of Service* (1989), pp. 327, 333; Horrox, *Richard III: Failed King?*, pp. 89, 94.
32. A.J. Pollard, *Richard III and the Princes in the Tower* (1991).
33. A.J. Pollard, *The Worlds of Richard III* (Stroud, 2001), p. 8.
34. Michael Hicks, 'Richard III as Duke of Gloucester: A Study in Character', in Michael Hicks, *Richard III and His Rivals: Magnates and Their Motives in the Wars of the Roses* (1991), p. 279.
35. Hicks, *Richard III: Self-Made King*, pp. 246, 260, 391-92.
36. *Richard III: A Medieval Kingship*, ed. John Gillingham (1993).
37. David Hipshon, *Richard III* (2011), p. 242.
38. Jasper Fforde, *The Eyre Affair* (2001), pp. 180, 182-83.
39. Kate Sedley, *The Midsummer Rose* (2004), p. 211.

Bibliography

Printed Primary Sources

The Anglo-Saxon Chronicles, ed. and trans. Michael Swanton (Phoenix Press, London, 1996).

The Chronica Maiora of Thomas Walsingham (1376-1422), trans. David Preest (Boydell Press, Woodbridge, 2005).

Chronica Monasterii de Melsa, ed. Edward A. Bond, 3 vols. (Rolls Series: London, 1866-68).

The Chronicle of Geoffrey le Baker, trans. David Preest (Boydell Press, Woodbridge, 2012).

The Chronicle of John of Worcester Volume III, ed. and trans. P. McGurk (Oxford University Press, Oxford, 1998).

Chronicles of the Revolution, 1397-1400, ed. and trans. Chris Given-Wilson (Manchester University Press, Manchester, 1993).

Keith Dockray, *Edward IV: A Source Book* (Sutton Publishing, Stroud, 1999).

Keith Dockray, *Henry VI, Margaret of Anjou and the Wars of the Roses: A Source Book* (Sutton Publishing, Stroud, 2000).

Keith Dockray, *Richard III: A Source Book* (Sutton Publishing, Stroud, 1997).

Early Common Petitions in the English Parliament, c. 1290-c. 1420, ed. W. Mark Ormrod, Helen Killick and Phil Bradford (Cambridge University Press for the Royal Historical Society, Cambridge, 2017).

Gesta Stephani, ed. and trans. K.R. Potter and R.H.C. Davis (Oxford University Press, Oxford, 1976).

Henry of Huntingdon, *The History of the English People 1000-1154*, ed. and trans. Diana Greenway (Oxford University Press, Oxford, 1996).

Knighton's Chronicle, 1337-1396, ed. and trans. G.H. Martin (Oxford University Press, Oxford, 1995).

Domenico Mancini, *De Occupatione Regni Anglie*, trans. Annette Carson (Imprimis Imprimatur, Horstead, 2021).

Matthaei Parisiensis, Monachi Sancti Albani, Chronica Majora, ed. Henry Richards Luard, 7 vols. (Rolls Series: London, 1872-83).

Memoriale Fratris Walteri de Coventria, ed. William Stubbs, 2 vols. (Rolls Series: London, 1872-73).

The Crowland Chronicle Continuations: 1459-1486, ed. Nicholas Pronay and John Cox (Alan Sutton for Richard III and Yorkist History Trust, London, 1986).

The Parliament Rolls of Medieval England, ed. Chris Given-Wilson *et al.* (Boydell Press, Woodbridge, 2005).

The Peasants' Revolt of 1381, ed. R.B. Dobson (2nd edition: Macmillan, Basingstoke, 1983).

Polychronicon Ranulphi Higden Monachi Cestrensis, 9 vols. (Rolls Series: London, 1879).

The Register of Thomas de Cobham, Bishop of Worcester 1317-27, ed. Ernest Harold Pearce (Worcestershire Historical Society, London, 1930).

The Reign of Richard II, ed. and trans. A.K. McHardy (Manchester University Press, Manchester, 2012).

Vita Edwardi Secundi, ed. and trans. Wendy R. Childs (Oxford University Press, Oxford, 2005).

William of Malmesbury, *Historia Novella: The Contemporary History*, ed. Edmund King and trans. K.R. Potter (Oxford University Press, Oxford, 1998).

Secondary Sources

Amt, Emilie, *The Accession of Henry II in England: Royal Government Restored 1149-1159* (Boydell Press, Woodbridge, 1993).

Appleby, John T., *John, King of England* (Alfred A. Knopf, New York, 1959).

Appleby, John T., *The Troubled Reign of King Stephen* (G. Bell and Sons, London, 1969).

Ashe, Laura, *Richard II: A Brittle Glory* (Allen Lane, London, 2016).

Ashley, Maurice, *The Life and Times of King John* (Weidenfeld and Nicolson, London, 1972).

Aston, Margaret, 'Richard II and the Wars of the Roses', in *The Reign of Richard II: Essays in Honour of May McKisack*, ed. F.R.H. du Boulay and Caroline Barron (Athlone Press, London, 1971), pp. 280-317.

Barber, Richard, *The Black Prince* (Penguin, Harmondsworth, 1978).

Barlow, Jill *et al*, *Edward II: His Last Months and Monument* (Bristol and Gloucestershire Archaeological Society, Bristol, 2015).

Barratt, Nick, 'The Revenue of King John', *English Historical Review* 111 (1996), 835-55.

Barron, Caroline M., 'The Deposition of Richard II', in *Politics and Crisis in Fourteenth-Century England*, ed. John Taylor and Wendy Childs (Alan Sutton, Gloucester, 1990), pp. 132-49.

Barron, Caroline M., 'The Tyranny of Richard II', *Bulletin of the Institute of Historical Research* 61 (1968), 1-18.

Barron, Caroline M. and Rosenthal, Joel T. (eds.), *Thomas Frederick Tout (1855-1929): Refashioning History for the Twentieth Century* (University of London Press, London, 2019).

Bingham, Caroline, *The Life and Times of Edward II* (Weidenfeld and Nicolson, London, 1973).

Boswell, John, *Christianity, Social Tolerance, and Homosexuality* (University of Chicago Press, Chicago, 1980).

Bradbury, Jim, 'Philip Augustus and King John: Personality and History', in *King John: New Interpretations*, ed. Church, pp. 347-61.

Bradbury, Jim, *Stephen and Matilda: The Civil War of 1139-53* (Sutton Publishing, Stroud, 1996).

Bradford, Phil, 'A Silent Presence: The English King in Parliament in the Fourteenth Century', *Historical Research* 84 (2011), 189-211.

Breay, Claire and Harrison, Julian (eds.), *Magna Carta: Law, Liberty, Legacy* (British Library, London, 2015).

Buck, George, *The History of King Richard III by Sir George Buck, Master of the Revels*, ed. Arthur Noel Kincaid (Alan Sutton, Gloucester, 1979).

Buck, Mark, *Politics, Finance and the Church in the Reign of Edward II: Walter Stapeldon, Treasurer of England* (Cambridge University Press, Cambridge, 1983).

Carpenter, Christine, *The Wars of the Roses: Politics and the Constitution in England, c.1437-1509* (Cambridge University Press, Cambridge, 1997).

Carpenter, David, *Magna Carta* (Penguin, London, 2015).

Carpenter, David, *The Struggle for Mastery: The Penguin History of Britain 1066-1284* (Penguin, London, 2003).

Carson, A.J. (ed.), *Finding Richard III: The Official Account* (Imprimis Imprimatur, Horstead, 2014)

Elizabeth Cary, *The History of the Life, Reign, and Death of Edward II, King of England, and Lord of Ireland with the Rise and Fall of his Great Favourites, Gaveston and the Spencers* (London, 1680; originally published under the name of Henry Cary, Viscount Falkland).

Chaplais, Pierre, *Piers Gaveston: Edward II's Adopted Brother* (Oxford University Press, Oxford, 1994).

Chibnall, Marjorie, *The Empress Matilda: Queen Consort, Queen Mother and Lady of the English* (Blackwell, Oxford, 1991).

Church, S.D., *The Household Knights of King John* (Cambridge University Press, Cambridge, 1999).

Church, Stephen, *King John: England, Magna Carta and the Making of a Tyrant* (Macmillan, London, 2015).

Church, S.D. (ed.), *King John: New Interpretations* (Boydell Press, Woodbridge, 1999).

Churchill, Winston S., *History of the English-Speaking Peoples*, 4 vols. (Cassell, London, 1956-58).

Clark, James G., *A Monastic Renaissance at St Albans: Thomas Walsingham and his Circle, c.1350-1440* (Oxford University Press, Oxford, 2004).

Cornelius, Michael G., *Edward II and a Literature of Same-Sex Love: The Gay King in Fiction, 1590-1640* (Lanham, Lexington, 2016).

Cronne, H.A., *The Reign of Stephen: Anarchy in England 1135-54* (Weidenfeld and Nicolson, London, 1970).

Crook, David, *Robin Hood: Legend and Reality* (Boydell Press, Woodbridge, 2020).

Crouch, David, *The Reign of King Stephen, 1135-1154* (Longman, Harlow, 2000).

Cuttino, G.P. and Lyman, Thomas W., 'Where is Edward II?', *Speculum* 53 (1978), 522-43.

D'Auvergne, Edmund B., *John, King of England* (Grayson and Grayson, London, 1934).

Dalton, Paul, and White, Graeme J. (eds.), *King Stephen's Reign (1135-1154)* (Boydell Press, Woodbridge, 2008).

Daniel, Samuel, *The Collection of the History of England* (5th edition: London, 1685).

Davies, James Conway, *The Baronial Opposition to Edward II: Its Character and Policy* (Cambridge University Press, Cambridge, 1918).

Davies, R.R., *The First English Empire: Power and Identities in the British Isles, 1093-1343* (Oxford University Press, Oxford, 2000).

Davis, H.W.C., 'The Anarchy of Stephen's Reign', *English Historical Review* 18 (1903), 630-41.

Davis, R.H.C. *King Stephen* (3rd edition: Longman, Harlow, 1990)

Dodd, Gwilym, *Justice and Grace: Private Petitioning and the English Parliament in the Late Middle Ages* (Oxford University Press, Oxford, 2007).

Dodd, Gwilym, 'Richard II and the Fiction of Majority Rule', in *The Royal Minorities of Medieval and Early Modern England*, ed. Charles Beem (Palgrave Macmillan, Basingstoke, 2008).

Dodd, Gwilym, 'Richard II and the Transformation of Parliament', in *Reign of Richard II*, ed. Dodd, pp. 71-84.

Dodd, Gwilym, 'Tyranny and Affinity: The Public and Private Authority of Richard II and Richard III', in *The Fifteenth Century XVIII: Rulers, Regions and Retinues – Essays Presented to A.J. Pollard,* ed. Linda Clark and Peter W. Fleming (Boydell Press, Woodbridge, 2020), pp. 1-16.

Dodd, Gwilym, (ed.), *The Reign of Richard II* (Tempus, Stroud, 2000).

Dodd, Gwilym, and Musson, Anthony (eds.), *The Reign of Edward II: New Perspectives* (York Medieval Press, York, 2006).

Doherty, Paul, *Isabella and the Strange Death of Edward II* (Constable, London, 2003).

Dunababin, Jean, 'Government', in *The Cambridge History of Medieval Political Thought, c. 350-c. 1450*, ed. J.H. Burns (Cambridge University Press, Cambridge, 1989), pp. 477-519.

Fletcher, Christopher, *Richard II: Manhood, Youth, and Politics, 1377-99* (Oxford University Press, Oxford, 2008).

Fryde, Natalie, *The Tyranny and Fall of Edward II, 1321-1326* (Cambridge University Press, Cambridge, 1979).

Gairdner, James, *History of the Life and Reign of Richard the Third* (2nd edition: Cambridge University Press, Cambridge, 1898).

Galbraith, V.H., 'A New Life of Richard II', *History* 26 (1942), 233-39.

Galbraith, V.H., 'Good Kings and Bad Kings in English History', *History* 30 (1945), 119-32.

Gill, Louise, *Richard III and Buckingham's Rebellion* (Sutton Publishing, Stroud, 1999).

Gillespie, James L., 'Richard II: King of Battles?', in *Age of Richard II*, ed. Gillespie, pp. 139-64.

Gillespie, James L. (ed.), *The Age of Richard II* (Sutton Publishing, Stroud, 1997).

Gillingham, John, *Richard the Lionheart* (Weidenfeld and Nicolson, London, 1978).

Gillingham, John, *The Angevin Empire* (2nd edition: Arnold, London, 2001).

Gillingham, John, (ed.), *Richard III: A Medieval Kingship* (Collins and Brown, London, 1993).

Given-Wilson, Chris, *Chronicles: The Writing of History in Medieval England* (Hambledon and London, London, 2004).

Given-Wilson, Christopher, *Edward II: The Terrors of Kingship* (Allen Lane, London, 2016).

Given-Wilson, Chris, *Henry IV* (Yale University Press, New Haven, 2016).

Given-Wilson, Chris, 'Richard II and the Higher Nobility', in *Richard II*, ed. Goodman and Gillespie, pp. 107-28.

Given-Wilson, Chris, *The Royal Household and the King's Affinity: Service, Politics and Finance in England, 1360-1413* (Yale University Press, New Haven and London, 1986).

Given-Wilson, Chris, '*Vita Edwardi Secundi*: Memoir or Journal?' in *Thirteenth Century England VI*, ed. Michael Prestwich, R.H. Britnell and Robin Frame (Boydell Press, Woodbridge, 1997), pp. 165-76.

Goodman, Anthony, *The Loyal Conspiracy: The Lords Appellant under Richard II* (Routledge and Kegan Paul, London, 1971).

Goodman, Anthony and Gillespie, James L. (eds.), *Richard II: The Art of Kingship* (Oxford University Press, Oxford, 1999).

Gordon, Dillian (ed.), *The Wilton Diptych* (National Gallery, London, 2015).

Gransden, Antonia, *Historical Writing in England I: c.550 - c.1307* (Routledge, London, 1974).

Gransden, Antonia, *Historical Writing in England II: c.1307 to the Early Sixteenth Century* (Routledge, London, 1982).

Green, John Richard, *A Short History of the English People* (Macmillan, London, 1882).

Green, Judith A., The Charters of Geoffrey de Mandeville', in *Rulership and Rebellion in the Anglo-Norman World, c.1066-c.1216*, ed. Paul Dalton and David Luscombe (Ashgate, Farnham, 2015), pp. 91-110.

Gundy, A.K., *Richard II and the Rebel Earl* (Cambridge University Press, Cambridge, 2013).

Haines, Roy Martin, *Archbishop John Stratford: Political Revolutionary and Champion of the Liberties of the English Church, ca.1275/80-1348* (Pontifical Institute of Mediaeval Studies, Toronto, 1986).

Haines, Roy Martin, *King Edward II: His Life, His Reign, and Its Aftermath, 1284-1330* (McGill-Queen's University Press, Montreal, 2003).

Haines, Roy Martin, *The Church and Politics in Fourteenth-Century England: The Career of Adam Orleton, c.1275-1345* (Cambridge University Press, Cambridge, 1978).

Hallam, Henry, *View of the State of Europe during the Middle Ages* (Revised edition: John Murray, London, 1871).

Halsted, Caroline, *Richard III as Duke of Gloucester and King of England*, 2 vols, (Longman, Brown, Green, and Longmans, London, 1844).

Hammer, Paul E.J., '"Absolute and Sovereign Mistress of her Grace?" Queen Elizabeth I and her Favourites, 1581-1592', in *The World of the Favourite*, ed. J.H. Elliott and L.W.B. Brockliss (Yale University Press, New Haven and London, 1999), pp. 38-53.

Hamilton, J.S., *Piers Gaveston, Earl of Cornwall, 1307-1312: Politics and Patronage in the Reign of Edward II* (Wayne State University Press, Detroit, 1988).

Hamilton, J.S., 'The Uncertain Death of Edward II?', *History Compass* 6/5 (2008), 1264-78.

Hanbury, H.G., 'The Legislation of Richard III', *American Journal of Legal History* 6 (1962), 95-113.

Hanham, Alison, *Richard III and His Early Historians, 1483-1535* (Oxford University Press, Oxford, 1975).

Hanley, Catherine, *Matilda: Empress. Queen. Warrior* (Yale University Press, New Haven and London, 2019).

Harriss, Gerald L., *Shaping the Nation: England 1360-1461* (Oxford University Press, Oxford, 2005).

Harvey, John, *The Plantagenets* (Batsford, London, 1948).

Heyam, Kit, *The Reputation of Edward II, 1305-1697: A Literary Transformation of History* (Amsterdam University Press, Amsterdam, 2020).

Hicks, Michael, *Edward IV* (Arnold, London, 2004).

Hicks, Michael, 'Richard III as Duke of Gloucester: A Study in Character', in Michael Hicks, *Richard III and His Rivals: Magnates and Their Motives in the Wars of the Roses* (Hambledon Press, London, 1991), pp. 247-79.

Hicks, Michael, *Richard III: The Self-Made King* (Yale University Press, New Haven and London, 2019).

Hicks, Michael, *The Family of Richard III* (Amberley, Stroud, 2015).

Hipshon, David, *Richard III* (Routledge, Abingdon, 2011).

Hollister, C. Warren, 'King John and the Historians', *Journal of British Studies* 1 (1961), 1-19.

Hollister, C. Warren, 'Stephen's Anarchy', *Albion* 6 (1974).

Hollister, C. Warren, *The Making of England, 55 BC-1399* (6th edition; D.C. Heath, Lexington, 1992).

Holt, J.C., *King John* (Historical Association, London, 1963).

Holt, J.C., *Magna Carta* (3rd edition: Cambridge University Press, Cambridge, 2015).

Holt, J.C., *Robin Hood* (Thames and Hudson, London, 1989).

Holt, J.C., *The Northerners: A Study in the Reign of King John* (Clarendon Press, Oxford, 1961).

Horrox, Rosemary, *Richard III: A Failed King?* (Allen Lane, London, 2020).

Horrox, Rosemary, *Richard III: A Study of Service* (Cambridge University Press, Cambridge, 1989).

Hume, David, '*The History of England from Julius Caesar to the Revolution in 1688*, 6 vols. (Harper and Bros., New York, 1879 edition).

Hutchison, Harold F., *Edward II: The Pliant King* (Eyre and Spottiswoode, London, 1971).

Hutchison, Harold F., *The Hollow Crown: A Life of Richard II* (Eyre and Spottiswoode, London, 1961).

Hutton, William, *The Battle of Bosworth Field* (Pearson and Rollason, London, 1788).

Jacob, E.F., *The Fifteenth Century, 1399-1485* (Clarendon Press, Oxford, 1961).

Johnstone, Hilda, *Edward of Carnarvon 1284-1307* (Manchester University Press, Manchester, 1946).

Jones, J.A.P., *King John and Magna Carta* (Longman, London, 1971).

Jones, Richard H., *The Royal Policy of Richard II: Absolutism in the Later Middle Ages* (Basil Blackwell, Oxford, 1968).

King, Andy, 'The Death of Edward II Revisited', in *Fourteenth Century England IX*, ed. James Bothwell and Gwilym Dodd (Boydell Press, Woodbridge,2016), pp. 1-21.

King, Edmund, *King Stephen* (Yale University Press, New Haven and London, 2010).

King, Edmund (ed.), *The Anarchy of King Stephen's Reign* (Oxford University Press, Oxford, 1994).

Kynan-Wilson, William, and Munns, John (eds.), *Henry of Blois: New Interpretations* (Boydell Press, Woodbridge, 2021).

Lachaud, Frédérique, *Jean sans Terre* (Perrin, Paris, 2018).

Lane, Samuel, 'The Deposition of Edward II: The Kenilworth Embassies', in *Fourteenth Century England XII*, ed. James Bothwell and J.S. Hamilton (Boydell Press, Woodbridge, 2022), pp. 65-77.

Lander, J.R., *Government and Community: England 1450-1509* (Harvard University Press, Cambridge [MA], 1980)

Langley, Philippa and Jones, Michael, *The King's Grave: The Search for Richard III* (John Murray, London, 2013).

Levin, Carole, 'King John and Early Tudor Propaganda', *The Sixteenth Century Journal* 11 (1980), 23-32.

Lewis, Matthew, *Stephen and Matilda: Cousins of Anarchy* (Pen and Sword, Barnsley, 2019).

Lloyd, Alan, *King John* (David and Charles, London, 1973).

Roger Lockyer, *Buckingham: The Life and Political Career of George Villiers, First Duke of Buckingham, 1592-1628* (1981).

Lutkin, Jessica A., and Hamilton, J.S. (eds.), *Creativity, Contradictions and Commemoration in the Reign of Richard II: Essays in Honour of Nigel Saul* (Boydell Press, Woodbridge, 2022).

McHardy, A.K., 'Haxey's Case, 1397: The Petition and Its Presenter Reconsidered', in *Age of Richard II*, ed. Gillespie, pp. 93-114.

McHardy, A.K., 'Richard II: A Personal Portrait', in *Reign of Richard II*, ed. Dodd, pp. 11-32.

McKisack, May, *The Fourteenth Century, 1307-1399* (Clarendon Press, Oxford, 1959).

McLynn, Frank, *Lionheart and Lackland: King Richard, King John and the Wars of Conquest* (Vintage, London, 2006).

Maddicott, J.R., *The Origins of the English Parliament, 924-1327* (Oxford University Press, Oxford, 2010).

Maddicott, J.R., *Thomas of Lancaster, 1307-1322: A Study in the Reign of Edward II* (Oxford University Press, Oxford, 1970).

Markham, Clements R., 'Richard III: A Doubtful Verdict Reviewed', *English Historical Review* 6 (1891), 250-83.

Markham, Clements R., *Richard III: His Life and Character* (Smith Elder, London, 1906).

Mathew, Gervase, *The Court of Richard II* (John Murray, London, 1968).

Matthew, Donald, *King Stephen* (Hambledon and London, London, 2002).

Montefiore, Simon Sebag, *Monsters: History's Most Evil Men and Women* (Quercus, London, 2008).

Morris, Marc, *King John: Treachery, Tyranny and the Road to Magna Carta* (Hutchinson, London, 2015).

Morris, Matthew, and Buckley, Richard, *Richard III: The King under the Car Park* (University of Leicester Archaeological Services, Leicester, 2013).

Mortimer, Ian, 'Sermons of Sodomy: A Reconsideration of Edward II's Sodomitical Reputation', in *Reign of Edward II*, ed. Dodd and Musson, pp. 48-60.

Mortimer, Ian, *The Greatest Traitor: The Life of Sir Roger Mortimer, Ruler of England 1327-1330* (Jonathan Cape, London, 2003).

Myers, A.R., *England in the Late Middle Ages* (Penguin, Harmondsworth, 1952).

Myers, A.R., 'Richard III and Historical Tradition', *History* 53 (1968), 181-202.

Norgate, Kate, *John Lackland* (Macmillan, London, 1902).

Oman, Charles, *A History of England* (Edward Arnold, London, 1895).

Oram, Richard, *David I: The King who Made Scotland* (Tempus, Stroud, 2004).

Ormrod, W. Mark, *Edward III* (Yale University Press, New Haven and London, 2011).

Ormrod, W.M., 'The Sexualities of Edward II', in *Reign of Edward II*, ed. Dodd and Musson, pp. 22-47.

Painter, Sidney, *The Reign of King John* (John Hopkins Press, Baltimore, 1949).

Petit-Dutaillis, Charles, *The Feudal Monarchy in France and England* (Routledge, Trench, Trubner, London, 1936).

Phillips, J.R.S., *Aymer de Valence, Earl of Pembroke, 1307-1324: Baronial Politics in the Reign of Edward II* (Oxford University Press, Oxford, 1972).

Phillips, Seymour, *Edward II* (Yale University Press, New Haven and London, 2010).

Pitts, Michael, *Digging for Richard III: How Archaeology found the King* (revised edition: Thames and Hudson, London, 2015).

Poole, A.L., *Domesday Book to Magna Carta 1087-1216* (2nd edition: Clarendon Press, Oxford, 1954).

Pollard, A.J., *Imagining Robin Hood* (Routledge, Abingdon, 2004).

Pollard, A.J., *Richard III and the Princes in the Tower* (Bramley Books, Godalming, 1991).

Pollard, A.J., *The Worlds of Richard III* (Tempus, Stroud, 2001).

Prestwich, Michael, *Plantagenet England, 1225-1360* (Oxford University Press, Oxford, 2005).

Prestwich, Michael, *The Three Edwards: War and State in England, 1272-1377* (2nd edition: Routledge, Abingdon, 2003).

Ramsay, James Henry, *The Angevin Empire* (Swan Sonneschein, London, 1903).

Rapin, Paul de, *History of England*, trans. Nicholas Tindal, 13 vols. (London, 1727).

Richardson, H.G., 'The Coronation in Medieval England: The Origin of the Office and the Oath', *Traditio* 16 (1960), 111-202.

Robinson, Chalfant, 'Was King Edward the Second a Degenerate?', *American Journal of Insanity* 66 (1910), 445-64.

Ross, Charles, *Edward IV* (Yale edition: Yale University Press, New Haven and London, 1997).

Ross, Charles, *Richard III* (Yale edition: Yale University Press, New Haven and London, 1999).

Round, J.H., *Geoffrey de Mandeville: A Study of the Anarchy* (Longmans, Green, London, 1892).

Rubin, Miri, *The Hollow Crown: A History of the Britain in the Late Middle Ages* (Penguin, London, 2005).

Saaler, Mary, *Edward II, 1307-1327* (Rubicon Press, London, 1997).

Saul, Nigel, *Richard II* (Yale University Press, New Haven and London, 1997).

Saul, Nigel, 'The Despensers and the Downfall of Edward II', *English Historical Review* 94 (1984), 1-33.

Schama, Simon, *A History of Britain, 3000 BC – AD 1603* (BBC Books, London, 2000).

Seel, Graham E., *King John: An Underrated King* (Anthem Press, London, 2012).

Seldon, Anthony, *Blair* (2nd edition: Free Press, London, 2005).

Speed, John, *Historie of Great Britaine* (3rd edition: London, 1632).

Spinks, Stephen, *Edward II: The Man. A Doomed Inheritance* (Amberley, Stroud, 2017).

Steel, Anthony, *Richard II* (Cambridge University Press, Cambridge, 1941).

Stenton, Doris Mary, *English Society in the Early Middle Ages (1066-1307)* (2nd edition: Penguin, Harmondsworth, 1959).

Stow, George B., 'Richard II and the Invention of the Pocket Handkerchief', *Albion* 27 (1995), 221-35.

Stringer, Keith J., *The Reign of Stephen: Kingship, Warfare and Government in Twelfth-Century England* (Routledge, London, 1993).

Strong, Roy, *Coronation* (HarperCollins, London, 2005).

Stubbs, William, *Historical Introduction to the Rolls Series* (Longmans, Green, London, 1902).

Stubbs, William, *The Constitutional History of England in its Origin and Development*, 3 vols. (Clarendon Press, Oxford, 1874-78).

Sumption, Jonathan, *Divided Houses: The Hundred Years War III* (Faber and Faber, 2009).

Taylor, John, 'Richard II in the Chronicles', in *Richard II*, ed. Goodman and Gillespie, pp. 15-35.

Tout, T.F., *The Place of the Reign of Edward II in English History* (Manchester University Press, Manchester, 1914).

Tuck, Anthony, *Richard II and the English Nobility* (Edward Arnold, London, 1973).

Turner, Ralph V., *King John* (Longman, London, 1994).

Turner, Sharon, *The History of England during the Middle Ages*, 3 vols. (2nd edition: Longman, Brown, Green and Longmans, London, 1825).

Tyrrell, James, *The General History of England*, 5 vols. (London, 1700-4).

Valente, Claire, 'The Deposition and Abdication of Edward II', *English Historical Review* 113 (1998), 852-81.

Valente, Claire, *The Theory and Practice of Revolt in Medieval England* (Ashgate, Aldershot, 2003).

Vincent, Nicholas, 'Isabella of Angoulême: John's Jezebel', in *King John: New Interpretations*, ed. Church, pp. 165-219.

Vincent, Nicholas, *John: An Evil King?* (Allen Lane, Penguin, 2020).

Walker, Simon, 'Richard II's Reputation', in *Reign of Richard II*, ed. Dodd, pp. 119-28.

Wallon, Henri, *Richard II*, 2 vols. (L. Hachette, Paris, 1864).

Warner, Kathryn, *Edward II: The Unconventional King* (Amberley, Stroud, 2014).

Warner, Kathryn, *Richard II: A True King's Fall* (Amberley, Stroud, 2017).

Warren, W.L., *Henry II* (Yale edition: Yale University Press, New Haven and London, 2000).

Warren, W.L., *King John* (Yale edition: Yale University Press, New Haven and London, 1997)

Watkins, Carl, *Stephen: The Reign of Anarchy* (Allen Lane, London, 2015).

Webster, Paul, *King John and Religion* (Boydell Press, Woodbridge, 2015).

Weiler, Björn, 'Kingship, Usurpation and Propaganda in Twelfth-Century Europe: The Case of Stephen', *Anglo-Norman Studies* 23 (2001), 299-326.

White, Graeme J., *Restoration and Reform 1153-1165: Recovery from Civil War in England* (Cambridge University Press, Cambridge, 2000).

Wilkinson, B., *The Later Middle Ages in England, 1216-1485* (Longman, London, 1965).

Index

Warren, W.L. (Lewis) (historian) 57
Wars of the Roses (1455-87) 129-30, 147, 162, 174, 180, 181
Warwick 73, 149
Warwick, earl of *see* Beauchamp; Neville; Edward (earl of Warwick)
Warenne, John de (earl of Surrey) 73, 76, 77, 79
Washington, George (US president) vii
Waterford 119, 124
Watkin, Carl (historian) 23
Weiler, Björn (historian) 21
Wendover, Roger of (chronicler) 45, 50
West, Sam (actor) 140
West End (London) 141
Westminster, abbey xiv, 38, 85, 109, 111, 112, 117, 127, 142, 155, 156, 161, 167
Westminster, abbey, dean of 127
Westminster, abbey portrait of Richard II 117
Westminster, Archbishop of 146
Westminster, parliament at 71-72, 75, 79, 84, 113, 114, 116, 121, 125
Westminster Chronicle xix
Westmorland, earl of 155
When Christ and His Saints Slept (novel) 28-29
White Boar, Fellowship of the *see* Richard III Society
White Princess, The (novel) 178
White Queen, The (novel) 178
White Ship Disaster (1120) 2
Whitty, Chris (UK chief medical officer) 142-43
Wight, Isle of 4
Wilkinson, Bertie (historian) 132
William I (the Conqueror) (king of England) viii, xiv, 2, 3, 34

William I (the Lion) (king of Scotland) 38, 42, 43
William I (the Bad) (king of Sicily) 34
William II (Rufus) (king of England) xx, 3, 4
William (son of Henry I) 2
William (earl of Salisbury) 46, 48
William Clito (nephew of Henry I) 2
William of Blois (son of King Stephen) 11
Wilson, Woodrow (US president) vii
Wilton (Wilts.) 9, 27
Wilton, abbess of 29
Wilton Diptych 117
Wiltshire 149
Wiltshire, earl of *see* Scrope
Winchelsey, Robert (Archbishop of Canterbury) 73
Winchester xiv, 7, 8, 11, 14, 27, 28, 44, 47, 48
Winchester, Bishop of 48; *see also* Henry of Blois
Winchester, earl of *see* Despenser
Winchester, Wolvesey Castle 8
Windsor (Berks.) 42, 45, 48, 71, 73, 123, 153, 161
Windsor, St George's Chapel 161
Wishaw, Ben (actor) 141
Within the Hollow Crown (novel) 141
Wolf at the Door (novel) 64
Woodville, Anthony (Earl Rivers) 154, 156, 168, 181
Woodville, Elizabeth (queen of Edward IV) 148, 149, 151, 153-54, 155, 156, 157, 160, 177
Woodvilles, family 148, 153-54, 155, 156, 175, 180, 181
Worcester 6, 11, 12, 45, 48, 49, 62, 80, 157
Worcester, Bishop of 78; *see also* Reynolds